GUNFIGHT AT MUSSEL SLOUGH

GUNFIGHT AT MUSSEL SLOUGH

Evolution of a Western Myth

Edited by Terry Beers

SANTA CLARA UNIVERSITY, SANTA CLARA, CALIFORNIA
HEYDAY BOOKS, BERKELEY, CALIFORNIA

Library of Congress Cataloging-in-Publication Data

Gunfight at Mussel Slough : evolution of a western myth / edited by Terry Beers.

    p. cm. — (A California legacy book)

ISBN 1-890771-82-1 (pbk. : alk. paper)

1. Mussel Slough Tragedy, 1880—Fiction. 2. Railroads—Design and construction—Fiction. 3. Mussel Slough Tragedy, 1880—Sources. 4. Kings County (Calif.)—Fiction. 5. American fiction--California. 6. Land tenure—Fiction. 7. California—Fiction. 8. Western stories. I. Beers, Terry, 1955- II. Series. PS648.W4G86 2004

813'.0108358--dc22   2004007249

Cover art © Comstock IMAGES
Cover Design: Rebecca LeGates
Interior Design: Philip Krayna Design, Berkeley, CA
Printing and Binding: Banta Book Group, Harrisonburg, VA

Orders, inquiries, and correspondence should be addressed to:

Heyday Books
P.O. Box 9145, Berkeley, CA 94709
(510) 549-3564, Fax (510) 549-1889
www.heydaybooks.com

Printed in the United States of America

10 9 8 7 6 5 4 3 2 1

Contents

Preface

In 1901, young Frank Norris published *The Octopus,* his quintessential "novel with a purpose." Meant to be the first of a trilogy of works exploring the intersections of American culture with material production, distribution, and consumption, Norris structured the novel around a real event, the Mussel Slough tragedy, an 1880 gunfight that erupted over a land dispute between farmers in the southern San Joaquin Valley and the Southern Pacific Railroad. By turning history into myth, Norris claimed the moral high ground, ultimately depicting both sides to be nearly powerless to check the relentless, almost preternatural power of business trusts because human greed and the lust for power work always in the interests of "the Octopus." Norris ended his novel with these words:

> The larger view always and through all shams, all wickedness, discovers the Truth that will, in the end, prevail, and all things, surely, inevitably, resistlessly work together for the good.

Even though contemporary readers do recognize Norris' right to fictionalize historical events in pursuit of "Truth," many still seem irritated that Norris' less-than-faithful version of the conflict between railroad interests and San Joaquin farmers has become the primary vehicle for our popular understanding of events at Mussel Slough, historical events that—if they were better known—would need no imaginative embroidery to demonstrate clearly the potential for misery whenever human weakness and shortsightedness meet unchecked corporate power. But without *The Octopus*—and, to a lesser extent, the novels of other writers who have dramatized the events at Mussel Slough—this important portion of California history might be even less familiar than it is. Of course, readers of Norris' fictionalized account might not ever discover the actual names of the participants, appreciate fully the complexities of the land disputes, nor even learn the fundamental facts of Mussel Slough geography. But these readers will learn something about the universal passions and compelling dreams of the men and women—farmers, speculators, capitalists, and merchants—whose lives were touched at Mussel Slough.

This book collects substantial selections from five novels that have given their own imaginative versions of Mussel Slough events. In order of publication, these novels are: W. C. Morrow's *Blood-Money* (1882), C. C. Post's *Driven from Sea to Sea; or, Just a Campin'* (1884), Josiah Royce's *The Feud of Oakfield Creek* (1887), Frank Norris' *The Octopus* (1901), and May Merrill Miller's *First the Blade* (1938). Alongside these selections appear other significant sources treating the conflict between the railroad and the settlers, including poems, photographs, maps, songs, editorials, and political cartoons, some of which became resources for Mussel Slough novelists.

I hope this book will deepen our understanding of how one of the most important events in California's history has inspired writers of fiction. More importantly, I hope this book will show how these novelists distilled from history the intoxicating liquor of myth, creating in the popular imagination a cautionary tale of good and evil, one that tells how California's cattlemen gave way to virtuous, God-fearing farmers; how unmerciful capitalists threw off challenges from cooperative citizen leagues; how innovative settlers—steeped in the agrarian mythos of the American family farmer—turned arid, desert homestead and railroad sections into a "garden of the sun," a garden that, for one brief moment, became the site of one of the bloodiest gunfights in the American West.

Terry Beers
December 2003

Acknowledgments

I was fortunate to have substantial help putting together this book. From Santa Clara University's Orradre Library, I wish to thank Leanna Goodwater, Associate Librarian; Anne McMahon, University Archivist; and Alice Whistler, Librarian, for their time and advice. They saved me many steps in the research process. Kristin Lenore, California Legacy Intern, helped with production.

Ray Silvia, Local History Librarian of the Fresno County Public Library, suggested sources for me to consider, as did author Bill Secrest. Robert David also deserves thanks. A Central Valley native, he did valuable legwork tracking down facts, as did Wm. Leslie Howard, who helped with online research.

William Greene, Archives Technician of the National Archives and Records Administration in San Bruno, helped me find material held by the National Archives. I am also grateful to the staff at the California Historical Society's North Baker Research Library.

The Carnegie Museum in Hanford, California, has been an especially valuable resource. Dan Humason of the Carnegie Museum Board of Directors made it possible for me to use material from their collections. I also wish to thank Docent Norma Silver and Carnegie Museum Director JoAnn Gibbons, who spent time showing me their collection. The enthusiasm they have shown for this project is much appreciated.

The Kings County Museum in Burris Park is, at this printing, no longer open. But before scarce resources forced the museum to close, I was fortunate to have access to its holdings, courtesy of Curator Stan Dolan and Docent Anna Mae Overton. Docent Joyce H. Hall took a special interest in the book, making arrangements for the reproduction of articles, photographs and political cartoons, and—most importantly—holograph copies of poems and songs about Mussel Slough and the irrigation ditches. To her I am greatly indebted.

I also wish to thank my colleague Juan Velasco for reading an early draft of the introduction and Heyday Books' Editorial Director Jeannine Gendar, who never fails to improve every project she works on.

Finally, I owe a large debt to Lisa K. Manwill, who helped greatly to improve the coherence of the book and give it needed polish.

Introduction

What I am inclined to think is that conditions were worse in California than elsewhere.
—Theodore Roosevelt, after reading *The Octopus* by Frank Norris[1]

On May 11, 1880—at Henry Brewer's homestead in the southern San Joaquin Valley district of Mussel Slough—seven men lost their lives during one of the deadliest shootouts in the history of the American West.[2] The gunfight at Mussel Slough marked the culmination of a titanic struggle between wholesome California farmers fighting for their homes and pitiless agents of the Southern Pacific Railroad intent on evicting them—or at least that is how the incident was sometimes portrayed in the muckraking fiction of the era:

> Approaching to within a few feet of the marshal, Erastus demanded to know if it were true that they had come to evict the settlers, and was told that they had.
>
> "You will not be allowed to do so," replied Hemmingway; "we redeemed these lands from the desert and gave them all the value they possess. They belong to us and we intend to hold them."
>
> The marshal replied that "he was doing only what the law and the court required of him, but that rather than use force he would abandon the attempt."
>
> But Crow and his gang thirsted for blood, and had been ordered to prevent any abandonment of the object for which they were sent.
>
> Scarcely had the words of the marshal issued from his mouth when Crow drew his revolver and fired at Erastus, thus giving the signal to the others of the gang, who at once followed his example and emptied their revolvers into the bodies of the innocent and almost defenseless men in front of them.[3]

Press reports depicting the tragic events at Mussel Slough convinced many that the Southern Pacific was even more rapacious than previously believed. But dramatizing the incident in novels, as did C. C. Post in *Driven from Sea to Sea; or, Just a Campin,'* offered an even more effective means for writers to attack the railroad monopoly and attempt to pry loose its stranglehold on commerce. The redoubtable, trust-busting president Teddy Roosevelt gave little credence to the colorful version of the Mussel Slough gunfight that Frank Norris created for *The Octopus,* but he still recognized one of the novel's fundamental themes: things were bad in California, especially if you were a farmer dependent upon the Southern Pacific Railroad.

Sensational as it was, the Mussel Slough gunfight was just as much the result of bad luck and misunderstanding as it was greed and heartlessness. In 1872, the Central Pacific—controlled by the "Big Four" of Leland Stanford, Charles Crocker, Mark Hopkins, and Collis Huntington—laid tracks into the southern San Joaquin to Goshen; a few years later, the Southern Pacific—also controlled by the Big Four—brought rail service into the heart of Mussel Slough country, establishing railroad towns in Hanford, Lemoore, and Huron.[4] In flyers and brochures, the Southern Pacific invited settlers to take up residence along its San Joaquin Valley lines on odd-numbered sections on either side of its tracks. These were the sections the Southern Pacific expected to patent from the federal government, a routine land grant that Congress offered railroads in order to spur new construction and subsequent development. Settlers believed that when the railroad officially held legal title to the land, it would in turn sell that land to them at the cost mentioned in the Southern Pacific's flyers and brochures for its least valuable, unimproved acreage: "The Companies sell ordinary agricultural, vineyard, and grazing lands, at from $2.50 upwards per acre, according to quality."[5] Despite the ominous use of "upwards," many of the settlers felt that any specific cost written into railroad flyers and brochures had contractual force. Moreover, Mussel Slough settlers counted on the idea—also mentioned in flyers and brochures—that whatever improvements they had made on railroad land would not be considered when the Southern Pacific set the purchase price for its acreage. Whatever the legal implications of the brochures and flyers, the availability of potentially valuable land at a low cost not only attracted legitimate farmers but also local land sharks more interested in turning real estate into quick profits than into sustainable family farms.

But when the railroad finally fixed prices for its Mussel Slough sections, many residents were dismayed to see prices far higher than the $2.50 an acre many had expected. Settlers believed one reason for the uptick was that the Southern Pacific ignored its pledge and included in its prices the value of settler improvements, especially the newly dug irrigation ditches. For its part the railroad claimed the increases were mostly due to the enhanced property values that the railroad itself brought to the region.[6] Just as disturbing to many Mussel Slough residents, the railroad also announced its willingness to sell to third parties if its prices were not paid by the settlers who had already claimed and improved the parcels.

Negotiations proved unsuccessful, despite the evident hopefulness of a group of leading Mussel Slough residents and Leland Stanford himself, acting in his capacity as an executive of the Southern Pacific. Court suits brought no relief for the settlers; the company was able to prevail against legal challenges to its ownership of the land and its right to set prices.[7] More disheartening to the Mussel Slough farmers, the Southern Pacific—with some justification—was widely believed to control not only the state's political parties but the courts themselves. Local attitudes toward the railroads hardened, and eventually the Southern Pacific resolved to begin selling its Mussel Slough tracts to third parties and move to evict those whom it often saw as squatters and speculators. The result was bloody.

Acting upon orders of a federal court, reluctant United States Marshal Alonzo Poole traveled to Hanford to evict farmers from two Mussel Slough parcels. He meant to install in their place two new purchasers, Mills Hartt and Walter J. Crow, a lethal marksman who could bring down wild geese in flight with a rifle.[8] As these men, the marshal, and a Southern Pacific land appraiser arrived in Mussel Slough country, news of their mission spread quickly. Many local residents were gathering at a public meeting in Hanford, expecting to be addressed by Judge David S. Terry, former chief justice of the state's supreme court, on the merits of their grievances against the railroad. When word of the marshal's arrival reached the meeting, members of the Settlers' League, a group formed to oppose the Southern Pacific's Mussel Slough policies, set out to stop the evictions. They found the marshal and his party at the homestead of Henry Brewer. Wishing to avoid a confrontation, Marshal Poole parlayed with the settlers, resisting their demands that he give up his weapon but respecting their difficult position. Nerves strained, a shouting match evolved between Hartt and Crow on one side and Mussel Slough settlers on the other. Then a skittish horse accidentally knocked the marshal to the ground, throwing the scene into confusion. Witnesses disagreed over who fired the first shot, but the aftermath was clear: in a matter of moments Mills Hartt was fatally shot at the scene, as were five farmers: James Harris, Archibald McGregor, Ivar Knutson, John E. Henderson, and Daniel Kelly. Walter Crow, who survived the gunfight, set off on foot through an adjacent field of wheat, apparently heading for the safety of his father-in-law's house. His body was later found beside an irrigation ditch, shot in the back. Five other farmers—members of the Settlers' League—were indicted and convicted of obstruction.[9]

In less than two years after the bloody Mussel Slough gunfight, most of the Southern Pacific holdings in the region had been either sold or leased, transactions motivated by a reduction in prices agreed to by Charles Crocker, by the availability of credit from the Southern Pacific, and by the railroad's unwavering defense of its property rights. Yet newspaper reports, editorials, magazine pieces, and political cartoons persisted in keeping the conflict before the public, often taking the side of the ostensibly embattled settlers of Mussel Slough—in defiance of the considerable economic power wielded by the Southern Pacific and despite the court verdicts against the five Mussel Slough residents, John D. Purcell, John J. Doyle, James N. Patterson, Wayman L. Pryor, and William Braden. Over time, however, the most effective vehicles for sustaining the incident in the popular imagination have been the fruits of novelists, authors who created their own fictional versions of the events at Mussel Slough. These writers explored the nature of social responsibility and deplored what they saw as the unchecked, immoral power of corporate trusts like the Southern Pacific, "the Octopus" controlling whatever its tentacles could reach. These imaginative versions of the Mussel Slough gunfight include those of W. C. Morrow, C. C. Post, Josiah Royce, Frank Norris, and May Merrill Miller. The facts of the tragedy at Mussel Slough were transformed into the popular fiction of the Mussel Slough massacre. The appeal of myth proved stronger than the appeal of history.

★   ★   ★

Novelists who take up historical events like the Mussel Slough gunfight navigate—often unconsciously—between two different versions of the past: that recorded in history and that celebrated by myth. Both history and myth rely on storytelling to offer their perspectives on the past. The former is rooted in facts and at its best supplements compelling storytelling with synthesis and analysis; the latter is rooted in our collective imagination and offers us, in the words of scholar Henry Nash Smith, the fusion of "concept and emotion into an image."[10] That is why fiction rooted in real events often risks unraveling the fabric of history in favor of weaving patterns from the imaginative threads of myth. Not just because the creative biases of the men and women who write such novels make it so, but because the myths that sometimes drive writers, lending them theme and purpose, can drive historical events, too.

How does this work? Ultimately serious history is a messy business, grounded in the quotidian intricacies of material life, politics, business, technology, and the caprices of human desire. Because history is inexhaustibly complex, historians know that whatever general conclusions they offer us will always be contingent, subject to the scrutiny of other historians who formulate different perspectives or unearth new sources that challenge prevailing views.[11] Myths—including myths ultimately grounded in history—often prove far more robust than contingent historical explanations because myths give no space to the ungovernable contradictions of daily events. They are extraordinarily powerful images that preserve our most cherished values, those which we believe—or want to believe—shape our culture.[12]

How else do we explain how a gunfighter like Wyatt Earp, hero of the shootout at the O.K. Corral, can remain an admired folk hero in the popular imagination despite the fact that some historians call the O.K. Corral gun battle "one of barefaced murder on the part of the Earps and Holliday"?[13] Whatever the merits of such assertions, the legend of Wyatt Earp is just too good to revise. It embodies the American myth of the romantic gunfighter, a fearless man who employs violence to defend personal honor or protect those weaker than he. For many of us, this mythologized Wyatt Earp is a mirror reflecting our own best instincts. If historians want to tell us otherwise, it's hard to hear them over the more stylish voices of film directors and novelists who reinterpret the legend, reinforce the myth, and reconfirm us in our deep-seated beliefs about the nature of American heroism. It's not that the myth is entirely false so much as that it emphasizes core values over inconvenient facts. It speaks to our appetite for clear-cut images of virtue.

And so does the story of the gunfight at Mussel Slough, one of the most colorful events in California's colorful past. With a little imaginative license, the history surrounding the shootout yields ample raw material for great storytelling: a sweeping arid landscape dwarfing human scale; men and women transforming that inhospitable terrain into independent family farms; and most of all, heroic, overmatched pioneers facing down agents of profit-minded, soulless capitalists. All of these elements organize around an appealing mythic image: the American yeoman farmer whose prosperity is secured by land carved from the public domain.

Like many other stories of the American West, the story of the Mussel Slough gunfight begins with the land. Mussel Slough country lies within the Kings River fan, about thirty miles south of Fresno and just west of Hanford within the Tulare Lake basin. The Kings River—originally named Rio de los Santos Reyes by Spanish explorers[14]—is one of five significant streams that carried snowmelt from the Sierra Nevada into the region and replenished various low-lying sloughs. Eventually the entire region drained into Tulare Lake, once the largest body of freshwater west of the Great Lakes.[15] As generations of water projects altered the watershed, Tulare Lake gradually dried up, its receding shoreline transformed year by year into San Joaquin Valley farmland. But the old natural outlines still exist, not quite erased by the press of human activity. Writes author Gerald Haslam:

> Viewing the basin from an airplane...reveals the unerasable impress of sinuous, disorderly shores that were once edged by a miles-wide band of tules; the old lake's shadow is still distinctly there—however divided, however settled, however drained and irrigated—waiting for the next wet year. On it has been imposed the world's largest and most productive agricultural chessboard: what geographer Alvin Urquhart describes as the geometry of ownership replacing geography of nature.[16]

Before human beings changed forever the character of the terrain, the Tulare Lake basin consisted of a diverse range of ecological zones, including prairie, oak woodland, chaparral, and marsh habitats. The Mussel Slough region itself was dominated by prairie land but also held occasional riparian areas where the gently sloping land was cut by stream or slough. The Coast Range to the west blocked much of the Pacific rainfall from reaching the region, and, without the moderating influence of marine air, seasonal variations in temperatures—then as now—could be extreme. Summer days were often hot, windless, and dry; winter days were often cool and depressingly damp, especially after a rain. On days like these, tule fog—named after the tall, wetland rushes—formed an opaque gray curtain when the chilly temperatures condensed the still, moist valley air. Shallow, marshy areas provided breeding grounds for mosquitoes, which often spread malaria among the people who lived in the region.

Originally these were Yokuts, the name of a number of distinct bands of native people who established individual territories but spoke dialects of a common tongue. Despite the enervating valley climate, all the individual Yokut groups—including the Nutunutu, who lived around Mussel Slough[17]—still found plenty of advantages to living in the Tulare Lake region. Chief among them was that the variation in ecological zones provided diverse and relatively stable resources. Besides acorns—a staple of many California native peoples—the Yokuts gathered grass seeds, tule bulbs, and wild blackberries. Throughout the region, they also hunted small game, including waterfowl that gathered in great numbers near Tulare Lake. Thomas Jefferson Mayfield, who lived among the Choinumne people when he was a boy in the 1850s, recalled that "there were about six kinds of geese in the San Joaquin when I first came here, and there were probably billions of them. I have seen the white geese with black wing tips flying so thickly that I am positive one band of them would cover four square miles of land as thick as they could land and take off again."[18] Regional streams provided further variety: fresh fish as well as mussels and clams. At that time, this abundance and variety of natural food sources helped make the area one of the most heavily populated regions in North America.[19]

The Yokut presence in the southern San Joaquin Valley certainly affected the character of that landscape, but only in limited ways, within what geographer William L. Preston calls "the opportunities afforded by basin environments and the constraints imposed by natural patterns and processes."[20] Although it would take several decades, the arrival of Europeans in the region changed the terrain far more deeply. During their reign over Alta California, the Spanish never really established a strong presence in the interior valley, partly because the region was so remote from their missions and presidios along the coast and partly because they lacked the human resources to expand into the area. They did, however, recognize the danger of leaving such a vast interior region unoccupied and susceptible to encroachment by rival powers. After the Mexican revolution in 1836, the Mexican government recognized the same problem and encouraged the establishment of cattle ranches in the interior valleys. Even so, only two land grants were issued for the Tulare Lake region and only one of those was ever occupied, the Rancho Laguna de Tache,[21] which helped establish—if only in a limited way—the business of raising livestock in the valley. The Yokut way of life was being erased by the commercial demands of a larger world. The process would soon be accelerated by the arrival of Americans.

American fur trappers—notably Jedediah Smith—had already visited the region in the 1820s and noted an abundance of beaver and other wildlife throughout the Tulare Lake basin. Just over two decades later, California's gold rush marked the beginning of a population boom in California, providing a financial incentive to expand cattle raising in the San Joaquin Valley and attract more Americans to the region. Ranchers—sometimes former forty-niners—often bought stock and let their cattle range over vast areas of the region. Soon after California became part of the United States, other Americans arrived in the Central Valley, surveyors working for the United States government. California—as well as other regions throughout the West—had to be measured and divided, and sections had to be assessed for their value in natural resources and their potential as farmland.

The old Mexican system of land grants depended upon perishable markers; "when Manual Castro received a grant, also known as the *Laguna de Tache,*" writes historian Wallace Smith, "the northeastern boundary was cited as being a certain oak tree."[22] Instead of relying on such natural features, the federal government meant to slice up California into familiar, already standard units, fitting the new territory to the edge of an almost seamless pattern already laid down across the East and Midwest. In 1785, the United States Public Land Survey began to map federal land based on an interrelated system of initial points and townships. On July 7, 1851, U.S. Deputy Surveyor

Colonel Leander Ransom established this same system in the new state, setting the point of the first meridian of California on the summit of Mount Diablo, east of Oakland and overlooking the Sacramento Delta.[23] From this point, the survey divided the state east and west in six-mile increments called "ranges," and north and south in six-mile increments called "townships." The crosshatch pattern that emerged formed a checkerboard of townships, each of which subdivided into thirty-six one-square-mile sections, themselves often subdivided further into quarter sections, or the 160 acres that became the statutory allotment of a homestead after the Homestead Act of 1862. So, for example, SW Quarter of Sec. 4, T18S R21E, corresponded to the 160 acres in the southwest quarter of section four in the eighteenth township south and the twenty-first range east of the Mount Diablo Meridian. These PLS coordinates include Henry Brewer's homestead, the site of the Mussel Slough gunfight.

Even today, the link between the survey lines and the shape of farms in the Central Valley is unmistakable. Writes author Andro Linklater:

> The valley runs roughly northwest to southeast, but the citrus orchards, lettuce fields, avocado groves, vineyards, and asparagus beds are all aligned strictly by the cardinal points of the compass, north to south, east to west. The yellow dirt tracks that form their boundaries appear at regular one-mile intervals following the surveyor's lines in a neat rectangular plaid.[24]

The survey sections allowed the federal government to fix precisely the position of its land grants, including the odd-numbered sections in the public domain lying within twenty miles of new railroad lines, parcels that were the capital incentive Congress gave railroads to extend transportation into new regions and invite settlement.[25] Soon immigrants—induced by the railroad's advertising and the promises of speculators—began to till the soil, feeling assured that they could eventually claim clear title to the land, perhaps by outright purchase from the railroad, perhaps by proving up a claim in even-numbered sections still open to homestead. Moreover, the nature of the congressional land grant to the railroad discouraged large land monopolies from forming: "Purchasers will not be limited as to the amount of vacant lands they can buy. It must be borne in mind, however, that 640 acres is the largest tract that can be sold in any one place, the Railroad sections not being contiguous to each other, or *adjoining*."[26]

Thanks to the Public Land Survey, the vast plain of the Central Valley was symbolically transformed. Instead of the wild realm familiar to the Yokuts and shaped by the curves of rivers and the arcs of mountains, the Great Valley became, in the collective imagination of immigrating Americans, a precise and familiar grid of sections whose boundaries paid no attention to physical landmarks or the natural sweep of the terrain. Human beings were imposing order on Nature, a typically American project well suited to a nation intent on its Manifest Destiny. This audacity is captured by May Merrill Miller in *First the Blade:*

> Edwin told Amelie she must imagine boundaries where there were none and draw a square for themselves to enclose a precise section. But Amelie could see no hope of geometry imposed upon this great expanse of dried grasses. And it seemed impudent that upon maps this desolate land was already banded by a checkerboard strip twenty miles wide with alternate section squares....Amelie laughed even as Edwin spoke of men's papers and plans. They could mean nothing in this vast valley forever set apart between barriers only the lost or foolhardy would cross.[27]

Despite the aridity of the region, available railroad sections were enticing to optimistic farmers, who soon outnumbered the cattlemen, some of whom were already ravaged by drought and the land's rapidly diminishing capacity to support grazing. Soon, passage of the No Fence Law forced ranchers to bear the responsibility of damages to crops caused by their stray animals searching for better grazing, affording the farmers additional rights on the land.[28] The stubborn Mussel Slough "sandlappers"—a pejorative term ranchers applied to Tulare basin farmers—wedded to their sections, confident in their property rights, and secure in their country's Manifest Destiny, were beginning to reshape the land in yet another way.

Many of the pioneers who settled in Mussel Slough country were intimately familiar with the intricacies of how local sections were surveyed, homesteaded, purchased, swapped, and even squatted upon.[29] Some no doubt appreciated fully the symbolic importance of the surveyed sections, land reclaimed by industrious, God-fearing farmers from savage Indians, irresponsible cattlemen, and eventually even indifferent and inhospitable Nature. And many of these pioneers felt an almost religious commandment, typical of westering Americans, to use the land and contribute to the commonweal. After the Mussel Slough gunfight, the Settlers' Land League, a group of Mussel Slough residents who organized to oppose the railroad policies,[30] published an "Appeal to the People" that grounded itself in a version of this idea:

> We have built up a prosperous, happy, intelligent Christian community; we have done all that honorable people could do peaceably to adjust the differences between us and the railroad company. We are faithful to all, and neglectful of none of the obligations we owe to the community, as well as the government in which we live. We have built about five hundred miles of main ditches, beside the side ditches, to make fruitful fields of a parched desert. We grow in abundance, besides the cereals, all manner of fruits and vegetables. We have added largely to the enumeration of the tax rolls of the State. We have contributed largely to its commerce. Our schools are largely attended and admirably kept; our churches have a large membership of devout worshipers. We feel we have built up communities such as are invaluable and indispensable to well-ordered society and to free and independent states.[31]

This statement by the Settlers' League stands as the Mussel Slough version of Manifest Destiny, especially its claim that the settlers had built communities founded on American principles "to make fruitful fields of parched desert."[32] The statement is reminiscent of an earlier influential expression of such ideas, found in the writing of Thomas Jefferson. In response to French inquiries about the new American states, Jefferson began a work in 1785 that would eventually be published as *Notes on the State of Virginia*. In it he urges that America steer clear of developing an economy too dependent upon manufacturing:

> We have an immensity of land courting the industry of the husbandman. Is it best then that all our citizens should be employed in its improvement, or that one half should be called off from that to exercise manufacturers and handicraft arts for the other? Those who labour in the earth are the chosen people of God, if ever he had a chosen people, whose breasts he has made his peculiar deposit for substantial and genuine virtue. It is the focus

in which he keeps alive that sacred fire, which otherwise might escape from the face of the earth....While we have land to labour then, let us never wish to see our citizens occupied at a work-bench, or twirling a distaff.[33]

Jefferson was in a position not only to write about the benefits of an agrarian democracy but also to help make it possible by lending key support to the public land surveys. Jefferson originally wanted to use decimal units, but in the ordinance that Congress passed in 1785, the grid system was pegged to traditional units of six miles square.[34] What mattered most, however, was that the grid system would allow land to be easily subdivided, and small parcels could be conveyed to individual landholders, a check against the large patents Congress some-times sold to persons interested in large-scale speculation, a practice anathema to Thomas Jefferson. As a result, the basis for Jefferson's vision of an agrarian republic became embedded in the public land surveys, and the foundation for conveying public property to private hands secured for American farmers the resources to realize their vocation as "the chosen people of God."

Confidence rooted in this vocation could persist in the face of intense discouragement. Mary E. Chambers—sister to Archibald McGregor, one of the slain Mussel Slough settlers—offered the *Visalia Delta* newspaper a précis of her experience after coming to the region, and her story captures the self-confidence of newly arrived settlers:

> The stock men looked upon [us] as intruders, and discouraged us all they could, telling us that we could do nothing on the land; that we would starve to death, as it was impossible to raise any-thing on the dry plains. These things, of course, we did not believe, as we looked on these stock-raisers as an indolent people, who had never made an effort to cultivate the soil; but we, with our energy and perseverance, would make the wilderness to blossom and bear.
>
> Alas, how swe flattered ourselves! We little imagined how our patience or perseverance would be tried, or how near the stock men's "starve to death" predictions would come on us.[35]

Chambers continues her story by recounting the sacrifices made by local families and focusing on their plans for designing and constructing irrigation ditches. The ditches themselves were not just a practical inno-vation; they became a symbol of the success of the Mussel Slough farming community, the means by which the farmers, Jefferson's "chosen people," would fulfill their desire and their obligation to "make the wilderness to blossom and bear."

Newspaper reporters also liberally infused their coverage of Mussel Slough events with the language of the yeoman farmer mythos, often reinforced with Biblical imagery. For instance, under the headline "Railroad Robbers," a *San Francisco Chronicle* report opined:

> "No citizen of California need be reminded of the many difficulties attendant upon the settlement of a new estate, and how both the soil and its surroundings seem sometimes to conspire against man in the prosecution of his work. It was not then a land of Goshen, flowing with milk and honey and fragrant with the perfume of roses, that these early immigrants found, but a land until then unoccupied and desolate, a land not fertile from want of moisture and unproductive from want of cultivation."[36]

Similar language appeared in the fiction about the Mussel Slough gunfight, underscoring the mythic image of the virtuous yeoman farmers of the San Joaquin Valley.

William Morrow, a former editor at the *Visalia Delta*, published the novel *Blood-Money* only two years after the Mussel Slough gunfight. Morrow's portrait of the local farmers underscored their wholesomeness, especially compared to the supposed idleness of the cattlemen who preceded the farmers in the region. Here, a local farmer named Newton explains the history of the region to a newcomer scouting land for purchase. Opening the new irrigation canals brought new challenges:

> "The first season the water came down there was hard work to make the ditches carry it, as they were continually breaking. Repairing these damages kept the men busy all the time and consequently the women and children had to work in the fields from morning till night. That woman you see in the house to the left cultivated thirty acres of corn with one man's assistance. My daughter and I dug a fence-ditch around our hundred and sixty acres of land, my daughter working as hard as I. I know another girl who helped her father in a similar manner; and you must consider that these were girls who had never been accustomed to such work."
>
> "Noble women!" exclaimed the stranger, with enthusiasm.

"Noble women, did you say? Ah, my dear sir! I can give you but a feeble idea of how noble these women of Mussel Slough are."[37]

The passage not only evokes the image of the virtuous Mussel Slough farmers—now supplemented by the generous inclusion of the region's "noble women"—but also mentions the familiar quarter-section parcel, the foundation of agrarian western America, almost an entitlement for "a people which preserve a republic in vigour."[38]

The passage also conveys the justifiable pride settlers felt in creating their system of irrigation ditches. These ditches etched yet another new pattern into the landscape, one that cut across section boundaries and gradually fell along natural elevation contours. The practical obstacles to their construction were daunting: without the aid of steam power, much of the earth had to be moved by hand or with the aid of earth-scraping tools pulled by draft animals; the sides of the canals were subject to collapse; small animal holes and previously unknown sinks could absorb the precious water after it was turned into the ditches from the Kings River, Cross Creek, or other local source. But Mussel Slough farmers overcame these problems by banding together into organized ditch companies, apportioning labor, and issuing stock certificates that recorded their individual rights to the water that flowed through their artificial rivers.

The Mussel Slough farmers were practical people, of course. When better ways to change the land came along—for instance, in the form of James Porteous' Fresno Scraper[39]—locals were quick to adopt them. But the images of the farmer digging a ditch with pick and shovel or moving earth with horse and buckboard nevertheless entered the collective imagination permanently. Such representations combined qualities of individual self-reliance and American perseverance with communitarian commitment. The completion of irrigation ditches was even marked with local celebrations and memorialized in songs. So in the eyes of many of these settlers, the railroad's apparent breach of promise not only threatened their livelihood, it attacked their pride and the natural satisfaction they earned by transforming the land from desert to garden. Seen in this light, the conflict with the railroad was only partly about money.

Hard to sympathize, then, with a railroad Octopus intent on squeezing every ounce of profit possible from the land it controlled and the transportation network it was constantly expanding. Its creed was summed up in a phrase associated with Collis Huntington:

"Charge all that the traffic will bear,"[40] an idea that conjures self-interest and greed rather than the self-reliance and generosity of spirit represented by the hard-working Mussel Slough farmers. It was even harder to sympathize with the Southern Pacific considering the influence it exerted through gift-giving and bribery of politicians and judges, not to mention the resources it spent to guarantee its views prevailed in cases before the courts, in decisions of railroad commissions, and in legislation passed in the state capitol and in Washington. However, the railroad really *did* have genuine interests to protect in the Mussel Slough region, and the decisions that emanated from its corporate agents were certainly not as arbitrary or as exclusively self-serving as they appeared to not only Mussel Slough farmers but also, it must be said, to many of the writers who mythologized them.

When it came to attracting the sympathy of the public, the Southern Pacific was at a considerable disadvantage compared to the small family farmer turning the soil in the southern San Joaquin. It helps little to know that Collis Huntington asserted the rights in common between the farmers and the railroad when he wrote that "the law of self-preservation and of self-defense was not made for individuals any more than for corporations."[41] Generally, the public—including the novelists who write for it—tends to favor the vulnerable over the powerful, often ignoring the irony that, at least in the case of the Mussel Slough farmers and the railroads, both sides shared many of the same values, including a healthy respect for the American dollar. In an 1873 speech to the men working in railroad shops in Sacramento, Leland Stanford made this point explicit: "Does Governor Booth sell at the same per cent of profit his sugar, pork, beans, bacon, lard, candles, soap, spice, coffee, whiskey, brandy, and other articles? So with the mechanic, the manufacturer, the farmer, and others. The market price governs. A farmer takes two and one-half cents for his grain as justly and as cheerfully as one and one-half cents, the cost of producing being the same."[42]

Maybe so. But even if they would concede the truth of Stanford's assertion and thus cast a softer light on the railroad, some of the Mussel Slough novelists still tended to exaggerate the farmers' blamelessness. In glossing over the misdeeds of the Settlers' League—for example, the occasional vigilante forays aimed at settlers unsympathetic to the

League—they placed the mantle of victim squarely upon the figure of the Mussel Slough farmer, and the railroad became the lone villain. The pursuit of moral clarity so required this arrangement, especially of the first novelists who transformed this history into myth.

The first novel to appear after the gunfight was William C. Morrow's *Blood-Money*, an 1882 work that takes a harsh view of the capitalist class and its treatment of Mussel Slough settlers. In 1884, C. C. Post published *Driven from Sea to Sea; or, Just a Campin'*, which offered an even harsher indictment of capitalists than did Morrow's novel. Both works were written by men who had experience as journalists, and while neither work ever achieved wide circulation (though Post's novel did go into a second edition in 1890), they make fascinating reading because they unabashedly advanced a common antimonopolistic point of view held by many reform-minded writers of the period. Their populist message was also made accessible to a wide audience because stock characters were clearly and simply drawn and the stories were conventionally plotted, blending muckraking zeal and a feisty willingness to challenge the railroads into an old-fashioned morality tale.

Today William Morrow (1854–1923) is usually remembered as a fabulist and horror story writer, his most lasting contribution a collection called *The Ape, the Idiot, and Other People* (1897), which along with other stories earned him "a secure reputation as an early master of horror."[43] But early in his career, during part of 1882, he worked as an editor at the *Visalia Delta*, which, according to historian J. L. Brown, gave him ample opportunity to gather information about the Mussel Slough incident.[44]

The main character of *Blood-Money* is John Graham, a Mussel Slough farmer tilling railroad land and supporting his aged grandmother. Although Morrow gives him moral backbone, he also tinges his Jeffersonian portrait of Graham with a hint of self-interest:

> By nature he was ambitious; but so unselfish and patient was he that no one knew of his dreams. He never complained, and his energy never abated. Although bashful and apparently timid, he was by nature utterly dauntless. A woman could frighten him, but a man could not.[45]

Graham is endeavoring to find a treasure stolen from his murdered father and thought to be buried under "Lone Tree," a local landmark. Part of his motivation for seeking the treasure is to secure his family's well-being and right a past wrong. But he is also aiming to please his fiancée, Nellie, who has been drawn to new friends belonging to the capitalist class, a relationship symbolized by gold when a formidable woman of the upper class gives Nellie an expensive bracelet "of rich, yellow woven gold, and the solid ends of the graceful spiral were set each with a handsome pearl and turquoise. It was the most magnificent piece of jewelry that had ever come under the wrapt gaze of Nellie."[46]

As Graham seeks the treasure, he also becomes more outspoken about the injustices done to the settlers by the railroad and predicts that the people will become the victims of "cold, cruel, grasping money."[47] Morrow creates a dramatic shootout set at Storer's ranch,[48] a scene that mirrors the actual Mussel Slough gunfight. In the end, Graham winds up in San Quentin prison, victim of false robbery charges engineered by the railroad capitalists. Nellie renounces her new friends—and, significantly, all the expensive gifts they have given her—and she marries Graham while he is still in jail. Despite the hopefulness with which the couple looks forward to Graham's eventual release, the book still ends with the capitalists unrepentant and in secure control.

Charles Cyril Post (1846–1906) had particularly impressive credentials as an antimonopolist journalist. According to literary scholar Gordon W. Clarke, Post served as editor of the *Saturday Express* of Chicago, an antimonopolistic paper, and as editor of *Roll-Call*, a left-leaning Chicago paper aimed at a labor audience. Besides his Mussel Slough novel, he also published another work of fiction, *Congressman Swanson* (1891) and a volume of "Metaphysical Essays."[49] The unhappy events depicted in his *Driven from Sea to Sea* are, in their cumulative effect, perhaps less plausible than those depicted in Morrow's *Blood-Money*, but the novel offers a harsher criticism and—it may be argued—a more expansive portrait of the extent of control capitalists exerted over California enterprise.

The main action of Post's novel surrounds the character John Parsons, who comes to California to make his fortune. A frustrated forty-niner, Parsons nevertheless remains optimistic, perceiving potential in the land available for pioneers in the new state. He settles his family on Northern California's Suscol Ranch—historically the site of a land dispute traced to a Mexican land grant—only to be ousted by a crooked land syndicate. "Only just a campin'," says

Parsons, as he and his neighbors leave their homes. "Only just a campin' where they thought to live always; that's what they're a-doin'; that's what I've ben a-doin' all my life."[50]

Bad luck prevails for the Parsons family. John develops their next home—in the foothills east of Sacramento—into a prosperous spread. But that land is eventually smothered beneath tailings from a hydraulic mining operation. In the meantime, Parsons' ward, Erastus Hemmingway, resolves to move to Mussel Slough to stake a claim and become sufficiently secure that he can marry one of Parsons' daughters, Lucy. After his marriage, Hemmingway is killed in the Mussel Slough gunfight; John Parsons dies of exhaustion and grief; and Hemmingway's widow and her widowed mother are left alone with scant resources in the still-harsh environment of Mussel Slough. Besides the constant barrage of misfortune heaped upon the Parsons family by unfeeling money men, three other features of the book underscore the indictment of capitalists prosecuted in the novel: extensive documentation cited by Post as the basis for his fictionalized treatment, his use of Walter Crow's true name (which contributed to the popular perception of Crow as a "tool" of the railroads[51]), and an extraordinary chapter devoted to an imagined conversation among railroad capitalists, characters clearly based upon the executives of the Southern Pacific, characters depicted as wholly unburdened of any shred of conscience for their greedy acts or any sense of responsibility for the misery they cause. Says one of the capitalists of the settlers, "They are everlastingly whining about being turned out of their homes. Why don't they go somewhere else and begin again? They ought to know by this time that they can't fight a rich corporation, such as we are."[52]

We can think of *Blood-Money* and *Driven from Sea to Sea* as muckraking novels of propaganda, but let's not forget that their authors were not indifferent to facts—after all, it was their interpretation of the material conditions of the Mussel Slough settlers that partly inspired these works. They did, however, let the complicated history linking the pioneers and the railroads recede into the background in order to transform the Mussel Slough incident into a cautionary tale showing why the power of the railroads must be broken. In doing so, these books sustain—if not strengthen—the myth of the virtuous pioneer farmers and the sections of land that they improved by the sweat of honest labor. And despite the conventionality of these works, their moral certitude still makes them compelling reading. In the fictional worlds inhabited by John Graham and John Parsons, evil exists and it is symbolized by the grasping need for money and power that characterizes the capitalist class.

After Morrow and Post, other Mussel Slough novelists brought more nuanced perspectives to their treatments of the gunfight. One of those writers was Josiah Royce (1855–1916), the distinguished California-bred Harvard philosopher and author of *The Feud of Oakfield Creek; A Novel of California* (1887). Royce was born and raised in Grass Valley and educated at the University of California and at Johns Hopkins, where he earned a doctorate. Between 1878 and 1882, he taught English at Berkeley, and then he moved to Harvard to become a professor of philosophy. A recurring theme in much of his work—whether history, fiction, or philosophy—was the importance of loyalty, which he favored, in the words of biographer John Clendenning, over "that form of individualism which seeks personal gain at the expense of social harmony."[53] Given Royce's interest in the cohesion of society and the commitment individuals must make to a chosen moral purpose, it was perhaps inevitable that California's land disputes—often the root of selfishness as well as sacrifice—would engage his attention.

Previous to publishing his only novel, Royce had written a history of California, *California, from the Conquest in 1846 to the Second Vigilance Committee in San Francisco: A Study of American Character* (1886). The distinctiveness of Royce's work is clear from its title. Royce was forthright in declaring the entry of California into the union as the culmination of a protracted "conquest" (an idea he knew Americans were loath to consider). He also focused on how men and women produced a social life and strived to create community loyalty even outside the umbrella of an effective local government. Trained as a scholar, Royce never undertook a project without doing thorough research. *The Feud of Oakfield Creek* is an almost unreadable work, heavy with exposition and—despite its "two bloody fights, three heroes, two heroines, several villains, and almost no morals"[54]—short on drama. Yet the book still bears the impress of Royce's thorough understanding of the difficulties and consequences of land disputes in the state, just as his California history had done before.

Unlike other novels inspired by the events at Mussel Slough, Royce's book is not set in the southern San Joaquin but in San Francisco and the East Bay region around Walnut Creek, near the site of an actual Contra Costa County land dispute.[55] The novel largely consists of events rooted in a personal feud between the wealthy Alonzo Eldon, president of the fictional Land and Improvement Company, and Alf Escott, an intellectual and onetime friend of the Eldon family. Escott became estranged from the Eldon family when Escott's daughter was jilted by Eldon's son, Tom. The enmity shared by the two old California pioneers is played out in a land dispute, wherein squatters on the land company's Contra Costa holdings receive support from the eloquent Escott, a kind of absentee squatter who sees that he can hurt Eldon by supporting the settlers in their claims. Although the main dispute involves a land company, not a railroad, as literary historian Irving McKee has noted, the events at Mussel Slough inspired the climax: "A band of settlers one May morning makes armed resistance to the United States marshal and a monopoly which has won legal title to the disputed lands; seven men are killed in the exchange of fire. A jumper named Buzzard, clearly the reincarnation of Crow, does the most effective work, accounting for at least six antagonists before he himself falls."[56]

Royce's book differs from some of the other Mussel Slough novels in more than just geography as it also makes less use of the symbolic image of Jefferson's virtuous farmer carving an agrarian paradise out of once-public lands. This is not to say that these characters don't appear in *The Feud of Oakfield Creek,* only that the focus remains almost entirely on the feud between Eldon and Escott. But when Royce *does* give us portraits of the settlers, they conform closely to the Jeffersonian ideal, showing that even from philosopher Royce, that agrarian image demanded respect. In the following passage, a leader of the settlers named Peterson addresses some of his neighbors before the climactic gun battle:

Boys,—I *should* say Noble Brothers (but, *darn* it! that's no matter), —news has just come that Alonzo Eldon, with his whole pack, has stopped outside in Carson's field. They're reconnoitering. Now, we mean to go out and meet 'em square and in full force, and show 'em what stuff we're made of. I say we're made of peaceable stuff, and have been all along; I say we aren't going to give up our rights; and I also say that we here are the last men in the State of California to violate the laws, unless we're driven to the wall. But if we are, boys, then the law of God is higher than that of man, and even the crushed worm will turn again and rend you.[57]

Peterson's speech makes plain two characteristics that Royce's farmers share with the characters drawn by Morrow and Post (as well as many of the historical persons who settled in Mussel Slough): the unquestioned belief that they enjoyed the grace of divine right in their cause, and their shared sense that this right was violated by the personal greed of strong-willed capitalists.

Yet is it the capitalists that oppress the settlers, or is it something more complicated and ultimately more sinister? Earlier in the novel, when discussing the dispute between the land company and the settlers, Eldon tells his daughter-in-law that if only his interests were at stake, he would seek a settlement with Escott and his cohorts for the sake of peace. But duty prevents him: "There are more interests than mine over there; there's more capital invested than mine. When, as its president, I defend the legal rights of the Land and Improvement Company, I'm acting not alone for myself, but for the capital of innocent shareholders, invested in those undertakings."[58] By insisting on the distinction between an individual human being—however well-heeled—and a corporation, Eldon complicates notions of responsibility and motive, legitimizing the corporation's rights in the name of the abstract interests of unnamed—and absent—individuals.[59] Now recall the capitalists' complaint in C. C. Post's novel: that the settlers "ought to know by this time that they can't fight a rich corporation, such as we are." In Post's novel—unlike Royce's—there is no distinction between the individuals who run the corporation and the corporation itself. As a result, readers are invited to place blame squarely on the shoulders of individual human beings instead of assigning it to an abstract, cor- porate entity—much as Californians were happy to blame Stanford, Huntington, and Crocker for the perceived wrongs done by the Southern Pacific Railroad. As a result, Post preserves a satisfying moral clarity but unfortunately such clarity comes at the cost of apportioning responsibility more thoughtfully.

William Morrow and C. C. Post were better storytellers than Josiah Royce but, not surprisingly, the Harvard professor might have seen more clearly into the moral issues embedded in California land dis- putes like those of Mussel Slough. Royce's work can be thought of as a novel of social conscience, one that goes beyond the propaganda of works like *Blood-Money* and *Driven from Sea to Sea* to consider more carefully the obligations and freedoms of the individual within a wider social order. The aim of such works is not to effect change through the simple vehicle of praise and blame—as in novels of propaganda—but rather to influence public opinion through urging a more thorough understanding of difficult issues. But marred by Royce's poor gifts as a fictional storyteller, *The Feud of Oakfield Creek*, with its more subtle approach, never quite succeeds. What it did do, however, was help prepare the way for Frank Norris, who combined his superior gifts as a storyteller with a penchant for the abstract in order to make *The Octopus: A Story of California* (1901) the most readable and compelling of the Mussel Slough novels.

Norris (1870–1902) was born in Chicago and studied in Europe, at the University of California, and at Harvard. Before writing *The Octopus*, Norris had been a correspondent in Cuba during the Spanish-American War, published short stories and essays—many of them on the art of fiction—and written several novels, among them *McTeague* (1899), which many readers feel is the equal to Norris' Mussel Slough book. *The Octopus* was meant to be the first in a trilogy, the "Epic of the Wheat," which would trace the production, distribution, and consumption of wheat as a means of understanding more deeply the forces at work in American lives. Unfortunately, Norris never completed the project. He died in San Francisco of a burst appendix, only thirty-two years old.

Experienced as a journalist, Norris had just the skills he needed to emulate his model, French writer Emile Zola, in whom Norris found the inspiration to attempt large scale, naturalistic works, works that explored how impersonal social and evolutionary forces could dictate the behavior of human beings. He was also driven by a firm desire to teach through his art. In "The Novel with a 'Purpose,'" published in 1902 in *World's Work*, Norris held that the best class of novel "proves something, draws conclusions from a whole congeries of forces, social tendencies, race impulses, devotes itself not to a study of men but of man," and that "it preaches by telling things and showing things."[60] *The Octopus* certainly embraced these ideas, and if readers have not been universally impressed with the integrity of the work—noting its lack of unity, its repetitions, its immature point of view[61]—they have almost always acknowledged the grandness and the sincerity of the attempt. And no one denies the brilliance of Norris' lush prose when he is at the top of his form. Whatever its drawbacks, *The Octopus* has never been out of print, and unlike the other Mussel Slough novels, it alone is solidly embedded in the canon of American letters.

The sheer scope of the novel is impossible to capture in summary. Norris uses the Mussel Slough struggle to provide the central conflict in the story—San Joaquin farmers face the railroad over a land dispute—but added to the mix are themes of romantic love, the nature and role of the artist, and the symbiotic relationship of human beings and the earth, "locked in a colossal embrace, at grapples with the throes of an infinite desire, at once terrible and divine, knowing no law, untamed, savage, natural, sublime."[62] All these motifs are tied together in the person of Presley, a dilettante poet who roams across the region in search of themes for his planned "Song of the West."

Like Royce, Norris depicted most of the principals in the land struggle as variously motivated; main characters emerge in the work plausibly, which makes readers *feel* the inevitable loss of life and land and care more deeply here than in any of the previously published Mussel Slough novels. Norris also employed the myth of the yeoman farmer within *The Octopus* in a more subtle fashion than in these earlier works: many of his characters do not embody the virtues of Jefferson's farmers so much as fail in the story because they do not have them. Instead of family farmers intent on establishing thriving and stable rural communities, Norris' farmers are aspiring "Big Men," out to reap huge profits from their Central Valley holdings. As such, these farmers hold much in common with the capitalists of the novel, especially Magnus Derrick, the charismatic leader of the San Joaquin farmers.

Early in the novel, Norris describes Magnus Derrick, the owner of the ten thousand acres of El Rancho De Los Muertos, as the "prominent man," the one other men looked to for leadership. A former forty-niner and a onetime candidate for governor, Magnus

> loved to do things on a grand scale, to preside, to dominate. In his good humor there was something Jovian. When angry, everybody around him trembled. But he had not the genius for detail, was not patient. The certain grandiose lavishness of his disposition occupied itself more with results than means. He was always ready to take chances, to hazard everything on the hopes of colossal returns.... The old-time spirit of '49, hap-hazard,

unscientific, persisted in his mind. Everything was a gamble—who took the greatest chances was most apt to be the greatest winner.[63]

Magnus' experience, luck, and charisma make him an impressive figure among his peers. But his bonanza-like attitude toward his land shocks the idealistic Presley when Magnus makes clear that he cares nothing for the railroad's legal maneuvers and rate increases so long as he can make a fortune in the meantime:

> It was the true California spirit that found expression through him, the spirit of the West, unwilling to occupy itself with details, refusing to wait, to be patient, to achieve by legitimate plodding....It was this frame of mind that Magnus and the multitude of other ranchers of whom he was a type, farmed their ranches. They had no love for their land. They were not attached to the soil.[64]

In *The Octopus*, farmers like Derrick are speculators in land and wheat, not the simple family farmers depicted by Morrow and Post. But even so, when Norris' farmers feel the railroad's land price squeeze, they form a league and do not hesitate to invoke the image of the underdog farmer, secure in their moral purpose. In response to railroad threats of higher land prices and eventual eviction, the farmers wail over the potential loss of their investment but justify themselves by asserting their attachment to their homes: "They can kill me. They can shoot me down, but I'll die—die fighting for my home—before I'll give in to this."[65] Painted with a bit of hypocrisy, Norris' farmers don't have a strong attachment to their land or any interest in the virtues of the agrarian life, yet when pressed, they do not hesitate to wrap themselves in the rhetoric of the agrarian myth—much as the actual farmers who formed the Mussel Slough Settlers' League had done. Because of that hypocrisy, it's no wonder that Magnus—who also stoops to political maneuvering and bribery, despite the promptings of his better nature—will face ruin. He strayed from the ideal, from the land. Not the quarter-section parcel for him, but the immense spread of land that he cannot possibly hold. Derrick fails partly because the forces of capitalism are arrayed against him, but mostly because of choices he has made himself.

Closer to the farmers depicted in earlier works is the character Buck Annixter, whose Quien Sabe Rancho abuts Derrick's spread.

The two landholders are partners in the construction of an irrigation ditch meant to water both their properties, and though Norris makes far less use of the symbolism of the irrigation ditch than previous writers, the project still represents the technological innovation of the farmers and the value they have added to their properties. But unlike Derrick, Annixter—college educated, keenly interested in the technology of farming—gains additional perspective as the story unfolds. He is a hard man, "one of the people, rough almost to insolence, direct in speech, intolerant in his opinions, relying upon absolutely no one but himself,"[66] but then he falls in love and marries young Hilma Tree, daughter of a tenet dairyman, and comes to look at the world and his place in it with new insight.

Self-reliance and directness are qualities Annixter shares with other characters in Mussel Slough novels, notably John Graham in *Blood-Money* and Erastus Hemmingway in *Driven from Sea to Sea*. Annixter also seems more committed to his land than the great Magnus Derrick, especially after his marriage. He tells Presley that Hilma has made him realize that

> a fellow can't live *for* himself any more than he can live *by* himself. He's got to think of others. If he's got brains, he's got to think for the poor ducks that haven't 'em, and not give 'em a boot in the backsides because they happen to be stupid; and if he's got money, he's got to help those that are busted, and if he's got a house, he's got to think of those that ain't got anywhere to go.[67]

Annixter's new community spirit, his self-reliance, his commitment to his land, and his interest in technology and innovation align with the familiar image of the Mussel Slough farmer, though Annixter's holdings far outstrip those of the typical homesteader and resemble more the holdings of large-scale purchasers. It is his death in the climactic battle that readers are likely to judge most tragic of all the characters in the various Mussel Slough novels.

To complement the San Joaquin growers, *The Octopus* gives readers portraits of the railroad men who challenge them. Easily the most hateful is S. Behrman, the small-minded, venal bureaucrat who enforces the rules and regulations of the fictional Pacific and Southwestern Railroad and who attracts the personal enmity of most of the San Joaquin farmers. Behrman eventually gets control of Magnus' property and then meets a grotesque death, oddly, fittingly, and memorably in the hold of a ship, drowned in a dusty sea of his own ill-gotten wheat. But the most interesting railroad man is Shelgrim, the head of the Octopus and the man whom most of the farmers assume is the controlling personality of the railroad and—through its abundant resources—the commissions and courts that regulate commerce and transportation in California. Near the end of the novel, Presley decides to confront Shelgrim: "Why not see, face to face, the man whose power was so vast, whose will was so resistless, whose potency for evil so limitless, the man who for so long and so hopelessly they had all been fighting."[68]

Shelgrim consents to see Presley and then surprises him. First, he makes a gesture of charity toward an unreliable employee, an act Presley never would have imagined; then, he unfavorably compares Presley's socialist poem "The Toilers" to the original painting that inspired it, a subtle, well-aimed criticism that mitigates some of the ignorance and brutishness Presley expected to encounter in his opponent;[69] and finally he surprises Presley by accusing him of naïveté because Presley believes that Shelgrim, as head of the corporation, has absolute power over the business of the railroad:

> You are a very young man. Control the road! Can I stop it? I can go into bankruptcy if you like. But otherwise if I run my road, as a business proposition, I can do nothing. I can *not* control it. It is a force born out of certain conditions, and I—no man—can stop it or control it. Can your Mr. Derrick stop the Wheat growing? He can burn his crop, or he can give it away, or sell it for a cent a bushel—just as I could go into bankruptcy— but otherwise his Wheat must grow. Can any one stop the Wheat? Well, then no more can I stop the Road.[70]

Like Royce, Norris makes a distinction between the body of the corporation—a soulless machine—and the person who is its head, a man with human vulnerability. Doing so emphasizes the impersonal forces at work in the conflict between the railroad and the farmers, making it more difficult to assign absolute blame to a particular person or group or to attribute conflict and misfortune to simple human greed. And since within the universe of *The Octopus* most of the farmers fall short of the democratic, agrarian ideal in the first place—in fact, characters like Derrick don't even aim for it—blame for the conflict must to some measure be apportioned to both sides and not just to the railroad men alone. Even with these complications and nuances, however, many readers have still read the novel as a depiction of virtuous farmers relentlessly and ruthlessly attacked by corporate interests. So powerful in the collective imagination is the agrarian ideal that it seems to guide us to that interpretation, regardless of the author's will.

Norris' "novel with a purpose" is certainly more subtle in its criticisms of capitalism than either Morrow's *Blood-Money* or Post's *Driven from Sea to Sea*. Like Royce, Norris saw that corporations and the individuals who run them and work for them are not the same entities. And he saw more clearly than earlier novelists that the often less-than-virtuous farmers must share some portion of the blame for the events that led up to the tragic gun battle. But it should be noted that Norris also had an advantage over previous Mussel Slough novelists: with the passing of time—two decades between the gunfight and the publication of *The Octopus*—some of the powerful feelings of injustice triggered by Mussel Slough had begun to fade, even though the railroad was still a powerful and sometimes oppressive force in California. Whereas Norris could still count on his theme to resonate powerfully with readers, he could also expect his audience to have enough perspective to appreciate his critical portrait of the bonanza wheat farmers, the men who had forsaken the agrarian ideal to gamble for enormous profits.

Like Norris, May Merrill Miller (1894–1975) brought yet another fresh interpretation of the Mussel Slough gunfight. Of all the Mussel Slough novels, *First the Blade* (1938) offers the most intimate portrait of the southern San Joaquin landscape and the domestic life led by the pioneers who settled there. Some events in the novel are drawn directly from pioneer experience, not surprising considering Miller was born and raised in Hanford and her grandparents were early California pioneers. Miller grew up, says J. L. Brown, "at a time when many of the earliest settlers were still living and usually in the mood to relate their experiences to good listeners."[71] Miller attended the University of California, the University of Minnesota, and the famous Bread Loaf Writers' Conference in Vermont, where she studied with western novelist Bernard DeVoto, presumably learning how to turn the various stories she heard growing up in Hanford into a unified work of fiction.

First the Blade is told from the perspective of a woman, Amelie Blansford, who comes of age in Missouri during the Civil War, travels to California, and there marries a man whose dreams eventually lead the couple to Mussel Slough. The real strength of this novel lies in the day-to-day portrait of pioneer living. Post and Morrow had idealized that life; Royce had alluded to it; Norris had indirectly lamented its absence. May Merrill Miller—granddaughter of pioneers and San Joaquin Valley native—gave it substance and verisimilitude, especially in domestic scenes largely left out of the previous Mussel Slough novels, which focus on male characters.

Not long after Amelie and Edwin Blansford arrive in the region, one of the local women decides to start a community garden near the headgate of the irrigation ditch the men are constructing. The idea catches on, not only because of the need for fresh vegetables, but because, says Amelie's neighbor Sigrid Halvorson, "if we go there each day to garden, […] it will help our men. They will know we have not given up. That should help more than the green things."[72] Where William Morrow had allowed one of his characters to extol the virtues of the women pioneers of Mussel Slough, Miller showed just how deeply the women were affected by the plans of the men, how the women supported them in their dreams, how they solidified their family partnerships: "Amelie knew now—she had discovered it while Sigrid and Mary stood before her—that she had leagued herself for certain with Edwin against this valley."[73]

As Amelie's husband gets more involved in the ditch company and in the dispute with the El Dorado Pacific Railroad, that partnership becomes harder for Amelie to sustain, but her commitment to her children and to the growing community of settlers help her weather the Mussel Slough crises. After the gun battle, Edwin, one of the settlers that perseveres to build a community out of the bloodshed, eventually thrives in the region. He becomes a businessman and director of a bank, and his rise to power is an example of how a business should be run; thinks a proud Amelie, "It was a good thing a bank could be small and not a great company like the El Dorado Pacific. One managed, not by agents, but by men who lived in the town, who wanted to care for their neighbors."[74] These were the neighbors who arrived in the region to realize the agrarian dream; now, after their battles—and despite their grievous losses—many were finally becoming secure.

Miller's novel risks sentimentality by evoking nostalgia for the past, a time when the region was alive with hope and settlers remade the arid landscape into an almost Edenic garden, when men and women worked together to build family and community. But the novel finally escapes sentimentality by balancing that nostalgia with gritty and detailed realism—the lack of resources, the malaria, the enervating climate. These challenges are drawn with so much detail that Miller's characters often seem more believable than the stereotypical farmers in some of the other Mussel Slough novels. And unlike these other books, *First the Blade* doesn't seize Mussel Slough as a cause but uses it as the core of a drama about idealism and constancy. The other books help us to see why laissez-faire capitalism must be checked, but this novel—with its less strident, domestic perspective—helps us to see in faithful detail what was really at stake: the ability of men and women to achieve the Jeffersonian dream together.

Scholar Richard Slotkin has written that "what is lost when history is translated into myth is the essential premise of history—the distinction of past and present."[75] The Mussel Slough novelists—William Morrow, C. C. Post, Josiah Royce, Frank Norris, and May Merrill Miller—colored history with their own desires and needs and drew upon mythic ideas to transform that history into a new story, a timeless one that sustains contemporary relevance by virtue of the values it preserves. This Mussel Slough myth has never been static. It has changed along with our culture. But the core values have remained the same: perseverance, self-reliance, and faith in justice and democracy, among them.

In an age of revisionist history and experimental fiction, the Mussel Slough novels represented in this collection—even the best of them—might seem hopelessly flawed. Some glorify the American farmer and demonize capitalist oppressors through simple stereotyping—as do *Blood-Money, Driven from Sea to Sea,* and even *The Feud of Oakfield Creek*—and others offer more complex characters but risk excesses of romance and nostalgia—as do *The Octopus* and *First the Blade.* Even so, these books still appeal to our longing for straightforward, moral story-telling that extols the loyalties of pioneer Americans. They evoke sympathy for the men and women whose values we still embrace, and they evoke indignation over their contemporaries—farmer or railroad baron—driven by love of power and wealth. And, given our uncertain times, renewing our acquaintance with these books— tempered with a healthy contemporary skepticism—is a welcome opportunity to understand better the mythic images by which Americans have measured justice. It is an opportunity to erase, at least in our imaginations, the distinction between past and present in order to celebrate enduring American principles.

Notes

1 Quoted in Owen Wister, *Roosevelt: The Story of a Friendship* (New York: Macmillan, 1923), 83.

2 Richard Maxwell Brown, *No Duty to Retreat: Violence and Values in American History and Society* (New York: Oxford University Press, 1991), 86. According to historian Richard M. Brown, the Mussel Slough shootout resulted in more deaths than any other gunfight in the region's history. He points out that the outcome—seven deaths—totaled more than twice the number of fatalities at the more famous gunfight at the O.K. Corral.

  Some accounts have put the number slain at eight. According to J. L. Brown, one settler, Edwin Haymaker, had received a superficial wound on the scalp that healed within the week. His subsequent death from pneumonia a month later caused some to include Haymaker among the Mussel Slough martyrs. J. L. Brown, *The Mussel Slough Tragedy* (1958; Lemoore, CA: Kings River Press, 2001), 72.

3 C. C. Post, *Driven from Sea to Sea; or, Just a Campin'* (Philadelphia and Chicago: Elliott and Beezley, 1884), 327–328.

4 Richard B. Rice, William A. Bullough, and Richard J. Orsi, *The Elusive Eden: A New History of California*. 3rd ed. (New York: McGraw-Hill, 2002), 235.

5 B. B. Redding and Jerome Madden, "Railroad Lands" flyer, Central Pacific Railroad Company and Southern Pacific Railroad Company, 1876.

6 These claims have become part of the Mussel Slough myth. Historian Richard J. Orsi points out that "...the railroad's prices, according to a recent survey of land transactions in the district during the 1860s and 1870s, coincided with those on unimproved lands changing hands on the even-numbered government sections, even among the squatters themselves. As early as 1874, before irrigation improvements were extensive, Henry Brewer, for example, subdivided his legal holding on the public section next to his railroad claim and sold sixty-three acres of it for $15.87 per acre." Rice, Bullough, and Orsi, 244.

7 See especially John A. Larimore, who discusses the court cases upholding the property rights of the Southern Pacific. According to Larimore, the railroad had the legal right to set prices for its land, a fact that should have been clear to Mussel Slough settlers except that they "failed to examine the evidence

closely. The railroad did make one definite statement about price and that statement in no way bound the company to any particular figure: 'When lands are ready to be sold, the Company sends a man...skilled in determining its true market value....His report is examined, and if found correct, a price is established....Further, there is but one price...that fixed by the Company.'" John A. Larimore, "Legal Questions Arising from the Mussel Slough Land Dispute" (*Southern California Quarterly* 58.1 [1976]: 75–94), 92.

8 J. L. Brown, *The Mussel Slough Tragedy,* 88.

9 Other settlers were also indicted but eluded capture, most notably Thomas Jefferson McQuiddy, a former Confederate cavalry officer who became the Settlers' League president and militia commander. Rice, Bullough, and Orsi, 241, 251–252.

10 Henry Nash Smith, *Virgin Land: The American West as Symbol and Myth* (Cambridge, MA: Harvard University Press, 1950), vii.

11 Some of these views can themselves become nearly mythical in their appeal. Historian Patricia Nelson Limerick has pointed out the tenacity in the public mind—despite the dissent of later historians—of Frederick Jackson Turner's idea that the frontier had "closed" once the West achieved a particular population threshold, thus marking a watershed moment, at least in Turner's version of western history. Patricia Nelson Limerick, *The Legacy of Conquest: The Unbroken Past of the American West* (New York: W. W. Norton, 1987), 31.

12 Or, as Richard Slotkin elaborates, myth "does not argue its ideology. It projects models of good or heroic behavior that reinforce the values of ideology, and affirm as good the distribution of authority and power that ideology rationalizes." Richard Slotkin, *The Fatal Environment: The Myth of the Frontier in the Age of Industrialization, 1800–1890* (New York: Atheneum, 1985), 19. Slotkin sees the Frontier Myth as the most enduring American myth, valorizing individualism, self-reliance, and Manifest Destiny. As such, it stands behind even the agrarian myth of virtuous yeoman farmers because the new lands of the West represent not only land needed for expansion of an agrarian republic but "a Frontier which promises complete felicity, the satisfaction of all demands, and the reconciliation of all contradictions." Slotkin, 70.

13 R. M. Brown, 72. Brown cites Ed Bartholomew as typical of historians who hold this point of view.

14 William L. Preston, *Vanishing Landscapes: Land and Life in the Tulare Lake Basin* (Berkeley: University of California Press, 1981), 14.

15 Gerald Haslam, *The Other California* (Santa Barbara: Capra Press, 1990), 30.

16 Ibid., 39.

17 Wallace Smith, *Garden of the Sun: A History of the San Joaquin Valley* (Los Angeles: Lymanhouse, 1939), 7. Says Smith, "The warlike Nutunutu lived between Cross Creek and Kings River and most of them congregated in the vicinity of Armona, Hanford, and Kingston; this territory was then a mass of swamps, sloughs, and overflow lands."

18 Thomas Jefferson Mayfield, *Indian Summer: Traditional Life Among the Choinumne Indians of California's San Joaquin Valley* (Berkeley: Heyday Books, 1993), 75.

19 Preston, 33.

20 Ibid., 46.

21 Ibid., 55.

22 Smith, 109.

23 Andro Linklater, *Measuring America: How an Untamed Wilderness Shaped the United States and Fulfilled the Promise of Democracy* (New York: Walker, 2002), 221.

24 Ibid., 222.

25 Despite the precision with which land could be surveyed, however, the process of conveying property granted to the railroads often took years, which thereby generated additional disputes between settlers and railroads. According to legal scholar David J. Bederman, "Since several years might elapse between a grant to the railroad and its construction, or between establishing a building route, it was almost inevitable that settlers would come onto the land and would be unaware that they were occupying an alternate tract given to a corporation. Inconsistent and ever-changing land office procedures and rules often delayed surveys, allowed the railroads to postpone selections of land, and so rendered settlement claims invalid." David J. Bederman, "The Imagery of Injustice at Mussel Slough: Railroad Land Grants, Corporation Law, and the 'Great Conglomerate West'" (*Western Legal History* 1.2 [1988]: 237–269), 249.

26 Redding and Madden.

27 May Merrill Miller, *First the Blade* (New York: Knopf, 1938), 382.

28 Preston, 90.

29 According to Orsi, "The Mussel Slough settlers actually included many groups, from honest farmers caught in the web of contradictory land policies to the land sharks haunting all American frontiers." Rice, Bullough, and Orsi, 238.

30 In its own words, the Settlers' League "was formed for but one purpose, and that purpose was, to enable us to present against the money power arrayed against us by the railroad an opposition which it is impossible for us to do as individuals." Settlers' Committee, *The Struggle of the Mussel Slough Settlers for Their Homes! An Appeal to the People*, pamphlet (Visalia: Delta Printing Establishment, 1880), 31.

31 Ibid., 30.

32 William Conlogue says this pamphlet was consciously designed to arouse sympathy for the farmers partly by sustaining "the myth of the poor farmer always battling the soulless corporation at a disadvantage." William Conlogue,

"Farmer's Rhetoric of Defense: California Settlers Versus the Southern Pacific Railroad" (*California History* 78.1 [1999]: 40–55; 73–76), 54–55.

33 Thomas Jefferson, *Notes on the State of Virginia*, ed. William Peden (New York: W. W. Norton, 1954), 164–165.

34 Linklater, 72–73.

35 Mary E. Chambers, "Pioneers in Mussel Slough: A Lady's Experience," *Visalia Weekly Delta*, 4 June 1880.

36 "Railroad Robbers," *San Francisco Chronicle*, 24 August 1879.

37 William C. Morrow, *Blood-Money* (San Francisco: F. J. Walker, 1882), 127–128.

38 Jefferson, 165.

39 James Porteous patented his first scraper in 1882, an improvement on the buckboard scraper, which was essentially a board drawn in an upright position to scrape and push soil. This upright piece had a tailboard attached that swung upward to dump the load. Porteous' creation was a C-shaped machine that had a blade along the bottom. It scooped dirt as it was pulled along but, unlike the buck scraper, this machine rode on runners and could be tilted to more easily dump the soil. American Society of Mechanical Engineers, "The Fresno Scraper" (Fresno, CA: American Society of Mechanical Engineers, 1991), 2.

40 According to Daniel Lindley, Huntington established a "general business theory that if a buyer protested loudly but still paid the asking price, the seller was charging all that the market could bear and therefore obeying the basic law of laissez-faire capitalism." Daniel Lindley, *Ambrose Bierce Takes on the Railroad: The Journalist as Muckraker and Cynic* (Westport, CT: Praeger, 1999), 61–62.

41 Quoted by William Deverall, *Railroad Crossing: Californians and the Railroad, 1850–1910* (Berkeley: University of California Press, 1994), 239.

42 Stuart Daggett quotes from Stanford's speech as partial illustration that the Southern Pacific had "acknowledged no duties other than those generally incumbent upon private business." *Chapters on the History of the Southern Pacific* (1922; New York: Augustus M. Kelley, 1966), 239.

43 Jack Sullivan, ed., *Penguin Encyclopedia of Horror and the Supernatural* (New York: Viking, 1986), 293.

44 J. L. Brown, "More Fictional Memorials to Mussel Slough," (*Pacific Historical Review* 26 [1957]: 373–376), 373.

45 Morrow, 11.

46 Ibid., 77.

47 Ibid., 150.

48 John Storer and Henry Brewer were partners holding a railroad section adjacent to Brewer's homestead where the historical gunfight took place. When the incident occurred, the marshal was actually seeking to evict Brewer

and Storer from their property in favor of Walter Crow, who had bought that land from the railroad. See J. L. Brown, *The Mussel Slough Tragedy*, 62.

49 Gordon W. Clarke, "A Significant Memorial to Mussel Slough" (*Pacific Historical Review* 18 [1949], 501–504), 501–502.

50 Post, 37.

51 The reputation of Walter Crow is one of the most interesting of all the persons involved in the Mussel Slough drama. After the tragedy, it was thought that Crow (as well as Mills Hartt) was a deputy marshal. But according to J. L. Brown, no evidence has been found in either the National Archives or in contemporary newspaper accounts to support the idea that Hartt or Crow were deputies. (J. L. Brown, *The Mussel Slough Tragedy*, 77.) Brown also points out that the misconception is reflected in the language of the state historical marker erected on the site: "Here on May 11, 1880, during a dispute over land titles between settlers and railroad, a fight broke out in which seven men—two deputy U.S. marshals and five ranchers lost their lives. The legal struggle over titles was finally settled by a compromise." California State Office of Historic Preservation, Landmark Number 245.

52 Post, 305.

53 John Clendenning, *The Life and Thought of Josiah Royce* (Madison: University of Wisconsin Press, 1985), 155.

54 So Royce described the book in a letter to editor Horace Elisha Scudder, September 25, 1886. John Clendenning, ed., *The Letters of Josiah Royce* (Chicago: University of Chicago Press, 1970), 202.

55 Clendenning notes that "a similar feud broke out in that area during the 1870s when a San Francisco lawyer, H. W. Carpentier, who had acquired a large part of El Sobrante de Castro, instituted suits of ejectment against squatters who claimed that they were living on public land." Clendenning, 159.

56 Irving McKee, "Notable Memorial to Mussel Slough" (*Pacific Historical Review*, 17 [1948]: 19–27), 24.

57 Josiah Royce, *The Feud of Oakfield Creek: A Novel of California Life* (Boston: Houghton, Mifflin, 1887), 465–466.

58 Ibid., 258.

59 See Walter Benn Michaels for a full discussion of literary depictions of the ontology of corporations and the legal theories supporting them. Walter Benn Michaels, "Frank Norris, Josiah Royce and the Ontology of Corporations," in *American Literary Landscapes: The Fiction and the Fact*, Ian F. Bell and D. K. Adams, eds. (London and New York: Vision Press and St. Martin's Press, 1989), 122–151.

60 Frank Norris, "The Novel with a 'Purpose,'" in *The Responsibilities of the Novelist and Other Literary Essays* (1903; New York: Haskell House, 1969, 25–33), 26, 27.

61 Ronald E. Martin argues that Norris tended to hold onto ideas uncritically and absolutely, a tendency that translated into an unreflective and naïve omniscience in his fiction. Ronald E. Martin, *American Literature and the Universe of Force* (Durham, NC: Duke University Press, 1981), 147.

62 Frank Norris, *The Octopus: A Story of California* (1901; New York: Penguin, 1986), 131.

63 Ibid., 64–65.

64 Ibid., 298.

65 Ibid., 274.

66 Ibid., 25.

67 Ibid., 467–68.

68 Ibid., 570.

69 Presley's poem is meant to recall Edwin Markham's immensely lucrative 1899 poem "The Man with the Hoe," which was inspired by his viewing of a painting by Millet owned by the Crocker family and which protested the exploitation of labor. James D. Hart, *A Companion to California* (New York: Oxford University Press, 1978), 260.

70 Norris, *The Octopus*, 576.

71 J. L. Brown, "More Fictional Memorials to Mussel Slough," 375.

72 Miller, 438.

73 Ibid., 438.

74 Ibid., 622.

75 Slotkin, 24.

Overlaid with a Sheen of Gold

Mussel Slough farmers staked their livelihood on an ambitious dream: making cheap desert land bloom with plenty. Sometimes these pioneers were dismayed by the initial disparity between their images of prosperous family farms and the rough everyday brutality of early pioneer life in the southern San Joaquin Valley. But as drawn by the Mussel Slough novelists, these characters continued to feel keenly their dream of success, a dream that seemed to them not only attainable but nearly assured. The railroad was offering its land to settlers at low costs, and the local watershed could provide enough Sierra snowmelt to water thousands of acres, once that resource was harnessed. All that was needed was dedication to the vision and a heavy investment of leadership and labor. Bonanza wheat farmers like Norris' Magnus Derrick and civic-minded visionaries like May Merrill Miller's Edwin Blansford provided the leadership; humbler men like William Morrow's John Graham and C. C. Post's Erastus Hemmingway provided the labor.

In Mussel Slough fiction, this golden promise of agricultural bounty also found symbols in the vast, flower-carpeted landscapes that briefly marked the San Joaquin's spring and in the initial booming yields of dry-land wheat farming. But for some characters—dispirited by the parched land, the enervating winds, and the wicked tule fogs that closed out the sun and heightened a foreboding sense of isolation—such transient symbols never inspired the same confident optimism. No matter how each character reacted to them, though, the almost insurmountable odds testing the pioneers became a crucial part of the Mussel Slough story. Overcoming obstacles made winning agrarian independence that much sweeter. So, too, the material well-being represented by family farms, small towns, and ever-more-efficient networks of transportation. This was the American dream planted into California's soil.

Depicting the pioneer men and women with great respect, Mussel Slough novelists underscored their admirable resilience and their unselfish willingness to sacrifice for friends and family. Against these pioneers, writers like Morrow and Post often set members of the capitalist class, caricatures of heartless men whose indifference to the plight of poorer individuals begins to look not merely uncaring and selfish, but disturbingly un-American. The capitalists' lust for power and wealth obstructs the more humble dreams of the poorer, more virtuous settlers so much that it even threatens the heart of the rural democracy valorized in these novels. Other characterizations, like those offered by Norris and Miller, depicted farmers and capitalists alike as susceptible to temptation, greed, and bad judgment. But always at the heart of the tales is the epic struggle over land and the depressing circumstances of the overmatched Mussel Slough pioneers—men and women just too stubborn to quit.

In this section, hard work, perseverance, and simple honesty characterize the Mussel Slough pioneers.

May Merrill Miller
"The Valley Far Away"

Transplanted Southerner Amelie Blansford, the main character of May Merrill Miller's First the Blade, *is comfortably settled with her husband Edwin on the Santa Clara farm belonging to Edwin's family. After Edwin travels to the Mussel Slough district to help an ailing brother, he becomes enthusiastic about moving his family to the southern San Joaquin and building a new life. He realizes this is his chance to "do something new." His own imagination full of dreams, he describes the valley from the vantage of Pacheco Pass, attempting to fire Amelie's excitement and make it burn as brightly as his own. For Amelie, "It was almost like being courted all over again."*

When Edwin came home, it was a warm night in April. How brown and ruddy and young he looked!—almost the same as that first time Amelie had met him, the day of the Blansford barbecue when he had returned from his two years of wandering. And he was glad to see her. He put his arms about her and held her to him until she laughed and asked him to let her go.

But he would not. It was almost like being courted all over again. He put his hand on her cheeks and turned her head. "I almost forgot what you looked like, Amelie. Next time you'll have to give me a picture."

"Oh, I hope there won't be any next time. I've been so lonely for you," she said. And then, as she saw a shadow cross his face, she added: "Tell me about it."

He blew out the lamp.

"Let's go outside," he said; "it's too warm here."

They went out on the side porch and sat on the steps, Edwin leaning his head against Amelie's knees.

Below them lay the square of shadows that was Amelie's garden, the old pear tree lifting its dark plume of shadow higher than the rest. Beneath it opened roses dotted the darkness, their fragrance a part of the night. Amelie sighed with happiness as she looked down upon them. Tomorrow she would show Edwin how much everything had grown this spring and how well she had cultivated the ground.

He was turning away from her now, but she kept her arm against the lean hard curve of his back as he sat with his chin in his hands.

"Amelie, you should have seen what I have seen. I thought of you and your little garden patch when I was on the road. Especially on the third day, when I reached the pass of the Pacheco. One moment I was riding between the higher hills, climbing, not knowing the way, the next—Amelie, I stood looking down from that high open place with the whole valley of the San Joaquin at my feet....It is a gigantic level valley, Amelie, between two long strips of mountains. Far across from me were the Sierras—three hundred miles I must have seen of those great blue mountains, with snow separating them from the sky. And between the Sierras and myself this wide valley....Oh, Amelie, you should have seen the flowers."

He flung out his hands as if, thought Amelie, he would push her own garden away—a child's toy too small to be bothered with, yet to be stumbled over.

"There wasn't anything regular, like your little plots of posies, but you could look away and see the hills at the foot of the snow peaks all poppies, each one lower than the rest until they spilled onto the floor of the valley—a whole range of poppies shining in the sun. And then there were other flowers. Some the color of cream, Amelie. Those were the marguerites, and others were lavender, the wild hyacinths, and there were rosy Indian paintbrushes and white sand lilies and yellow buttercups and blue lupines and the blue and pink larkspur they say will kill the cattle. And on the hills, Amelie, and in the valley too, each color was separate in great patches, miles and miles spreading away from you, with a spot of pink here and blue there and white beyond, each distinct except at the very foot of the Sierras, because your eyes could not keep so many colors separate so far away.

"And when I started riding down the Pacheco into the valley—I tell you, there is no place in the world where grasses grow like that. On my horse, Amelie, the wild oats were shoulder-high...and the alfilaria—" she thought of the ferny grass that sometimes came to her shoe-tops—"it reached to my stirrups, so thick I often had to go round it.

"Coming down through the Pacheco, I saw several deer and one bear looking so surprised at me I just laughed and watched him go away. And farther west, on the floor of the valley, where it was so quiet except for the bees buzzing over the flowers, I thought I heard something—I was not sure. I looked to the north and saw nothing, I looked to the west, I looked to the south, and there was a patch of gray and pure white—a herd of antelope, three hundred there must have been, and every one standing still, staring at my horse and at me. They are small, Amelie, with tiny white feet and horns not like a deer's, but sort of a question—just beginning. And they just stood looking at me with their big black eyes, hundreds of black eyes in the gray, eyes larger than any doe's—and them so small. And not a sound, not a sound—and their eyes so still.

"Then they started to run. That was what I had heard. The grass was shorter where they fled across it; their hoofs were so small and the grass so soft you might have missed it, you might not have heard them, you might not have seen them—and when they were gone, you could not believe that they had been....I was riding all alone...."

He was silent. Amelie too could hear the small hoof-beats on the new grass.

"How could you find your way?"

He laughed. "You couldn't get lost, Amelie. That valley was a sea of grass and wild flowers, and the mountains the shore line to guide you, the lower ones at the west behind me and the high ones to the east, and myself going to the south, and then eastward to King's River and Tulare Lake.

"After several days going to the south, when I reached Kings Crossing, the last stage station at the river, Martin had told me to look for a huge sycamore tree, east of the river, out on the plains. 'The lone sycamore,' they call it. It is a landmark for everyone. It has two trunks and is larger than most, and you can see it for miles, there are no others near by. So I located it and rode toward it. Think of it, Amelie, almost three hundred miles from here I found my way to one tree....Then I went still farther south to Tulare Lake, where the stockmen live along the river.

"You have seen Tulare Lake on every map of California, Amelie, down the middle of the San Joaquin, a blue bag tied and hanging by a string. The string is green when you come to it, a line of willows along the river of the Kings.

"That is where the stockmen live; Martin was there. He was with an old stockman they call Uncle Amos Jordan, who lives in an old adobe built like Father's. Uncle Amos was the first man to settle there; a trader and explorer named Jedediah Smith went through and Hudson Bay trappers earlier than that, but they took out beaver and otter skins and did not stay; pigs they were, Amelie, there isn't a beaver left. There are only a handful of stockmen there at the lake now, about a dozen. There isn't a town, only the trading post at Kings Crossing, except Visalia. They have to go to Stockton with four-horse wagons each summer and bring back a year's supplies. But they have plenty of everything—all they need. They live like lords."

◆

John Muir
"THE RANGE OF LIGHT"
FROM *MOUNTAINS OF CALIFORNIA*, 1894

Making your way through the mazes of the Coast Range to the summit of any of the inner peaks or passes opposite San Francisco, in the clear springtime, the grandest and most telling of all California landscapes is outspread before you. At your feet lies the great Central Valley glowing golden in the sunshine, extending north and south farther than the eye can reach, one smooth, flowery, lake-like bed of fertile soil. Along its eastern margin rises the mighty Sierra, miles in height, reposing like a smooth, cumulus cloud in the sunny sky, and so gloriously colored, and so luminous, it seems to be not clothed with light, but wholly composed of it, like the wall of some celestial city. Along the top, and extending a good way down, you see a pale, pearl-gray belt of snow; and below it a belt of blue and dark purple, marking the extension of the forests; and along the base of the range a broad belt of rose-purple and yellow, where lie the miner's goldfields and the foot-hill gardens. All these colored belts blending smoothly make a wall of light ineffably fine, and as beautiful as a rainbow, yet firm as adamant.

When I first enjoyed this superb view, one glowing April day, from the summit of the Pacheco Pass, the Central Valley, but little trampled or plowed as yet, was one furred, rich sheet of golden compositæ, and the luminous wall of the mountains shone in all its glory. Then it seemed to me the Sierra should be called not the Nevada, or Snowy Range, but the Range of Light.

May Merrill Miller
"With Patience It Must Be Made"

Seasons change in the San Joaquin Valley. When Amelie Blansford—in the company of her husband and family—first beholds the vast landscape from the vantage of Pacheco Pass, the scene contrasts markedly with the one described by her husband when he stood near the same spot. After spending a night near the pass and enjoying the memorable hospitality offered at a vaquero rodeo, Amelie is unprepared for the disappointment she feels when she first beholds the Central Valley, marked by "this ugliness that breathed off diabolic heat one could see." Her frustration becomes even keener as she travels through the desolate valley landscape and realizes how great a challenge she and her family have undertaken, especially as she learns about the improbable schemes to lay out local irrigation ditches as part of the overall plan to create a community of small family farms.

A fter a few paces Edwin stopped the horses.

"This is the summit," he said. "There is the San Joaquin Valley."

For a moment Amelie could not believe it. She moistened her lips in numb fright. She was tricked, as the Negroes had said when they thought they had been bewitched.

Nothing but barren brown vastness, not a tree, not a blade of green...how far...forever...down at their feet, so far away, yet near... an ugly, barren, desolate unending expanse of brown valley.

"It's so wide," Edwin was saying, "they're hard to see, for all the heat waves, but the mountains are there across from us."

She looked to the sky where the tall mountains should be. There were no mountains at all....Finally she saw them, a low blue hurdle. So far...with something unseen yet seen, iridescent, twirling swirls shimmering between...and beyond them, only if you strained to see, that far-off edge of palest blue, an almost imagined line of white between it and the sky.

"But the flowers," Amelie cried, "and the tall grasses!"

"Why, Amelie," he said, "you couldn't expect the wild flowers this time of the year."

Of course not....

She told herself she had been foolish, but her eyes filled, hidden by her bonnet. The way he had said it—as if this valley were not as others. She had never forgotten that night on the porch when his back was a lean hard curve under her hand and he had looked scornfully down upon her own roses dotting the dark, telling her of the miracle of a whole valley of flowers.

"When do they bloom?" she asked faintly.

"Oh, if it's a wet winter, in February or early March. Dry years, they tell me, there's scarcely any."

"And how long do they bloom?"

He was lifting the reins.

"Oh, good years, about two weeks—maybe a little longer."

Amelie looked straight ahead. After all, it was her own fault, being so stupid. Only the trip had been long—bad enough to leave home and her garden, but at least she thought she was coming to beauty, not barrenness, not this ugliness that breathed off diabolic heat one could see.[...]

Two days later they came to Kings Crossing. The green ribbon they had been seeing for a day and a half was near now, a quiet river bordered with willows, with a ferryboat moored ready for their crossing.

"Just think," Edwin said, looking back at the blue mountains to the east, "all this water comes from the Sierras."

Amelie wanted to laugh and cry out: "What for?" Of what use was this placid river with here and there a stagnant branch of black slough, a river with no perceptible value save to cut this ugly barren land in two?

On the bank above this river crossing was the town that would be theirs. It formed an elbow of shacks with upright fronts where the river turned. Three saloons. Two stores. A hotel, the only two-story building in the place. In front of the largest store a stage was standing; it was the first one Amelie had seen, although they had stopped once before at a station, a house and barn alone on the plain; Edwin had told her there were more of them, a day's journey apart. This stage could carry fourteen passengers, Edwin told her proudly, and express besides. Just under the top and over the doors and windows was lettered: "San Francisco, Visalia, Los Angeles, Yuma, El Paso, Ft. Smith, St. Louis." Amelie ached at this last name and the thought that this bead of a stage and others like it were strung along a road leading at last to a white house on a green hill she had known. Some people could leave this valley, then...but for herself she held no such hope, only an increasing knowledge of its arid length and breadth and the memory of the wild horses lost beneath the pass of the Pacheco. She looked enviously at the portmanteau of one of the gentlemen passengers, flushing at the sight of her own sprawly carpet-bag bulging with diapers.

"Come inside, Amelie." Edwin led her into the store. She met the proprietor, Albert Weinstein, a broad and beaming Jew, and his son, Eli. She looked around the shelves—cans of sardines, oysters, jars of Leibig's extract, shotgun shells, plug tobacco, a few bolts of cloth, a string of garlic and one of chili peppers hanging on a nail. Lucy discovered, jumping delightedly, some peppermint lozenges in a jar.

"They're pretty old, Mrs. Blansford. The Indians buy them."

But Amelie, sniffing the stale sweetness, bought some for Lucy, and soon Lucy was prancing happily with the wonted mound of bee-stung upper lip.

Upon the floor stood sacks of white beans, sacks of butter beans, sacks of rice, barrels of flour, and a few single plows. Edwin touched one of the shares with his foot.

"They're for the Sandlappers, Mr. Blansford," Albert told him. "You'd be surprised to know how many are coming in."

"Sandlappers?" Edwin repeated stupidly, as if Albert were making sport of him.

Albert laughed apologetically. "I forgot, Mr. Blansford. There were a few families drifted down here last fall, but mostly they started coming last spring after your trip. You see," he included Amelie, "they're settlers, Mrs. Blansford, dry farmers coming in here to settle on the railroad land. We call them Sandlappers because they are all so poor and settling on such a small patch of ground—we've named them after a scrawny little bird you'll be seeing on the plains, always sticking its beak in the sand, scratching for food and finding next to nothing."

Edwin stood silent. Amelie knew by his face that he was not liking the news he was hearing, but Albert, glad of company, kept on:

"We wonder every time we see one of them pulling up here in his wagon, asking about plows and seed, how he expects to live."

"That's what we all wonder," young Mr. Eli interrupted. "One man with a family and a single plow and a sack of barley sets himself down on a half section. It would cost him two thousand dollars to bring in fence for a single acre—most of them are lucky if they have a couple of hundred for a grub stake. And after they get their little patch of barley planted they've got to figure how to keep the cattle from trampling it down. You know yourself, Mr. Blansford, the stockmen have had this valley to themselves too long to expect them to keep herds away from scattered fields. But even if they did, we have so many dry years there's no counting on a crop. Now they tell me the Sandlappers have started some wild scheme of digging a ditch to get river water to their land—it will take that handful of folks forever, with no money and only picks and shovels to dig with. They're scratching gravel all right. Sandlapper's a good name for them."

"But railroad land—I don't understand."

"The El Dorado Pacific's '67 survey, Mr. Blansford. It goes right through this valley—a twenty-mile strip, ten miles on either side of the right of way, every odd-numbered section."

"But the El Dorado Pacific's never laid a tie in all this time," Edwin objected. "That map was laid out in the overland excitement. The El Dorado Pacific will never come through here—it's stock country. That's all it ever can be."

"I know, but the El Dorado Pacific's been advertising, especially up Stockton way—you'd be surprised how many poor devils are coming into the valley, even if they can't get title until the railroad's completed, if ever."

Outside, Edwin sought the dodger pasted near the door which young Mr. Eli indicated. "The El Dorado Pacific's bait for Sandlappers," he laughed.

"Well, I'll be damned," Edwin whispered, reading: "'Land covered with timber $5.00 per acre, pine $10.00.'...God knows there's no timber in this valley. 'Most is offered at $2.50...price not to be increased on account of any improvements which the settler may have made...title to be given when patents are issued and the road completed.'...We will file on a homestead, Amelie—we don't have to buy ours from any railroad drawn on paper. I want my land now."

Back in the wagon they left the river behind, but it soon curved, straightening again to make a green line parallel to their own course, which lay south again over the dusty level plain and the thin beaten grasses.

In the late afternoon Amelie noticed a slight change on the horizon, which for days now had been a straight unbroken line. This looked like a single sagebrush, low and round.

Edwin exclaimed: "Now we are there, almost. It is the lone sycamore, Amelie, the only tree on the plains for miles and miles. I found Martin by it. It's the landmark for us all."

They traveled on, half an hour, an hour; the tree appeared no larger. But closer now, it became a great shadow in the twilight.

Finally the wagon was abreast of it—a very large double-trunked sycamore. Perhaps it had been two trees once, you could not tell; the two white trunks dappled with gray were together now at the base, higher, the barest separation of space between them. It was the largest sycamore Amelie had ever seen. In its shadow cattle rested. In all this land, save for the low line of river willows, only one tree. And by it one steered one's course in this roadless plain.

"We will soon be at the Jordans'," Edwin said, turning the horses west.

It was almost dark when the line of river willows became actual again so that Amelie could mark the curved outlines of single trees.

"We are not far from the lake," Edwin said, "but it's too dark to see it."

A little farther, suddenly the lights of a house. Dogs running barking to meet them.

"Get down, Amelie."

Edwin lifted her in his arms over the high wheel.

Upon the ground she looked back. She could still see the giant tree against the sky, with a first star appearing.

C. C. Post
"Desolation"

In Driven from Sea to Sea; or, Just a Campin' C. C. Post ranges well beyond events at Mussel Slough in order to indict the disinterested forces of capital that shaped business practices—and ruined lives—throughout California. As the novel unfolds, Erastus Hemmingway's legal guardian, John Parsons, watches his small but prosperous farm disappear beneath a river of mud created by hydraulic mining operations. Soon after, Erastus leaves his adopted family to seek fortune in the sparsely populated Mussel Slough district, where he seeks to escape the ubiquitous forces of unchecked capitalism and realize his own dream of self-sufficiency and personal independence. Drawn partly by cheap railroad land, he's willing to depend upon his own strength of character to succeed. He knows he'll have to struggle against the herdsmen who already live there, and he's also daunted by "the Herculean task of digging an irrigating ditch upwards of twenty miles long." But the chance to "convert a desert into a garden" is just too good to miss.

Erastus was six days in making the journey to Mussel Slough, and a desolate looking country he found it.

For miles and miles, at this season of the year, not a green thing appeared upon which to fasten the smallest hope of ever changing the waste into fertile fields of grass and grain.

The settlers already there seemed upon the verge of starvation. But three or four inches of rain fell during the entire year, and for months at a time the soil was unmoistened even by dew. Those who possessed a little money when they came, had expended it in futile efforts to produce a crop, and all were now dependent for the means of subsistence upon small patches of ground near the lake, distant in many instances from four to seven miles from their claims.

Even these patches had to be constantly guarded from droves of ravenous and half wild cattle belonging to the herdsmen who gave them little attention, and who were illy disposed toward any attempts at inclosing or cultivating the land which, although seemingly little better than a desert, at certain periods of the year produced a thin growth of wild alfalfa upon which their stock fed, being in the main driven to better pastures as the dry season advanced.

These patches of ground were made fertile by their nearness to Lake Tulare, and by being but little above the level of its waters.

Veritable oases in the desert these spots seemed, and upon them the settlers raised the few bushels of corn and beans and vegetables which formed their sole means of subsistence while prosecuting the work of redeeming their claims by the herculean task of digging an irrigating ditch upwards of twenty miles long, by means of which they were to obtain water from the river above them, and convert the desert into a garden.

But if these oases furnished garden spots for the settlers they were also desired by the herdsmen, for a few of whose cattle they supplied pasturage the year round, and being without the means of fencing them in, the protection of their little crops meant a constant watch upon the cattle, and one which consumed the entire time of some member of each family.

Owing to the lack of feed, but few were able to keep teams, and that they continued the unequal contest for their homes can only be understood when it is known that of all the rich farming lands of the State, not an acre remained for pre-emption or purchase except at second-hand, and as a rule, in large bodies, being held by corporations or individuals who claimed it under pretended grants from Spain or Mexico, given before California was ceded to the United States, or by act of Congress since that time. So that this barren, sandy plain offered the only hope for poor men in California of obtaining a portion of the inheritance of the race.

Besides, they had confidence that, once irrigated, it would produce abundantly, and well repay all their labors by future yields of fruit and grain.

All efforts to induce men with capital to invest in the enterprise of cutting the ditch, and depending upon the sale of water privileges for reimbursements, had failed,—the idea that any amount of water could render the sand of the plains fertile being scouted as visionary, the land being judged not worth paying taxes upon,—and the settlers had undertaken the task themselves, all unaided, and had been two years at work on the main ditch when Erastus Hemmingway arrived in the community.

So dreary and forbidding was the outlook that he felt tempted to leave again immediately, but knowing that no land remained open for pre-emption elsewhere in the State, at last decided to stay and cast his lot with those who were so manfully struggling to overcome the difficulties by which they were surrounded.

Guided in part by the advice of such acquaintances as he had made since his arrival, he located a claim of one hundred and sixty acres, and made arrangements to live for a time in the family of a settler who was on a claim adjoining his own, agreeing to pay a small sum weekly for such food and accommodations as they could offer.

Of the half dozen men who accompanied Erastus to the Slough, not one had the hardihood to remain. All were too much discouraged by the outlook, and either returned to the old neighborhood or sought places for rent in other portions of the country.

When he had staked out his claim, Erastus hitched up and drove across the country until he found pasturage, and a rancher who was willing to let the colts run with his own stock until such time as the light rains, which might be expected to fall a few months later, should revive the seemingly dead grass of the Mussel Slough country. He then returned to the Slough on foot, and went to work with his fellow settlers upon the ditch, which was their only hope.

For weeks and months he worked in company with these men, many of whom had worked through all the weeks and months of the two previous years; ill-fed—often without bread of any kind for long periods at a time, sleeping upon the ground almost as frequently as in a bed, working at night as well as by day, their families camping in wretched little huts at the lake watching the patches of vegetables and corn upon which their very existence depended.

When the rain came and vegetation started up, the colts were brought down from their pasture and made to do a portion of labor on the ditch; their young master taking the best care of them possible under the circumstances.

May Merrill Miller
"Mists of Laguna De Tache"

Thick, cottony tule fog became familiar to long-term Mussel Slough residents. Named for the rushes that grow in marshland throughout the Central Valley, tule fog forms a bone-chilling, gray blanket that covers valley lowlands when high humidity combines with low temperatures and still air. To Amelie Blansford, the heavy dankness of the fog is unsettling. After moving into what she hopes will be just a temporary home—a cabin set by a putrid slough—Amelie struggles to maintain her cheerfulness despite the clammy interior of the one-room cabin situated too close to the foggy slough ever to dry out. The chill never dissipates and soon Amelie realizes her worst fear when her infant daughter, Helen, develops chills and a fever. To Amelie, it almost feels like the Mussel Slough landscape has launched a personal assault on her and her family, as if the land itself is the main antagonist against which she and the other pioneers must test their will.

Edwin apologized for the cabin by the slough the day after. "It's a damp place here; Uncle Amos would be glad for you to stay with them—but I know how you feel and we'll be back with the lumber for our own house before you know it."

She did not mind when he said it this time. She was grateful for privacy after weeks of the wagon and the watchful hospitality of the Jordans.

"Oh, I'm so glad to be here and have the children alone. It really isn't more than a mile to the ranch house. I can walk it easily.

"Only, Edwin," she added, "I know you can't hurry much coming back from Stockton with such a heavy load—but come as soon as you can. I'm worried about Helen; she's so cross and it isn't like her at all."

Edwin went over to the baby's basket and looked down upon her, his arms around Amelie's shoulders.

Helen's face, framed in the pointed contrary wisps of hair which would not curl, was thinner than when her basket had lain on the sunny porch above Amelie's garden, but when she saw her father she lifted her arms to him and rewarded his attention with her four-toothed welcome. She laughed aloud and Edwin chuckled with her.

"Shucks, she'll be all right, Amelie—it's just the long trip."

Amelie sighed, hoping he was right.

"Well, keep Jerry with you," Edwin warned when he was finally ready to start, tying up the young shepherd dog the Jordans had given them, "and go over to Uncle Amos's if you get worried, and be sure and make a fire if you get cold."

"But it's so nice and sunny."

"Indian summer." He looked at the sky. "It can't last forever."

She watched them drive away in the empty wagon. Edwin was taking Zeke; he said it was better not to travel alone and Zeke could help with the loading.

How long one could see them—how large the wagon looked, crawling across the dry plains toward the sycamore, and even past it, until it was lost in the heat swirls ascending in continual motion from the still brown land!

Amelie shrugged at the remembrance of Edwin's warning: this burning earth at the end of summer could never know cold again. But when she went into the cabin, still blinded by the sun outside, the one room was dark and clammy. That was because the cabin was in a swale so close to the foggy slough, never really getting dried out, Edwin said. Well, they wouldn't be here long.

The wagon had been so crowded, yet when Amelie looked around the cabin now she was dismayed to see how few things they had brought after all. Their own New Improved Franconia stove Edwin had pushed in a corner, saying it would be best to use the small rusty stove already set up for the few weeks they would be here in this cabin. A wooden box nailed on the wall, the only shelf, held most of Amelie's dwindling supply of groceries. A square table of split willow logs, Amelie's leather trunk, the boxes of blankets, the children's mattresses and Helen's basket, one cane rocking-chair, the mahogany bureau with the mirror not yet set back upon it, looked lost and lonely, but the bed that was the replica of the Emperor Napoleon's, set up in one corner of the cabin, not only almost filled but dominated it.

That afternoon Amelie walked along the slough with Roger and Lucy. It reached almost to their doorstep, a withered arm of the river, an unamputated wound of black water. Willows grew here, but not so thick, so soft, as along the flowing stream—here their roots bent and twisted in enlarged joints above the low stagnant water.

The stale smell of it assailed Amelie's nostrils.

"This is a nasty place," she said.

She made Roger and Lucy promise not to descend those rotted slopes to the black slimy water. But as they turned she saw Lucy gazing speculatively toward the green algæ scum. "It looks like green meringue on boiled custard," she said, "doesn't it, Mamma?"

"Boiled custard! It's black," Roger answered in scorn.

"I mean burnt boiled custard."

But to Amelie it was six feet of water her children could drown in. She knew as they walked back to the cabin that she would have to keep her eye on Roger and Lucy every minute.

That night when Amelie lifted the lids to make the fire for supper, her hands were cold. Though the first smoke rose through the cracks almost at once and soon every line of the rusty round lids glowed in a red pattern, still she was cold.

At supper Amelie tried to feed Helen. Amelie was sorry to start her on cow's milk so suddenly, but her own was giving out much sooner than she had expected. Helen had a surprising strength now as she arched her back at the taste of the new fare. She clenched her four teeth against every offering. She looked up at her mother, trusted till now, in bitter surprise. She screamed until lines ran down from her mouth like an old lady's.

She was still hungry, Amelie knew, when she had induced her to drink all that she could. Amelie sighed. Helen's stubbornness would give way later when Helen was hungry enough, but she needed the new food now.

That night after the children were in bed Amelie sat by the lamp until, looking up, she realized there were no shades to pull over the windows. No one to look in, of course, but she found two quilts and hung them over the square-headed rusty nails fastening the window frames. Everything in the hut was rusted. It must get damp here, as Edwin had said.

For the first time Amelie was afraid.

"There isn't a thing to worry about," she told herself. "Plenty of women have stayed alone in cabins like this." Only it was the first time in her whole life; always before someone else had been in the house—Angela snoring in her room, Zeke out in the tankhouse, and if Edwin went to the lodge, he was always home by midnight.

That night Amelie slept, but she was awakened once by her own dream. From a circle of starving Indians an Indian girl clad in doe-skins was pointing an accusing finger straight at her. Then Amelie was lost, entrapped in mists enveloping her, choking in her throat. When she awoke she saw only part was dream, the rest reality, for the cabin was filled with damp. She pulled the quilt away from the window. All the world was pigeon gray. It was the fog of which Edwin had told her. "It rises from the lake," he had said.

Amelie had loved the twilight mist of the Santa Clara coming in from the sea. But not this heavy dankness wrapping the world with the stench of the stagnant slough.

When morning came, there was no sun. All day long the fog persisted and the cold. Amelie kept a fire in the stove until it was red-hot, but it was a cook-stove, not a heater, and a few feet away she and the children were cold.

Amelie read to Lucy and Roger. When Edwin had told Amelie at the last there was not room for the heavy box she had so carefully packed, she left it with her stack of *Godey's* without a word. Now she was bitter at Edwin and longed for every volume.

She read Lucy's Mother Goose until she was dizzy, and all Roger's *Chatterbox.* Finally she went to the leather trunk, from which she had thought to use nothing. She smiled when she found Mr. Abbott's *Home* and the tiny blue volume of Mr. E. A. Poe's *Complete Poems with Original Memoir* from that birthday so long ago.

That afternoon and the next day she struggled with these. *Annabel Lee* brought memories of the absent namesake, but *The Raven* was fine, doubly eerie in this cabin. Lucy and Roger liked *Home* better than Mr. Poe's verses, finding pleasure the author never intended in Mr. Abbott's accounts of disobedient girls and rude boys.

By the next day Amelie did not mind the fog, the fussing of Lucy and Roger, the whining dog, anything except Helen. If she would only eat. But she buried her head in Amelie's shoulder at the sight of the cup. As Amelie held her closer she felt the baby's hot breath on her cheek, and, listening to the quick breathing, caught a sandpaper rasping that continued.

Amelie decided to go over to the Jordans' and, wrapped in her cloak, left the cabin. But outside in the gray world—no sky, no river trees, only fog—she knew she could not find her way. If Mrs. Jordan did not come soon, Amelie would untie the dog and trust him to lead her to the ranch house, but she would not leave the children yet. She unpacked the red *Ladies' Household Guide,* but its Sickness Hints did not hint much that was helpful.

When Mrs. Jordan did come over, the sound of her step startled Amelie.

"You poor thing," Mrs. Jordan said, "alone in this fog. It's come early this year. It's hard to get used to, and I'm not yet, though I've been here close to twenty years....You'd best come back with me."

But when she saw the sleeping baby with her knees drawn up and nostrils dilating in quick breaths she said: "It's cold out there."

Amelie looked out the windows at the mists sweeping downward. She knew it was useless, but she would ask.

"Is there a doctor anywhere?"

"Yes—that is, usually—at Kings Crossing. Dr. Ennis stays there, but when Amos came back day before yesterday he said Dr. Ennis had gone to San Francisco to get bleached out—you know, he takes cocaine, and about once a year he goes up to get cured. It helps him for a while. Have you any quinine?" she asked after a moment.

"Yes, but you couldn't give a little baby like that quinine," Amelie protested.

"Oh yes, you can—mine cut their teeth on it. Chills and fever, chills and fever, that's what she has."

She showed Amelie how much to give, pinching it with a practiced finger from the yellow druggist's box and laying it out in a spoon. "Give her that when she wakes up. Keep her warm. I'll be back early in the morning."

Amelie did give Helen the powder, forcing it between her four teeth tightly clenched against it.

By night Amelie was terrified. The baby lay with gray face and blue-shadowed lips, not caring whether Amelie held her or not. Amelie heated an iron, wrapped it, and tucked it in at the foot of the basket. She tended the cook-stove but though the lids were red-hot, the baby, a few feet away, was no warmer.

Amelie did not stop to put quilts over the windows tonight. Anyone who saw this light would be welcome. But there were no visitors and no sounds save the whining of the dog tied outside and, farther off, the forlorn echoing yelps of raiding coyotes.

Toward morning, when Helen's skin seemed moist, Amelie dropped on the bed fully clothed, soon forcing herself to awaken at the hungry complaints of Roger and Lucy, to make a new fire. The cook-stove had begun to rust again; it was sweating all over, dripping red beads of moisture, witness to continuing fog. The kindling was damp. Amelie blew at the rusty teeth of the damper in front, almost baring her own teeth in hate of it.

There was no need to try to feed Helen. Amelie opened the red *Ladies' Household Guide,* studying it again and again. But it suggested terrifying possibilities and medicines Amelie did not possess.

By afternoon Amelie was glad to have Mrs. Jordan, who had come over that morning, go home. By night Helen was flushed and burning, her lips dry. She was no longer quiet, but cried out as if perplexed, her face faintly colored and twisted under contrary wisps of hair, her small fists clutching at nothing. Amelie wrung out a crash cloth in basin after basin of cool water, smoothing it back and forth over the small curved back where the tiny vertebræ whitened the loose skin like a Christmas string of popcorn.

How thin she had become in these few days in this valley! She was never like this at home.

Amelie stopped sometimes to run her hands over Helen's cramped feet and the knees drawn up so tightly, but she kept at her task, dipping water with the tin dipper, filling the basin again and again.

She prayed—not on her knees—only conversational entreaties. Her hands were busy; she dared not stop; but she gazed about the unfamiliar room filling again with fog—or was it smoke from the fire?—and past it, looking for help when there was none.

She brought the lamp closer; now Helen whistled strangely as she breathed faster and faster through her four teeth fixed in a grimace that was not a smile. Amelie gripped the lamp steadily until she had set it safely down. She would be afraid to lift it again.

Finally, when Amelie's eyelids were stinging and her hands, wringing the washcloth, numb, she saw she must get more water.

She opened the door wide into the night. She had to leave the rectangle of light cast out the open doorway to go to the end of the cabin to the pump, but the sight of the light on the ground was reassuring, even though dimmed by mists sweeping over it. Amelie tried not to look back at the great humping shadows of slough willows crouching in the heavier fog behind her. She breathed deeply in the cooler air, but only caught in her throat the dank putrid stench of the stagnant slough.

She worked the rickety pump. The handle was almost off. Up and down, up and down—only that wheezing gasp when no water is coming. In response the frogs by the slough started croaking.

There never was a white house under the oaks....

Why don't You listen? Why don't You help? I've asked You, I ask You again.... There isn't any help, even the water won't come....

There—a stream of it at last, sputtering into the bucket with a great rush, splashing over. Amelie left the pump handle in mid-air and ran toward the light.

When she ran into the cabin and looked at Helen she knew. She lifted the baby, calling her name, blowing breath into blue lips, pulling arms high—all the things she had heard—but the head with the wispy straight hair fell limply against Amelie's breast and Amelie gave up trying, holding the baby against her...rocking...rocking...holding her tighter....

She kept rocking, her teeth clenching her lower lip.

When I hold her like this I can't believe it…if I ever put her down it will be true.…

Finally she remembered Martin and the curved lounge. And Tommy.

She stood up and laid the baby down on her own bed.

"There's things to do," Ellin had said when Roger had brought Tommy home in the small wagon.

With lye soap Amelie scrubbed the table of split willow logs, wormed by sap veins, knife-scarred. Everything must be the best one could do.…She went out for fresh water, no longer afraid of the night. She found a clean sheet…Hester and the chest in the room under the ridgepole…only one must not think, just do what must be done.…She knelt on the floor until she found in her leather trunk the christening robe, all patterned with wheat sheaves in Aunt Cordelia's best stitches above the hemstitched hem…the others will just have to wear a plainer dress—of course there will be others—but you can never love them as you do this one.…

Finally Amelie was done, and tonight's straight bed ready, but the cold warning calmness throughout these new tasks persisted.… Something…

The blue-eagle spread and Tommy's stony hands folded upon it.

The blue-eagle spread Great-grandmother McNeil had woven in tidal Carolina was still in Missouri, but Amelie did have the quilt that woman's daughter had pieced on higher land toward the west—the True-Lover's-Knot quilt from Amelie's and Katy's bed in the ridgepole bedroom, which Ellin had sent just last Christmas—"I want you to have it, Amelie."

Amelie had kept it for best. She undid it now out of its brown paper wrappings and camphor and was about to leave it half folded, but when she thought of Roger and Lucy awakening in the morning, she covered the table entirely.

She blew out the lamp.

Everything had been attended to. Pain was freed.

Amelie tore off her clothes and put on her nightgown with cold fingers. It was one of the best of her Trousseau C, but it could not warm her as she lay weeping at last for a four-toothed child who would smile from her clothes-basket no longer.

Later, into this first release of sorrow a new pain crept. Soon her eyes were dry and her body a cold arch of bitterness. Her head was burning and her whole being divided as she tried to find some comfort and could only alternate between blaming herself for not knowing more of nursing and Edwin for bringing Helen to this valley. She could not remember texts, only the stone church at home and the people in it, not the Reverend Mr. Hewey's words, only how he always came to your house when you needed him.

She tried to say it was God's will, but she did not believe it. She was probably lacking in being able only to think of Him as a middle-aged Farmer and a Presbyterian Deacon loving His daughter but letting her make her own mistakes. How could He want to take a baby who had just cut her fourth tooth and was learning to wave good-by. "Helen, thy beauty is to me..." Of course her hair was straight, but she might have had a fever sometime and her hair come in curly. "Homely babies make pretty ladies." That was what was intended, that growth should be more than a promise....

In the dim light the true-lover's knots on the white covering were redder than they should be. Something about the old quilt reproached Amelie. She caught her breath at the sight of it.

Katy and the room under the ridgepole...and before that this same quilt in Mother's and Father's room, and earlier still, other women, back to that one on the Nantahala who pieced those true-lover's knots onto cloth she wove on her own loom. What did she think?—she bore children and lost them, her man took her on journeys too, west over the mountains—how did she go on, and those others, how did they bear it?...

Suddenly Amelie knew.

She was cold. She went to the children's mattresses and lifted the sleeping, half-protesting Roger and Lucy into her own bed to lie beside her. She must have them near her tonight.

Roger of the kilts and the wandering legs that must be watchfully kept from the slough. Almost old enough for school. Where would he carry the new lunch-box he wanted so badly? Could there be any school at all? Lucy sighed in her sleep. Lucy of the yellow curls who had lost Annabel Lee, Lucy who must have sweets and peppermints. The warm scent of the sleeping children swept over Amelie, and all their needs. She buried her face against Lucy's unheeding curls.

Amelie knew she could sleep then, but she opened her eyes once more. The true-lover's knots on the old quilt were very clear. Amelie's heart warmed as she thought of Ellin sending it to her. Ellin had known Amelie would need it some day.

Surely there must be some pattern continuing....My grandmother wove this to cover herself, yet to be passed along. She is gone now with all her despairs and losses, yet this one pattern of beauty she made is here now—for me....It will be Lucy's quilt some day.

But now it was Amelie's. Too briefly covering another, it would be her own again. Hers to receive and to give. It was almost as if she could touch it as she used to as she fell asleep.

Frank Norris
"The Nourisher of Nations"

Norris' The Octopus: A Story of California opens after impressive ranches in the southern San Joaquin are already well established. Even so, the limitless stretches of the great valley still retain the power to overwhelm the merely human scale defined by section boundaries and railroad tracks. The vast scope of the valley landscape fires the imagination of one of the novel's main characters, the poet Presley, as he seeks inspiration for his planned "Song of the West." Here, in exuberant prose, is the valley as Presley sees it, expressed in an over-the-top mixture of the metaphorical and material. For Presley, the "whole gigantic sweep of the San Joaquin" is the great mother, sleeping the "sleep of exhaustion, the infinite repose of the colossus, benignant, eternal, strong, the nourisher of nations, the feeder of an entire world."

Toward four in the afternoon, Presley reached the spring at the head of the little cañon in the northeast corner of the Quien Sabe ranch, the point toward which he had been travelling since early in the forenoon. The place was not without its charm. Innumerable live-oaks overhung the cañon, and Broderson Creek—there a mere rivulet, running down from the spring—gave a certain coolness to the air. It was one of the few spots thereabouts that had survived the dry season of the last year. Nearly all the other springs had dried completely, while Mission Creek on Derrick's ranch was nothing better than a dusty cutting in the ground, filled with brittle, concave flakes of dried and sun-cracked mud.

Presley climbed to the summit of one of the hills—the highest—that rose out of the cañon, from the crest of which he could see for thirty, fifty, sixty miles down the valley, and, filling his pipe, smoked lazily for upwards of an hour, his head empty of thought, allowing himself to succumb to a pleasant, gentle inanition, a little drowsy, comfortable in his place, prone upon the ground, warmed just enough by such sunlight as filtered through the live-oaks, soothed by the good tobacco and the prolonged murmur of the spring and creek. By degrees, the sense of his own personality became blunted, the little wheels and cogs of thought moved slower and slower; consciousness dwindled to a point, the animal in him stretched itself, purring. A delightful numbness invaded his mind and his body. He was not asleep, he was not awake, stupefied merely, lapsing back to the state of the faun, the satyr.

After a while, rousing himself a little, he shifted his position and, drawing from the pocket of his shooting coat his little tree-calf edition of the *Odyssey*, read far into the twenty-first book, where, after the failure of all the suitors to bend Ulysses's bow, it is finally put, with mockery, into his own hands. Abruptly the drama of the story roused him from all his languor. In an instant, he was the poet again, his nerves tingling, alive to every sensation, responsive to every impression. The desire of creation, of composition, grew big within him. Hexameters of his own clamoured, tumultuous, in his brain. Not for a long time had he "felt his poem," as he called this sensation, so poignantly. For an instant he told himself that he actually held it.[...]

As from a pinnacle, Presley, from where he now stood, dominated the entire country. The sun had begun to set, everything in the range of his vision was overlaid with a sheen of gold.

First, close at hand, it was the Seed ranch, carpeting the little hollow behind the Mission with a spread of greens, some dark, some vivid, some pale almost to yellowness. Beyond that was the Mission itself, its venerable campanile, in whose arches hung the Spanish King's bells, already glowing ruddy in the sunset. Farther on, he could make out Annixter's ranch house, marked by the skeleton-like tower of the artesian well, and, a little farther to the east, the huddled, tiled roofs of Guadalajara. Far to the west and north, he saw Bonneville very plain, and the dome of the courthouse, a purple silhouette against the glare of the sky. Other points detached themselves, swimming in a golden mist, projecting blue shadows far before them; the mammoth live-oak by Hooven's, towering superb and magnificent; the line of eucalyptus trees, behind which he knew was the Los Muertos ranch house—his home; the watering-tank, the great iron-hooped tower of wood that stood at the joining of the Lower Road and the County Road; the long wind-break of poplar trees and the white walls of Caraher's saloon on the County Road.

But all this seemed to be only foreground, a mere array of accessories—a mass of irrelevant details. Beyond Annixter's, beyond Guadalajara, beyond the Lower Road, beyond Broderson Creek, on to the south and west, infinite, illimitable, stretching out there under the sheen of the sunset forever and forever, flat, vast, unbroken, a huge scroll, unrolling between the horizons, spread the great stretches of the ranch of Los Muertos, bare of crops, shaved close in the recent harvest. Near at hand were hills, but on that far southern horizon only the curve of the great earth itself checked the view. Adjoining Los Muertos, and widening to the west, opened the Broderson ranch. The Osterman ranch to the northwest carried on the great sweep of landscape; ranch after ranch. Then, as the imagination itself expanded under the stimulus of that measureless range of vision, even those great ranches resolved themselves into mere foreground, mere accessories, irrelevant details. Beyond the fine line of the horizons, over the curve of the globe, the shoulder of the earth, were other ranches, equally vast, and beyond these, others, and beyond these, still others, the immensities multiplying, lengthening out vaster and vaster. The whole gigantic sweep of the San Joaquin expanded, Titanic, before the eye of the mind, flagellated with heat, quivering and shimmering under the sun's red eye. At long intervals, a faint breath of wind out of the south passed slowly over the levels of the baked and empty earth, accentuating the silence, marking off the stillness. It seemed to exhale from the land itself, a prolonged sigh as of deep fatigue. It was the season after the harvest, and the great earth, the mother, after its period of reproduction, its pains of labour, delivered of the fruit of its loins, slept the sleep of exhaustion, the infinite repose of the colossus, benignant, eternal, strong, the nourisher of nations, the feeder of an entire world.

Frank Norris
"The Plowing"

In the early years of agriculture in the Central Valley, the success of the wheat crop didn't depend upon irrigation; it depended upon rainfall, fifteen inches enough to assure a rich harvest. Wheat was once California's largest agricultural product, but eventually foreign competition, the collapse of prices, soil exhaustion, and—with irrigation—the eventual dedication of land to other crops all combined to cripple California wheat. Yet in its time, according to historian Donald J. Pisani, California wheat farming was a bonanza business, heavily mechanized and heavily reliant on rapid technological innovation.[1] Frank Norris represented this kind of mechanization in The Octopus *in this memorable passage set on the Quien Sabe Ranch describing the work of a phalanx of gang plows, "thirty-five in number, each drawn by its team of ten." One of these teams is driven by itinerant shepherd Vanamee, Presley's friend. The passage pays tribute to the innovation and the scale of the big wheat farmers, which stand in marked contrast to the struggling hand-tool operations run by the smaller, more humble farmers of the region.*

The evening before, when the foreman had blown his whistle at six o'clock, the long line of ploughs had halted upon the instant, and the drivers, unharnessing their teams, had taken them back to the division barns—leaving the ploughs as they were in the furrows. But an hour after daylight the next morning the work was resumed. After breakfast, Vanamee, riding one horse and leading the others, had returned to the line of ploughs together with the other drivers. Now he was busy harnessing the team. At the division blacksmith shop—temporarily put up—he had been obliged to wait while one of his lead horses was shod, and he had thus been delayed quite five minutes. Nearly all the other teams were harnessed, the drivers on their seats, waiting for the foreman's signal.

"All ready here?" inquired the foreman, driving up to Vanamee's team in his buggy.

"All ready, sir," answered Vanamee, buckling the last strap.

He climbed to his seat, shaking out the reins, and turning about, looked back along the line, then all around him at the landscape inundated with the brilliant glow of the early morning.

---

[1] Donald J. Pisani, *From the Family Farm to Agribusiness: The Irrigation Crusade in California and the West, 1850–1931* (Berkeley: University of California Press, 1984), 8–9.

The day was fine. Since the first rain of the season, there had been no other. Now the sky was without a cloud, pale blue, delicate, luminous, scintillating with morning. The great brown earth turned a huge flank to it, exhaling the moisture of the early dew. The atmosphere, washed clean of dust and mist, was translucent as crystal. Far off to the east, the hills on the other side of Broderson Creek stood out against the pallid saffron of the horizon as flat and as sharply outlined as if pasted on the sky. The campanile of the ancient Mission of San Juan seemed as fine as frost work. All about between the horizons, the carpet of the land unrolled itself to infinity. But now it was no longer parched with heat, cracked and warped by a merciless sun, powdered with dust. The rain had done its work; not a clod that was not swollen with fertility, not a fissure that did not exhale the sense of fecundity. One could not take a dozen steps upon the ranches without the brusque sensation that underfoot the land was alive; roused at last from its sleep, palpitating with the desire of reproduction. Deep down there in the recesses of the soil, the great heart throbbed once more, thrilling with passion, vibrating with desire, offering itself to the caress of the plough, insistent, eager, imperious. Dimly one felt the deep-seated trouble of the earth, the uneasy agitation of its members, the hidden tumult of its womb, demanding to be made fruitful, to reproduce, to disengage the eternal renascent germ of Life that stirred and struggled in its loins.

The ploughs, thirty-five in number, each drawn by its team of ten, stretched in an interminable line, nearly a quarter of a mile in length, behind and ahead of Vanamee. They were arranged, as it were, *en echelon*, not in file—not one directly behind the other, but each succeeding plough its own width farther in the field than the one in front of it. Each of these ploughs held five shears, so that when the entire company was in motion, one hundred and seventy-five furrows were made at the same instant. At a distance, the ploughs resembled a great column of field artillery. Each driver was in his place, his glance alternating between his horses and the foreman nearest at hand. Other foremen, in their buggies or buckboards, were at intervals along the line, like battery lieutenants. Annixter himself, on horseback, in boots and campaign hat, a cigar in his teeth, overlooked the scene.

The division superintendent, on the opposite side of the line, galloped past to a position at the head. For a long moment there was a silence. A sense of preparedness ran from end to end of the column.

All things were ready, each man in his place. The day's work was about to begin.

Suddenly, from a distance at the head of the line came the shrill trilling of a whistle. At once the foreman nearest Vanamee repeated it, at the same time turning down the line, and waving one arm. The signal was repeated, whistle answering whistle, till the sounds lost themselves in the distance. At once the line of ploughs lost its immobility, moving forward, getting slowly under way, the horses straining in the traces. A prolonged movement rippled from team to team, disengaging in its passage a multitude of sounds—the click of buckles, the creak of straining leather, the subdued clash of machinery, the cracking of whips, the deep breathing of nearly four hundred horses, the abrupt commands and cries of the drivers, and, last of all, the prolonged, soothing murmur of the thick brown earth turning steadily from the multitude of advancing shears.

The ploughing thus commenced, continued. The sun rose higher. Steadily the hundred iron hands kneaded and furrowed and stroked the brown, humid earth, the hundred iron teeth bit deep into the Titan's flesh. Perched on his seat, the moist living reins slipping and tugging in his hands, Vanamee, in the midst of this steady confusion of constantly varying sensation, sight interrupted by sound, sound mingling with sight, on this swaying, vibrating seat, quivering with the prolonged thrill of the earth, lapsed to a sort of pleasing numbness, in a sense, hypnotised by the weaving maze of things in which he found himself involved. To keep his team at an even, regular gait, maintaining the precise interval, to run his furrows as closely as possible to those already made by the plough in front—this for the moment was the entire sum of his duties. But while one part of his brain, alert and watchful, took cognisance of these matters, all the greater part was lulled and stupefied with the long monotony of the affair.

The ploughing, now in full swing, enveloped him in a vague, slow-moving whirl of things. Underneath him was the jarring, jolting, trembling machine; not a clod was turned, not an obstacle encountered, that he did not receive the swift impression of it through all his body, the very friction of the damp soil, sliding incessantly from the shiny surface of the shears, seemed to reproduce itself in his finger-tips and along the back of his head. He heard the horse-hoofs by the myriads crushing down easily, deeply, into the loam, the prolonged clinking of trace-chains, the working of the smooth brown flanks in the harness, the clatter of wooden hames, the champing of bits, the click of iron shoes against pebbles, the brittle stubble of the surface ground crackling and snapping as the furrows turned, the sonorous, steady breaths wrenched from the deep, labouring chests, strap-bound, shining with sweat, and all along the line the voices of the men talking to the horses. Everywhere there were visions of glossy brown backs, straining, heaving, swollen with muscle; harness streaked with specks of froth, broad, cup-shaped hoofs, heavy with brown loam, men's faces red with tan, blue overalls spotted with axle-grease; muscled hands, the knuckles whitened in their grip on the reins, and through it all the ammoniacal smell of the horses, the bitter reek of perspiration of beasts and men, the aroma of warm leather, the scent of dead stubble—and stronger and more penetrating than everything else, the heavy, enervating odour of the upturned, living earth.

At intervals, from the tops of one of the rare, low swells of the land, Vanamee overlooked a wider horizon. On the other divisions of Quien Sabe the same work was in progress. Occasionally he could see another column of ploughs in the adjoining division—sometimes so close at hand that the subdued murmur of its movements reached his ear; sometimes so distant that it resolved itself into a long, brown streak upon the grey of the ground. Farther off to the west on the Osterman ranch other columns came and went, and, once, from the crest of the highest swell on his division, Vanamee caught a distant glimpse of the Broderson ranch. There, too, moving specks indicated that the ploughing was under way. And farther away still, far off there beyond the fine line of the horizons, over the curve of the globe, the shoulder of the earth, he knew were other ranches, and beyond these others, and beyond these still others, the immensities multiplying to infinity.

Everywhere throughout the great San Joaquin, unseen and unheard, a thousand ploughs up-stirred the land, tens of thousands of shears clutched deep into the warm, moist soil.

It was the long stroking caress, vigorous, male, powerful, for which the Earth seemed panting. The heroic embrace of a multitude of iron hands, gripping deep into the brown, warm flesh of the land that quivered responsive and passionate under this rude advance, so robust as to be almost an assault, so violent as to be veritably brutal. There, under the sun and under the speckless sheen of the sky, the wooing of the Titan began, the vast Primal passion, the two world-forces, the elemental Male and Female, locked in a colossal embrace, at grapples in the throes of an infinite desire, at once terrible and divine, knowing no law, untamed, savage, natural, sublime.

May Merrill Miller
"The Sierra Ditch Company"

Edwin Blansford is enthusiastic because the irrigation ditch—a community project meant to assure individual success—is finally about to be opened. His jubilation is so contagious, even Amelie feels his joy. But when the ditch is opened and the water drains off into an unknown underground riverbed, Amelie confronts a new worry: the bleak future of her children. As her family's resources dwindle and neighbors begin to move away, the Blansfords' dreams of creating a prosperous farm seem no match for the reality of the harsh terrain. Yet Edwin and Amelie will stay, the two of them in league "against this valley," the two of them united by their resolve to endure hardship rather than give up on Edwin's dream.

I t was after New Year's when the rain finally came, but it was only a sprinkle and then there was no more for weeks. The grain did not entirely dry up, but most of it would not be fit to cut.

It had been so long since Amelie had seen Edwin jubilant that she was surprised when he came home from the ditch one night late in February whistling.

He put his arm about Amelie as she stood over the stove. When he kissed her so happily, she recalled how long it had been since he had grasped her impulsively like this. The meat-fork in her hand fell to the floor.

"What ever in the world!" she laughed as he danced her around.

"We're going to turn the water in the ditch tomorrow," he said, rubbing his hands together. "There's been snow in the Sierras even if we haven't had any rain, and these last few warm days have brought the river up. It's risen twelve feet since Monday. It's high enough to turn in the headgate. Those men will have that little strip of ground between the river and the headgate lifted out early in the morning— it will just be like taking a spoonful of frosting off a cake. I'm going to set the alarm for four o'clock."

"How far will you run the water?" Amelie asked. "Clear to the end?"

"No, just a little ways, the gates aren't all in. The ditch isn't finished even to Moore's, let alone Connery's or us. But we'll put in some fields of corn close to the river and each of us will share in the crop. That will see everybody through until next year. It's just the beginning, Amelie, by next fall the ditch ought to be done right through our place and Whitney's too, and then we will all have water for our own fields. I can hardly believe it, it's been so long."

The next morning Amelie did not hear Edwin when he got up. She awakened to the smell of coffee. It was not yet light, the windowpanes were dark as the surface of a deep pool, but the flames of the cook-stove glowed through the open damper windows across the front of the stove, lighting the room with its familiar red-toothed smile. The lamp on the table was turned very low.

Edwin must have heard her start to rise, for he tiptoed over to the bed at once.

"Lie still," he smiled as he pushed her back upon the pillow and pulled the quilt around her shoulders. "It's time for children to be sleeping."

She followed his glance over to the bed in the corner. Lucy's arm was flung out—she would keep uncovered—almost touching the baby in the clothes-basket beside her. Roger had his own cot now and was only visible as a gently moving roll of blankets.

"You sleep too, Amelie."

Because she knew it pleased Edwin, Amelie lay quietly. But when he had finished his breakfast she whispered to him, asking him to tell her good-by.

When he came over to the bed, she reached up to put her arms around his neck. He laid his cheek against hers. "When you do get up, Amelie," he whispered, "just remember that the Sierra Ditch is officially opened."

Amelie was so happy all day she could not find enough to do. With Roger off to school, it would be a good day to wash Lucy's hair. She combed out the yellow curls and heated the water on the stove. She had to dip the bucket down several times for water; the well was lower since yesterday.

All day long she added to her tasks; she was surprised at her own energy. The Mission rose bush by the door had grown a few long sprays. It should bloom this summer. She dug around its roots on her knees. She took everything out of her leather trunk and put the things back again. She could touch them now without despair. Even though most days she was lonely, the sight of the leather trunk often producing an added stab of homesickness, today Edwin's triumph filled the room for her. She folded her wedding dress and the white brocade and the green riding habit away again. She did not even open her old black book except to think with a pang how near that past war had come to breaking her friendship with Letitia. She did not unclasp the catch on Jason's daguerreotype. She did not open the calf-bound album. Herself and Katy in striped socks and round hats were too far away. She wished Edwin would come back early.

But Edwin returned late. When, through the window, Amelie saw him walking toward the cabin she stood perfectly still. Something dreadful must have happened. He was as stooped as an old man. The Edwin of this morning was gone. She ran to the doorway.

Edwin lifted his face and stood with his foot on the doorstep, not seeming to care if he ever stepped upon it. "We turned in the water," he said tonelessly. "Ten o'clock it was. The men made quick work of it. But, Amelie, when we did turn it in—" he stopped. She wanted to help him, but she could not. "The water only flowed a little way. Then it made a hole for itself and went no farther. We stood there and listened and you could hear it flowing underneath the ground, echoing at one place if you put down your ear, gurgling at another, and at the end just rushing like a hidden waterfall. And there was nothing, just plain ground beneath us, nothing we could see, only we could hear that water running. Then the ground began to get spongy. We kept on trying to fill up the hole until noon, but there wasn't any use. All of a sudden Tim Connery's team started to mire; the horses were clear up to their flanks in a minute. It took six horses and ten men with chains to pull those two out. By that time we saw it was no use; probably it was an old underground bed of the river we were pouring water into and it would just go on forever. So we pulled down the headgate. We turned back the water."

He climbed the steps and brushed past Amelie as if he were walking in his sleep. Amelie was afraid to grasp his hand as he went by.

Later, when they had gone to bed, he spoke again. The flat tones hurt her, as if he were dead and still could speak.

"We'll have to hire an engineer," he said. "First we had Orrin and he laid the lines true enough for most of us, but when Horace Whitney and the others came in, we saw they wanted a real survey, so we had that assessment and hired a surveyor. But he only ran his lines on the top of the ground—only an engineer can tell us what's under the ground and how to keep from running our ditch down to China. Amelie, what if the whole ditch is like that, three miles of it done, perhaps more holes? I don't see how any of the men can pay for another assessment. They are discouraged and ready to stop, but we can't give it all up now. We'll have to help. I'll get paid back in ditch shares for whatever we put in."

Amelie lay very still. She was sorry for Edwin, but a new fear was added to those she had known before. She listened to the children's quiet breathing. You had to think of them. It would be foolish to pour more hard metal dollars down a subterranean river running one knew not where, and then be paid back with more paper shares in that useless stream. But she must not say anything. Not now.

The next day Edwin came home with the news that Lem Hancock was packing his wagon and telling the boys they could have all his shares in the God-damned ditch and welcome. He was going to pull out while he had a little flour and cash money before he had to feed on jack-rabbits. And Janet Gordon was begging Harry to take her and her furniture back East and the poor boy had almost given in. And Edwin said he was trying to tell all of them not to pull up now—at least not till the engineer came to tell them what to expect and where to dig.

That afternoon Sigrid Halvorson and Mary Connery came to see Amelie. Sigrid stood by the table, tall and quiet, with something old yet new in her face.

"We want you to send to San Francisco for us," said Sigrid, "for seeds, please—seeds of the turnip, of the onion, of the lettuce, and of the everything we can plant now. Please to write and send right away."

Mary Connery explained. It was Sigrid's idea. Sigrid and herself and all of the women they had talked to—except Janet, poor thing; all she could do was to dust her furniture—were going to have a vegetable garden. They would ask all the neighbor women to join them.

There was not a great distance between the river and the headgate, where the water had been turned in, but there was enough for a fair-sized garden on either side of the new take-in. The water was right there to stay; no underground hole in the take-in, only past the headgate. Each one could have a plot and surely something green before long.

"And we think"—Sigrid looked squarely at Amelie—"if we go there each day to garden, some of us, that it will help our men. They will know we have not given up. That should help more than the green things."

Amelie wrote the letter. Sigrid said she would walk to town with it.

For there was a town. The stakes set out last year to mark a town site on the empty plain had not been in vain. Nueva Esperanza had its beginning in a railway station, two saloons, and a store, which, while not as diversified as Weinstein's at Kings Crossing, at least boasted a post office.

Amelie watched Sigrid go; in a few steps she was striding far past Mary. Sigrid would walk the nine miles, five to Nueva Esperanza and four back to her own house, before supper. She wore no hat. As far as Amelie could see Sigrid crossing the plain, the sun was shining on her coronet of braided golden hair.

Nueva Esperanza and this tall woman who was used to mountains walking toward it. It was the woman and not the town that brought new hope to Amelie.

For Amelie knew now—she had discovered it while Sigrid and Mary stood before her—that she had leagued herself for certain with Edwin against this valley. At least for the present. Leave it sometime, perhaps, only there is no time to think of that now. But do not leave it defeated.

Sigrid knows. You must not do that to a man or to yourself.

◆

Mary E. Chambers
"PIONEERS IN MUSSEL SLOUGH"
FROM THE *VISALIA WEEKLY DELTA,* 1880

Eds. Delta:—As there is great excitement at the present time over the Mussel Slough railroad land, and the position the settlers thereon have taken, and having lost a brother (A. McGregor) in the late fearful slaughter, in justice to his memory I would like to state a little of my own experience since coming on these lands. If you will give me space in your columns, I will make it as short and concise as possible, that the people may see whether we can be classed as *squatters* on these lands or not.

In the fall of 1869 we were living in Placer county; my husband at that time being in the employ of the Central Pacific railroad company. Being away from home all the time I was anxious that he should get land somewhere and settle down, and make us a home. At that time we heard of this land in Tulare being forfeited by the railroad company (see decisions of Sec. Browning, July 14, 1868, also of Sec. Cox, Dec. 2 and 11, 1869), and that it was to be thrown open for homestead and preemption settlement. I therefore persuaded Mr. Chambers to go and locate, and in November, 1869, he came here and located on railroad lands; then came back, bought an outfit, and moved his family December 26, arriving in Tulare January 7, 1870.

I shall never forget my first impression of the country. I was so discouraged with the looks of it that I did not want to look out of the wagon. Nothing but cattle and horses, sheep and hogs, till it looked like one vast corral, with no more appearance of vegetation than a well swept floor. And this was the country we were to make a home in. If some one would only say go back! But, no; I had urged the move, and was too determined to say "go back;" so we settled, and commenced living with great discouragements. We had never farmed any before. We brought all our farming implements from Stockton. Everything here was at a very high price, having to pay at the rate of 3 cents per pound freight; bacon was 37 ½ per pound, common brown sugar, 25 cents; tea, $1.25; coffee, 2 ½ pounds for $1; beans, 10 cents per pound; and everything else in proportion. The stock men looked upon as intruders, and discouraged us all they could, telling us that we could do nothing on the land; that we would starve to death, as it was impossible to raise anything on the dry plains. These things, of course, we did not believe, as we looked on these stock-raisers as an indolent people, who had never made an effort to cultivate the soil; but we, with our energy and perseverance, would make the wilderness to blossom and bear.

Alas, how we flattered ourselves! We little imagined how our patience or perseverance would be tried, or how near the stock men's "starve to death" predictions would come on us. The first year, the few families that were here all went to the lake to farm, taking up the little patches of moist land as the waters receded, and each putting in his little piece of grain or corn. The first grain we put in, we had to go to Banta's station—a distance of 140 miles—for seed, taking eight days to make the trip. This we put in, making hay, which we harvested with the greatest care, saving it for our horses to eat while putting in the next season's crop, and depending on salt grass and corn fodder to keep them until that time. We then went to Mr. Daniel Rhoads, who was very kind to the settlers, and begged a sack of corn, which we planted. Here let me mention, that in bringing home the corn a nail in the bottom of the wagon tore a hole in the sack, and when lifted out of the wagon one third of the corn was gone. This was a great loss to us, as we counted every grain a sack of corn.

We took buckets and pans and tracked the corn back for four miles and picked it up. After planting and sowing we were obliged to herd stock day and night to keep off the wild cattle, which were starving and ready to devour anything green in sight. And the trouble did not end here—after harvesting we had to guard it until fed to our own stock. In the latter part of July, or the first of August, of the same year, we moved on to the quarter section of land adjoining the one we now occupy, my brother, Arch McGregor, taking up the one we are now on. He took this up in preference to government land (of which there was plenty to be taken at that time) because it joined ours. He made application at the railroad company's office, B. B. Redding being their agent, and I suppose it is still on file, at the time asking for instructions about the land, what steps were necessary to be taken to hold it, etc. The answer came back for us to go and improve it, and the price of the land would be the same as other unimproved land in the neighborhood.

There would be no advantage taken on account of improvements. So, having faith in their word, we went on putting on what improvements we were able. By this time we found nothing could be done without ditches, so we made our first effort to get a survey, which cost each settler $3.50. Though small the sum may seem, yet it was quite a tax for us to raise in cash. From this effort came what is known as the Lower Kings River ditch. This, I can tell you, was a great triumph for the people. We were so delighted over the prospect of water that women and children ran out to see the first water come in the ditch. This ditch was seven or eight miles long; so every one for that year, who was not fortunate enough to live on the line of the ditch, rented of their more fortunate neighbors, giving one-third, and some even one-half of their crops, as rent. That year the crops were very small, the ditch not carrying sufficient water, and the dry land taking up so much. The men not understanding irrigating had to work day and night to get a little stream of water on their land.

Many men had to go away and leave their families and land to earn something for their support. Mr. Chambers left us here and went back to work for the company, and was gone for fourteen months, while I cooked, took care of the sick and washed for those who could pay me. So we worked along for three years, many getting discouraged and leaving before this. Then the People's ditch was started. This gave us hope again, as this ditch, if put through, would go through our place and give us water. But what an undertaking! Twenty-seven miles of ditch, and to be built by men without a dollar and a living to make the while. Who was to do this? These very men who are termed by this company as squatters (a name I have always associated with an idle, worthless person who would rather enjoy what belonged to others than his own,) were the men who built this ditch, and who have made a success of it; but who can say at what cost! I have known men, when they were working on those ditches, to grind corn in their coffee-mills to make their bread, and take their frying pan with them and depend on catching fish for their meals. Just let this great corporation think of that a moment. Think what it has cost the poor settler for the *faith* he placed in their *word* and for bringing these lands under cultivation. At this time, when we had prospects of water, we were still uneasy about the land, as we were desirous of putting out an orchard and some other improvements.

So we wrote again to the railroad land office, and received a circular stating the land would be $2.50 per acre for plain land, and from $5 to $7 for timber land. This put us at ease. We went on adding to the land as we were able. For the first five years, all that we ever sold that was raised here was two tons of corn, which we exchanged in part pay for a horse. We put in five successive crops without ever raising anything; and not until the water came in the Last Chance ditch did we raise anything on our place, and that being the sixth crop, we saved out of two hundred acres of wheat only ten, that being all we could get water for. Three years ago they sent their land grader here. Up went our land from $2.50 to $22 per acre. And why? Because we had a house, barn, orchard, alfalfa pasture, flower garden, ditches, and a well cultivated farm. Our ditch interests cost us about $1,500, and now, just as we are getting our heads above water, here comes the demand, $22 per acre or leave the land. They well know that if put off the land we cannot take what belongs to us away. They don't offer to pay us for improvements. If we cannot buy, what shall we do? We offer to pay them *double* for the land, but no! They will not take *treble* for it. Are we to walk out of our homes and leave them to strangers without even a murmur?

We appeal to the people for sympathy. Let each one suppose himself in our position. Let either one of the railroad lords suppose himself, wife and children in our position. What would they do? Quietly leave? I think not. It is not natural to suppose so. Who is to take care of the widows and orphans they have made? Is it the railroad company. At their door lies this murder. No, not them. The poor settler has it to do, and there is room in his heart for them all. In conclusion, let me say that the company has represented us as land-jumpers, squatters, and as a people capable of any kind of misdemeanor, when we have made a country, built towns, churches and school houses, and made our old enemies, the stock men, respect us, and express their sympathy for us. How did the company take advantage of us? Did they send the parties that were to be dispossessed word that they would be here on that day to dispossess them? No! But, after an agreement with the settlers to await the decision of the higher courts before undertaking to dispossess them, they came like thieves, in the night. Coming in after most of the farmers' bed time, and on the day of our picnic, when they supposed that everyone would be at the picnic, and they could murder the few who would offer resistance. They themselves would be protected by the *law,* and would put the settlers' goods in the road, and leave, as they did at Mr. Braden's door step, four cartridges, to intimate what he might expect if he dare come back after they had dispossessed him. There being no one there, they met with no resistance. They next went to Brewer's. By this time it was known what was going on, and some men left their families on the picnic grounds, others were halted on the road. My brother was on his way to the picnic in company with two ladies. When he left them, some friend suggested that he take a pistol, but his answer was, "No, we will settle this without arms;" and I have been told by an eyewitness that at the time of the shooting there were only four pistols there, and some had no ammunition. How could it be otherwise! Men do not carry guns to picnics or church; although Poole and Clark assert they were surrounded by forty armed men.

The arms did not appear until after the slaughter. But I have no doubt that *one* pistol held in a man's face at such a time would look like *forty*. It was *not the pistols*, it was *what they saw in men's faces* that frightened them. And then to think of these "terrible leaguers!" What did they do with their sworn enemy, Clark, the grader? They furnished him with a body guard and saw him safely out of the country. Who ever heard of such forbearance! If there was any manhood in Clark would not he come out on the side of the settlers, and openly confess that he owes his life to them for saving him from an excited populace? There were no acts of violence committed by these people, and none intended. Just suppose it had been the directors of this company that had been killed, instead of the settlers. Flags would have been flying at half-mast; there would have been a wail from our state, and the capital would have been draped in mourning. Is there no *justice* for us poor settlers? we who have bankrupted ourselves trying to make this country what it is to-day. Why is it that we cannot buy these lands at their figures? Because, take off what belongs to us, and the land is not worth it. Let them pay us for what is *ours* and we will be glad to leave. Many families have left in the past year, broken down in health and with empty pockets.

Nine years ago we put in a garden where the Lemoore flouring mill now stands, and I walked back and forth, taking care of the garden, getting up at four o'clock in the morning and walking those five long miles, hoeing and weeding my garden and back home again to dinner. I don't say this in a boasting way, but just to show what struggles we made to get along; and my experience is only that of many others. Talk of poor oppressed Ireland, and the miseries of the landlord system. Why, Ireland never had such landlords as these. I do hope that Providence will open a way for us out of this trouble, and make these landlords feel the injustice they have done these people; and that there will be a speedy and amicable adjustment of our troubles.

Mary E. Chambers,
Grangeville, Tulare co., Cal.
June 4, 1880

May Merrill Miller
"Seed Corn"

Despite their early hopes, Edwin and Amelie are almost as desperate as their neighbors. When a stockman offers the sandlappers a sack of corn seed, they swallow their pride and accept the offer. What follows is a fictional account that closely parallels Mary Chambers' historical one.

By Christmas there was no need to drive away the cattle. The wheat had grown scarcely taller than the wild grasses. Another dry year.

There was no Christmas program at the school. Roger and Lucy were disappointed. Amelie unwrapped the Christmas parcel from Uncle Michael, wishing he had sent apples instead of trinkets.

By February the plains were as dusty as summer. Then a driving rain descended. Almost two weeks of it. But it was too late to save the grain—it was only a part of the dust and the powdered shriveled grass.

When Edwin told Amelie a few days later that Uncle Amos Jordan himself had gone to Banta for a wagon-load of seed corn for the settlers, she failed to share his enthusiasm. Uncle Amos had said he was sorry the Sandlappers had come to the San Joaquin of the stockmen, but he could not see the ditch-diggers and their families starve even if his own cattle must. So he had offered each one of them a sack of corn for seed. It would ripen early with another rain or two. It ought to tide the families over until summer. It was worth trying. They could pay him later.

Amelie found herself grimly resentful when Edwin told her he was going out to harness the horses to go for his own sack that afternoon. She knew now, about the money. Edwin and Amelie were no better off now than their neighbors. The provisions Edwin had apportioned to his own family were almost used up. The coffee was gone long ago. Only beans and part of a barrel of flour and jerky from the Jordans' were left. And Edwin could not persuade any store—even those at Kings Crossing—to accept gilt-edged certificates of the Sierra Ditch Company in exchange for flour.

Amelie was bitter as she stood in the doorway looking at the dried thorns of the Mission rose. It had lived when slips from tender roses had died, but even it could not stand last summer's drought. The padres had been right to leave this valley to the horned toad and the Devil. You could not expect even a thorny rose to grow where horses went wild and even Indians were lost.

Amelie shut her eyes and thought of the garden of roses and clove pinks, wallflowers, and violets she had left under the old lean pear tree. February—pomegranate petals scarlet against the sky. She felt sick with longing to see it all again. It was wrong to live in this horrible room behind her with knot-holes and cracks mocking her every time she faced them. She and Edwin and the children could still go back to the Santa Clara…Edwin's father would help them…another house…another garden…but Mrs. Conley would give her slips from the garden that had once been her own, things would grow fast….

A sack of corn was keeping her from her garden.

Amelie tried to remember last year's spring when she hoed with Letitia in the women's garden by the river. But now there were only short days and cold when Edwin pulled on shirt and pants and boots and went out into the dark to persuade his neighbors to dig a ditch, though there was no water to fill it. She tried to remember Edwin's greening grain-field, but now there was only the square deserted scorched raft of it on the stagnant plain miasmic with camphor weed's green scum. Useless, it thrived.

When she heard the rattle of the wagon and saw Edwin actually starting for Jordans', Amelie wanted to run out to the road to call him back. For this act of Edwin's was decisive; when he returned with the seed corn he would plant it, harvest it, and another year would be on its way.

For one moment thoughts dark as a flock of blackbirds settled on the field of her mind and then flew away. "I hope something happens to the corn….If he does not plant it, we cannot stay here much longer."

Then at once she tried to forget the sinister instant in which, almost with a curse, she had sought to weave a spell against Edwin's purpose. It bothered her that this had happened, to be going about her usual tasks and then have a flash of this kind come to her, so different from what she really wanted to think, yet with an eerie truth.

She started back from the doorway toward the stove to tend the fire, but she sank down upon a chair instead. Here was another certainty she was trying to deny. Outside the door the camphor weed reminded her it was spring, eighteen months since Isobel was born. She had hoped it would not be so soon.

Children should not come this way. She should not sit upon the vast ocean of fecundity as a sea-gull sits upon a wave, giving herself up to nature. She knew she wanted to control this thing, just as Edwin would find it needful to put gates across the ditches to hold back the water, making the land crop only when he wished. The nausea swept over her like a wave—not so much nausea as a distinctive weakness. She trembled when she arose from the chair.

Often that afternoon she stopped to rest. Around her the boards of the walls seemed to stand, each one by itself, like the posts of a corral. She decided this was because the late afternoon sun seemed to strike lower until each crack was not only visible but an entrance where the red battle of light speared into the room.

She went to the doorway again to look at the children. The three of them were safe enough: Isobel close to the doorway, Roger and Lucy at least a mile and a half away the other side of Whitney's toward the lone sycamore. The tree was still farther, but when there was nothing else to see, the children and the tree seemed to be together. Amelie wondered if she would ever get used to letting the children roam like that, with no fence, no yard, just three steps and then the plain as far as they could see.

She let them play longer than usual before she called them in to supper. Edwin was late in coming; they must eat without him.

She put the children to bed; still he had not come.

When she did hear him drive the horses to the barn and finally come into the kitchen, she was shocked by the wrecked look on his face. It was as bad, worse even, than on that day when the water, first turned into the ditch, disappeared into the hidden underground river.

"What has happened?"

He sank down upon the chair by the table and curved over it like a hunchback. His face was gray as she had never seen it.

"I lost the corn."

She stood still. The flock of blackbirds, the wishes she had made, come back upon her. She could not speak.

"It was the last sack Jordan had. I should have gone earlier, but the men told me he would save it for me, and he had. I didn't want to leave the ditch. Now everybody but us has theirs in the ground. Well, ours is in the ground too. When I sent to get it out I found a nail had come loose in the tail-board. I had torn a hole in the sack. The sack was still there, but the corn had spilled out a little bit at a time between the boards. The crows will have it by morning."

He could not go on.

This was the end. They could not stay here now. Without the corn they were lost. Two hundred miles to Stockton, a hundred and forty to Banta—no, it was impossible. The memory of the Santa Clara garden came again to Amelie, but seeing the shame of defeat on Edwin's face, she thought now only of this final catastrophe for him. She knew theirs was not the extremity of desperation of the other neighbors— Edwin could go back to the Santa Clara; his father, his brothers, would welcome and help him—that was what made the present harder: it was more difficult to keep on striving with this alternative of placid plenitude always before them than to be forced on such a course by starvation. But if Edwin returned to the easy fields, they would not be those he had won for himself and for her. He and she would be forever poor in spirit and their children after them. That was what it came to; she was ashamed she had been thinking only of a blossoming garden, not what soil its roots must feed upon. And as she looked at Edwin sitting before her, his arms folded in a dejection so rare to him, she thought what a load it must be for a man to carry always, this wife, these children, this house, these decisions, and so seldom she realized it, taking his care for her for granted.

She gave him his supper.

He looked down at the jerky and the beans, the same as yesterday and every day. She put the cup of parched barley tea beside his plate.

"My God, Amelie"—he pushed the cup away—"I am so sick of this. It tastes just like cistern-water the rats have got into."

"Yes, I know."

How she hated herself as she put the dishes away! Maybe God was punishing her for that blinding instant when she had hoped something would happen to the corn. She thought of it lying on the ground, lost to them, and their fields bare while the others grew stalks and tassels. The neighbors would share with them later as Edwin had with them, but it would be too late. The one foe Edwin could not fight was inaction; he would leave the valley rather than submit to it. She looked at Edwin again. Now she knew. That gray face of his was like Tommy's on the cot so long ago. The look of death. A pity rose in her for him as it had for Tommy.

Suddenly she turned to him.

"Edwin, I know what we can do. Oh, I know you will say I'm crazy, but listen. Let's hitch up the horses again and take a lantern and go after the corn. We'll just pick it up, even if it takes all night."

He looked at her and away again. He did not bother to answer.

"Edwin, please listen. We can start right out. What if we don't find it all? We can just go till we get tired, every single grain we pick will be a stalk of corn by summer."

"No, Amelie, there just isn't any use. I'm so tired I've got to roll in."

"No, please, Edwin, let's try it anyway. No one will know."

She caught him looking in surprise at her, his own face dark with disbelief. But he took up his hat and put on his coat, lit the lantern, and went out into the night.

She wondered, as she put the quilts over Roger and Lucy and Isobel, that she felt so oddly light, with no concern for them, no, not the slightest. One part of her told her they might wake up and be frightened to find themselves alone with Zeke gone to the ditch; one part mocked at her that she who had trembled at the threat of Vasquez and Procopio should leave them; yet she knew that she would. She enjoyed for the moment the frenzy of entire singleness of purpose.

Edwin drove the wagon up to the door. She knew by the way he sat over the seat that he was as tired as the horses that had to be prodded to start.

Ten miles ahead of them, and the night was dark. And she knew she had persuaded Edwin to come on what he must think was an impossible mission. He was just doing this to please her. She shook her head when he asked her to sit on the seat beside him.

"I've been in the house all day, I need to walk. I'll just walk along in front with the lantern and pick up the corn, and when I get tired, I'll drive."

She took the lantern from him and turned it higher. She knew that she must find a start of grain or he would turn back.

She swung the circle of the lantern in front of her. On and on, no sign of anything. They had already passed Horace's and Letitia's cabin. Their dog had run out and barked. Amelie was glad they had not come to their door. Once Edwin said: "Oh, Amelie, what's the use?" but she pretended not to hear. She swung her lantern, watching the ground at each step. This dust was so light, how could she ever see anything in this blackness?

Suddenly it leaped out at her, yellow as butter separated into tiny particles. She picked up the first grain.

It was remarkable how evenly the grain had fallen, a little to one side of the center of the road, soon she could actually tell by the tracks ahead just about where to look.

Step, step, step, step—six times and stoop, yes, that was it.

Her back began to hurt. She remembered then what she had forgotten. "Never mind," she thought, "I am strong, it is not as if it were the first time." And she went on.

The smell of the earth in the dark came to her. The camphor weed, pungent, like ammonia smelling-salts. She needed it.

As she reached up after stooping she could not avoid seeing the stars. Soon they too began to look like grains of corn. She was dizzy. She looked back. Quietly, quietly the wagon came; two or three creaks of the wheels, the horses stopped, then started again. Edwin was bent over in his hunched curve. The houses were lost.

It was no lighter, but she was used to the dark.

She looked back again toward the house they had left. The children alone. No, nothing could happen except this task that made her so fiercely exultant.

"This must be what it is like," she thought, "when men work with the land, pitting themselves against it. No wonder Edwin is too tired to read at night, no wonder he is too tired to talk to me, only to be quiet, only to forget until morning what the land does to you." This was a battle she herself could enlist in. She remembered how she had longed to go to war with Tommy and Jason. Wide hoop skirts were supplanted now by dragging percale, black slippers by brogans with copper tips, the rebel flag for the moment forgotten, the only standard a raveling whip with which to spur on the half-fed horses.

She looked back at Edwin and then at the seed rattling in her pail. Not enough—not enough.

The spot in the middle of her back grew larger; pain caught her in a circle around her waist. No, she would not give up. Tired, but even in that discomfort there was quiet peace like that of the fallow land that waited for their seed. She and Edwin were together. Together they would find the seed for this land.

Soon she realized she could walk no farther. She waited for Edwin and the wagon.

"I will drive now; look how much it makes."

She showed him the quarter of a peck of corn she had gathered.

So they went on, she in the wagon now, her feet swinging, or, when she had to change her position, slumping to brace herself against the footboard, her shoulders hunched over as Edwin's had been, the loose lines lying over the patient horses.

Always the great sycamore ahead of them; they had not come more than four miles. And then as she watched, the moon showed an unbelievable red edge, then rose higher. Of all the times she had seen it, never this far south in the sky before, and it could not be, but it was, directly behind the lonely sycamore, the old branches and the new in silhouette against this ashy scarlet circle of the moon.

She called to Edwin. He stopped to watch it, the horses stood in their tracks. Never, never, had she seen it like this, that landmark where the road turned, that solitary tree she and Edwin and every other settler who ever came to the San Joaquin looked for; it had been a welcome before, but never a welcome like this. She decided one must watch very late to see it.

Edwin walked faster now. Four steps instead of her six, stoop, and go on again. How much faster he could go! Hope had swept his strength back as if by magic. Like a boy again, how happy he is after a quarry!

She loved him. It was good to be away from the house and the children and to know that she loved him.

The moon made everything lighter. Amelie could see no color, only gradations from the road, which was white now, to the low smudges of river willows.

She took another turn at the picking, but she was too tired. As she climbed back again, the tendons in her legs pulled at her back; she felt she could not climb into the wagon. But she did, lifting the lines when Edwin stumbled down.

Suddenly she saw Edwin stop.

"Look, Amelie!" he cried. "Drive closer, but be careful!"

She drove the horses to one side of the road to see what he wished to show her.

There in a golden heap lay the first corn that had been spilled.

Edwin picked it up in handfuls. Amelie watched him run it through his fingers and back again. In the light the kernels shone like river pearls. Unmindful of the dust, he scooped them into the sack, laughing as he did so.

"This is one time we cheated the crows."

Amelie was tired no longer. She climbed down from the wagon to be nearer. She felt the cool kernels herself. How many, how lavish to hold all this seed!

Finally Amelie watched Edwin take a piece of cord from his pocket and tie it around the sack before he lifted it to the wagon and placed it under their foot-rest where they could watch it.

"It won't escape again," Edwin assured her.

They were safe then. A tithe of the seed had been given to the roadway, but the rest was secure. Amelie felt oddly light as Edwin started to help her to the axle.

"Edwin—"

He held the lantern nearer to her face.

"Amelie, you look dreadful. Are you sick?"

"No, I just seem awfully cramped. Let me walk a little."

But she could not stand; she leaned against him.

"I've got to lie down a minute." She turned to the ground beside the road.

"Not here, Amelie, we can get home in just a little while—or you could lie in the bed of the wagon."

"No, it's too splintery," she gasped. "Just for a moment—I just have to, Edwin, I just have to stretch out."

She dropped on the ground beside the road. The moon shone above her, the tree was not lost, and the stilled horses and the wagon and Edwin loomed larger than ever. Reassured that they would stay, she shut her eyes. She sighed and lay with her arms flung wide upon the unplowed ground.

She could not believe it when Edwin's voice sounded above her, his hand on her shoulder.

"Amelie, I'm sorry to wake you up, but it isn't good for you to lie there too long."

She could not move. About her dried grasses clashed and in her ears she heard their rustling. Close to the ground the pungent green camphor weed assailed her nostrils with sharp bitterness, acrid potency continuing when tender grasses could not withstand the drought. For the first time this seemed miraculous. Its stinging stench helped her to awaken. It was helping now. She breathed of it deeply.

Her back was gripped in a vise. She could not move within this iron shell holding her fast. Gradually motion came to her. She felt the contours of the ground beneath her and drew away from them. Bit by bit she moved her muscles. She could still feel Edwin's hand on her shoulder. She opened her eyes to him, knowing she would never forget his face at this moment. He lifted her in his arms and helped her to her feet.

With his arms still around her, Edwin drew Amelie to the wagon. "The horses are so tired; we ought to go back."

The horses turned happily and trotted for the shelter which had been denied them in this strangely halted journey.

When Edwin and Amelie reached their door the plain was lightening toward dawn. Inside, the children lay as they had left them, one arm of Lucy's flung out, her hand hanging limply.

Edwin pulled off his clothes as fast as he could and was at once asleep. But Amelie undressed more slowly. She wanted to sit a moment on the edge of the bed in the midst of this crowded cabin. Between the wall-boards the morning light fenced them in, upright saplings of light thrust in a stockade against the plain outside.

As Amelie undressed she noticed that her feet were resting upon her leather trunk. It was in the way, right out where the children could stumble on it. She pushed it under the bed.

This time it was Edwin's head that lay heavy on her shoulder, not hers on his. As he slept, his breath caught now and then as Roger's did when he yielded to sleep after tears. Wonderful to have him here, not afraid to rest now. The light of day was coming in between the boards, lighter, lighter still. She had no need to sleep, not with Edwin beside her. It was sweet to lie together, to know she had given him the seed for this strange unconquered land he loved.

Lyman Brown Ruggles
"SETTLERS' DITCH SONG"
FROM THE ALTA *ADVOCATE*, N.D.

Oh, we've now got done our ditching,
And now let's have some fun,
We'll celebrate and jubilate
O'er the labors we have done.

The work was long and tiresome,
But we pushed it right along,
So we'll celebrate, then irrigate,
And this shall be our song,

Then blow, ye winds, aye-ho,
Let fall the rain and snow.
Through old Cross Creek and the Settlers' Ditch
The water now may flow with melted snow and rain,
And we'll all get rich with the Settlers' Ditch
To grow the golden grain.

Then honor to the pioneers
Who first conceived the plan
To use the waters of Cross Creek to irrigate the land.
With Urton for the engineer, and the rest to lead the way,
They laid the grade where the ditch was made
For they saw that the thing would pay.

May Merrill Miller
"And the Gates Shall Be Opened"

After months of hard labor, the shareholders in the Sierra Ditch Company are about to open the headgates once more, just as their seed corn has ripened and their hearts are gladdened by spring wild flowers in fulsome abundance. Amelie is finally able to see the valley as Edwin had first beheld it: "And the sun rose and the sun set and the miracle continues." The settlers—whose hard work and perseverance have placed their dreams of family farms within reach—now plan a picnic to celebrate their changing fortunes. But soon rumors of new trouble emerge, and the settlers reexamine their land claims in light of the title supposedly held by the El Dorado Pacific Railroad.

The seed corn had no sooner been planted than a rain came, and another until it was as if all the waters held back these last three years were falling upon the earth. If it kept on, the stockmen said, the valley would be covered with a flood like that of '62, when the river was so high one could go from Kings Crossing right across the low plains to Visalia in a rowboat. This final deluge was withheld, but the corn, the first the Sandlappers had tried to grow, pierced through the wet earth with myriad green blades.

For the first time since Amelie had come to the valley, all the wild flowers blossomed. Not one feeble tint laid upon the drying grass by Indian paintbrushes, but orange poppies, lavender wild hyacinths, cream and yellow marguerites, rose, blue, and purple larkspur, and the ethereal white sand lilies that bloomed only in good years, sometimes withholding any sign for seven seasons. Pale ponds of bluebells mirrored the sky. Great gray bushes speared with blue lupines tangled in green-needled alfilaria and button mallow. Black-spotted mauve bird's-eyes, sweet white four-o'clocks, deep yellow buttercups, and lighter creamcups circled in great separate swirls, white-foamed with daisies. But the poppies were the ground swell of it all—when she looked far off the other hues became pastel foaming eddies caught in that great molten sea. For poppies flowed upon the valley to the dikes of the mountains—the brown earthworks of the Coast Range to the west, the blue white-painted Sierras halting the flux to the east. And the sun rose and the sun set and the miracle continues.

Isobel, walking this spring, often became entangled in a mass of flowers as high as herself. From the doorway Amelie, watching her, would look out upon the startling pasture, the river willows only a green hedge now for a garden.

This was the way Edwin had seen the valley that first time. He reminded her of it jubilantly; she believed it now. The scent of the flowers was borne into the cabin day and night, the doors could not shut against it; only darkness stilled the hum of the bees, increasing each day until the valley echoed with the sound.

The corn grew so fast one could almost see it lengthening, standing sharp and defiant, marking each settler's house with a green square. There was no need to guard it, the satiated cattle roamed where they were first herded, seeking no further delight than the lush alfilaria bedded in the flowers.

There were no more wagons going to Stockton for supplies; there was credit now for anyone at the small store in Nueva Esperanza; Frank Bailey was content to wait for his pay. And the El Dorado Pacific freight that came to Nueva Esperanza three times a week carried boxes of tinned oysters and sardines, bolts of cloth, shoes, and coffee, tea, tobacco, and spice. The heartened men returned to the ditch, all of them, even those who had scoffed most. And those who had kept on digging when the others had lost faith welcomed the deserters back. The ditch came closer now to Edwin's place, the great even gash of it cut through his field, and beyond to Horace Whitney's and to the last newcomers'—Pierre Lamonde's, Dan Fleming's, and Wade Norris's. There were no shifts now, everybody worked, every day. Amelie could hear Zeke singing before sun-up when he left with Edwin, both of them returning, happy and hungry, only when it was dark.

When the warmer weather came, the snows melted, for the Sierras, blue so long, with just a penciling of white, were covered with snow now far down the slopes. Amelie could see those far-off valley markings on clear days. The men were afraid the river would flood beyond all bounds, but the waters rose discreetly and flowed bank-high without spilling a single drop. The take-in was a small lake, the waters swirled around the headgate as if they protested being withheld until they were freed to pour into the waiting ditch.

In a month now, Edwin told Amelie one day early in April, the headgate would be opened and the waters turned into the main ditch. They must all work until then, for the men had been so discouraged by the dry years they had not even started to dig the smaller ditches branching across their own fields from the single trunk.

The members of the Sierra Ditch Company were proud of their membership now, Edwin told her, and had voted unanimously to celebrate the opening of the ditch by a picnic on May Day. And it would be no ordinary picnic. It would be advertised from Fresno to Stockton. They would get the Fresno band for the dance—a hundred and fifty dollars, but what of it?—they would charge three dollars a ticket; people would come.

Amelie, seeing Edwin so jubilant, could not quite match his own relief. Only a few weeks ago she had helped him seek the seed for this greening. It was too overwhelming. Success ripened quickly like the tall tasseled corn coming into ear.[...]

Early as they were, there were other teams at the headgate, the horses tethered at the bright pine hitching-racks, built for today. Edwin carried Amelie's basket to the tables set in the shadow of the river willows, while the children were soon playing with red-headed Connerys, jocund dark Schumachers, a whole tribe of black-haired bashful Lamondes, flaxen Halvorsons, and the Moore assortment of twins.

Letitia was already there, trying to keep up with Ulysses. For Ulysses was a wanderer. He wandered now around the picnic tables and out toward the river, Letitia after him. He was a big boy, tall and sturdy for a little over two years and beginning to chatter with a loquaciousness that puzzled his reticent Yankee mother and father. Horace and Letitia were harvest native to the stony limited soil of white-wintered Franklin County, Massachusetts, but Ulysses had been nurtured in a sunnier different valley. There was nothing spare or reticent about Ulysses. He was running away from his mother again, seeking the excitement and the clankety-clank of the men playing horseshoes under the farther willows. He would not wear a hat, and, bareheaded, grinned back at his pursuing mother, his small grimacing face triumphant.

Long-limbed Letitia finally caught him and brought him back, rewarding him shamelessly with a piece of cake and hovering over him, holding him until his hair was neatly parted and combed anew, even though he was ready to play again and continue his wandering.

"If that child keeps on growing, you'll have a hard time keeping up with him," Amelie laughed, knowing it pleased Letitia, but was the truth as well.

A little before noon the women covered their picnic baskets, leaving them on the new tables, and took their children by the hand, while the knots of men under the farther willows stopped telling stories and pitching horseshoes and, putting on their coats, their voices stilled, became silent as, with their hats in their hands, they walked bareheaded to the headgate by the banks of the river.

There were no benches; everyone stood to see the headgate opened.

The River of the Kings was wide here, bank-full between long lines of willows on either side, growing so low, feathery sprays of leaves almost dipped into the water. As far as the eye could see, the green willows stood, round, alike, symmetrical, as if they had marched from the east and from the west to stand on these banks to watch, as these people were watching now, the miracle, in this wide barren valley of the arid San Joaquin, of this vast flow of water, melted from the snows of the distant blue Sierras, passing through this last great channel before it poured into the lake of the Tulare. And it flowed as it must have flowed always, serenely, with only a swirling eddy now and then circling and floating on like a leaf, no current disturbing the one great equal tranquil flow that was motion, yet was a silence.

But here on this eastern bank was a halting of this stream on its imperturbable way to the lake of the Ta-chis. Here where Amelie and her neighbors stood was a notch cut by men's shovels, filled now with water, the triangle of the take-in pointing toward the headgate, waiting, latch unlifted, to bed its share of this river.

All the neighbors and their children crowded on either side of the take-in forming the outer sticks of this unfolded fan of mica-silted water. For the River of the Kings was not clear, but bore in May the false gold of silt that glittered in circles of light falling through the shade cast by the nearest willows.

How splendid the neighbors were this morning, the men and boys in Sunday suits, the women and little girls in new dresses! But they were Sigrid and Mary and Letitia and the rest in these garments Amelie had not seen before today, even though the last time she was here at this take-in each of them wore copper-toed brogans as she did and carried a hoe and helped one another tend a patch of ground planted to potatoes and peas and turnips. And she knew that she and they, as well as the men, had set their mark upon the banks of this river, for even last spring's dried grasses could not hide the trenches and rows of those common gardens. Amelie must take heed of them now, on this uneven ground, standing as the other women stood, the broods of little children hanging to their mothers' skirts, the toes of their shiny tasseled new shoes almost in the water.

Amelie was proud of Edwin as he stood there by the great timbered framework of the headgate with his hat off, making the first speech. She had never heard him speak in public before, she had not known that he could. But of course he had been Regal Commander of the Lodge in Las Flores, probably that was where he had learned. It was interesting to be this far from him, to be watching him demonstrating his gift to the others. How black his hair was, how kind and happy his black eyes! He looked so young today, almost as young as when they used to ride together along the San Francisquito. She loved him. They were still young together. She would prove it to him. There had been less tenderness these last few months with first anxiety and then all this planning for victory taking its place. This lifting of the headgate would bring new waters to them too. The child within her stirred. Never mind. As this child had a youth of its own in the darkness within her, her youth and Edwin's was a living stirring thing. They owned this present triumph together. She had helped him. It was good to know that. She smiled at him, but he did not see her.

It was gratifying to see Edwin turning his words from his neighbors for a moment to those strangers who were here already from Visalia and Fresno and Stockton, witnesses to the importance of the Sierra Ditch Company, speaking assuredly of capital stock and shares and cubic feet of water. When he had done he called upon the president of the Sierra Ditch Company for a few words.

There was something splendid about Arne this morning—more than his Sunday clothes, something about him standing by the headgate waiting to speak, his fine handsome head lifted, his blue eyes steadfast, that rooted Amelie to the ground. And there was something splendid about Sigrid too, standing so tall, watching Arne, with her golden braids wound around her head as some other woman must have stood by a blue fiord when her man set out in high-prowed ships for Iceland and Greenland and that farthest impossible greater land where the wild grapevines were turning.

And there was something splendid about each neighbor this morning, standing on the banks of this halted water to hear what Arne would say—even Tim Connery...something happy for Tim...home at last, no landlords, no walking in the ruts behind a cart knowing you can never own one, with only a crooked stick in your hand and a crooked lane turning to a thatched roof that must always be another's—something happy and splendid about freckled red-headed Tim, his face unguarded, trusting, triumphant....And scarred, meek Orrin, who had sought for gold in his youth and found only the slow painstaking way to make sluices for water burdened with mica, fool's gold, as he had built them now for this river....And young Harry and Janet, who would soon have a new roof of their own and room under it for the lyre-based tables and the ribbon spindles and the shell-blocked desk that would need no longer to be piled one on top of the other where it was so hard for Janet to dust them....And Jed Fassett no longer scowling, and Jessie sweet-faced for once—how could you judge her, how do you know what these years of percale and copper-toed brogans have done to her with no excursions to be taken save with her tongue?...And the newest neighbor, Pierre Lamonde, still a little strange with his broad-waisted wife, Marie, and all their dark brood decked out today with slender golden chains linked around their necks and the tiny gold crosses Vasquez had left in the plush-lined drawer in Kings Crossing, afraid to steal, sold by Eli Weinstein in his new store in Nueva Esperanza at a bargain to make room for new up-to-date stock....And August and Minna Schumacher, so clean, with their little ones' red cheeks polished like winter apples...and kind Rhoda, so good to Janet, and Ralph, who would no longer need to fill sacks with white-bellied catfish to peddle in Visalia for cash money for flour...and gaunt Horace and Letitia forgetting their austere Yankee selves, unashamed in happiness, with restless-footed Ulysses between them....Something rose in Amelie's throat as she saw her neighbors all together, herself close beside them, yet with her own ground to stand on...in this clear morning light, splendid somehow, our neighbors...how far they have come to meet in this common task in this desolate land we have conquered!

There was not a sound, not a breath in the willows, only her eyes could mark the peaceful flowing of the River of the Kings. But Amelie found herself turning from the river, as the other watchers turned, to follow Arne's glance. For he was looking past all of them where Arne always lifted his eyes—to the east. Amelie followed his gaze past the nearest river willows. There was a break in them. The blue Sierras with this year's widened white crests seemed very near— nearer than any day before—framed thus by the trees.

"We have waited," Arne said slowly, "yust for this one hour. We have believed the Lord who set the snows upon the mountains would share them with us and not forget His promise yet. 'And by the river upon the bank thereof, on this side and on that side, shall grow all trees for meat, whose leaf shall not fade, neither shall the fruit thereof be consumed: it shall bring forth new fruit according to his months, because their waters they issue out of the sanctuary.' Today we see His bounty. When we turn this water upon our land, yust let us not forget Him who sent us this blessing."

They would have a church, and a pastor too, in Nueva Esperanza soon, Edwin had promised. But Amelie knew when the pastor came he could not return truer thanks than Arne, who had planned to be a minister once, but who had become a ditch-digger with a shovel in the San Joaquin Valley. Amelie lifted her head and looked back at Arne proudly.

Arne's words hung in the quiet still air that was acrid with the smell of the willows. Lucy's moist hand clung to Amelie's, Isobel's smaller one fast within her other.

Overlaid with a Sheen of Gold

Amelie watched Arne lean over now to the headgate at his feet; balancing himself, arms outspread, Ralph Walker walked across the frame to the other side to stand by Orrin Moore, solemn and proud, ready to help with his own handiwork. With Edwin, they pulled out the cross-piece. Then Arne held up his hand for a sign and they lifted the whole gate of boards, leaving it high.

The withheld waters rushed into the void. One huge shining silty moving mass, a momentary crashing waterfall, then released, pouring and thrashing down through the wooden flume-box into the way cut for it in the dry valley earth. Amelie's eyes followed the running tongue of water, the ditch bed dry before it, until it reached to the next gate, with a group of men standing ready; then it too was opened—and on to the next, and the next and the next, men standing waiting by the gates as far as she could see.

Silently now the waters poured from the great River of the Kings into the Sandlappers' ditch. There was plenty; the banks were full.

Amelie looked once more toward the blue Sierras. She could see the constant snow upon them. Her eyes were wet as she turned again to her neighbors, silent beside the controlled waters.

◆

Ambrose Bierce
"ODE TO THE CENTRAL PACIFIC SPADE"
FROM THE SAN FRANCISCO *WASP*, 1884

Precursor of our woes, historic spade,
What dismal records burn upon thy blade?
On thee I see the maculating stains
Of passengers' commingled blood and brains;
In this red rust a widow's curse appears,
And here an orphan tarnished thee with tears;
Upon thy handle sanguinary bands
Reveal the clutching of thine owner's hands
When first he wielded thee with vigor brave
To cut a sod and dig a people's grave—
(For they who are debauched are dead and ought,
In God's name, to be hid from sight and thought.)
Within thee, as within a magic glass,
I seem to see a foul procession pass—

Judges with ermine dragging in the mud
And spotted here and there with guiltless blood;
Gold-greedy legislators jingling bribes,
Kept editors and sycophantic scribes;
Liars in swarms and plunderers in tribes.
They fade away before the night's advance,
And fancy figures thee a devil's lance
Gleaming portentous through the misty shade,
While ghosts of murdered virtues shriek around thy blade!

C. C. Post
"There Ought to Be a Law"

Silas Ensign, originally a workman employed by the Hydraulic Mining Company, has become John Parsons' son-in-law. Here he outlines his ideas about the evils of land ownership by corporations, including the railroads that "get their charters from the people on the plea of being public highways." Ensign's complaints underscore the gulf between the giant corporations—which are driven solely by their interest in large profits—and the small family farmers—who are driven by their vision of a simple, agrarian life, a dream secured by their land and by their hard work.

Ensign's ideas are reminiscent of those of the land-reform economist Henry George, who in 1871 charged that land monopolization was "the blight that has fallen upon California, stunting her growth and mocking her golden promise, offsetting to the immigrant the richness of her soil and the beneficence of her climate." [2]

Ensign remained with the family nearly a week, and every day endeared himself more and more to his wife's parents. It was in order that they might become better acquainted with him and thus not feel that they were giving their daughter to one so nearly a

---

[2] Henry George, "The Effect of Land Monopolization," 1871. In *California Heritage: An Anthology of History and Literature*, John and Laree Caughey, eds. (Los Angeles: Ward Ritchie, 1962), 331.

stranger that he remained. During his stay he helped all he could to put the place in better shape, and as the rains did not fall during the entire week, the two men were enabled to do much towards making things look more cheerful.

A shed for the horses was built out of lumber bought for that purpose by the former owner, but never erected. The broken places in the fence were repaired; the grape vines staked and tied up, and portions of the over abundant growth of fruit trees cut away.

It was really wonderful, the change which these little improvements made in the look of the place. But then they had the sun, and the sun with a very little assistance in the way of setting leaning fences and gates upright will, in a few days, make a great change in any picture first seen when wet and sodden by long continued rains.

As the two men worked they talked,—talked of the wrongs of the farmers and the laboring and business men of the cities; of the causes of so many losses and so much poverty and suffering and of the possible or impossible remedies.

"There ought to be a law to prevent corporations from ownin' land they don't need an' can't make no use on, 'cept to make them that does want to use it pay for the privilege," said Mr. Parsons, as they were at work repairing the fence. "No man can't be really free unless he has a home of his own, and here gover'ment has gone an' give half the State to corporations, an' how is the next gineration to git homes, I'd like to know.

"An' other corporations are washin' down the mountains an' a fillin' up the valleys; spilin' the finest lands; chokin' up the river, an' destroyin' the homes of honest folks jest as ef gold was of more value than bread. I've tried hard to get somethin' ahead agin old age come a creepin' on to us, and to give the youngsters a start when they left us, as Jennie is a doin' now, and here's what it all amounts to; a bit of land not much better than wild on the side of a mountain. The land God made, an' all the improvements that is on to it never cost a thousand dollars when they was new, and that ain't as much as my wife had when I married her; so we've got nothin' at all to show fer a lifetime of hard work an' savin'.

"So fur as we're concerned, mother n' me I mean, it don't make much difference any more. We're gettin' old and shan't last much longer; but ef you an' Jennie ain't no luckier than we hev been, and there ain't no change for the better in things, I'm afeard you won't have even sich a shanty as we've got to die in, and your children won't be no better than slaves. Ye see it holds to reason that ef things don't git no better they must git wus, fer every year the corporations an' the rich folks is a gittin' more an' more of the land, an' of everything else, an' the more they git the easier it is to git more, an' by an' by they'll hev it all, an' them as hain't got nothin' an' can't get nothin' will hev to do as they say or starve."

"I don't exactly understand where the wrong starts," replied Ensign, "but I know there is a great wrong somewhere. The ownership of land by corporations, and by others who only wish to play at dog-in-the-manger, is one cause for the existing condition of things, but there must be others.

"Some way or other the larger portion of all the wealth which the people create gets away from them while they are exchanging it among themselves. I don't know how, but it does. If it didn't there could not possibly be rich people who have never worked.

"The merchant buys the goods of the manufacturer and sells them to those who consume them, thus saving much time which would be wasted if each individual was forced to go to the manufacturer for every article purchased. The merchant is therefore a valuable member of society—he helps the producers to make an exchange of wealth, and is fairly entitled to receive pay for what he does. But there are the national banks, I don't see how they help any; and every particle they consume or hoard up is so much taken from the wealth which belongs to those who produce it. It seems to me that those who produce wealth ought to have wit enough to devise some means of exchanging it among themselves without paying a bank for the privilege. And every once in a while there comes a panic, and thousands of business men are ruined, and thousands of laboring men thrown out of employment, and then they get desperate and try all kinds of sharp tricks to catch up again. Now if nobody is benefited by these panics, some way ought to be devised to prevent them, and if anybody is benefited by them they are the fellows that ought to be watched and not allowed to have any hand in the making of the laws, for it is natural to suppose that they would legislate in their own interest and not in that of the laboring and business portion of the community.

"Then there are the railroads; they get their charters from the people on the plea of being public highways. The people build the roads and then the companies charge just what they choose for transporting the people and their goods from one part of the country to another, and if it is goods that they transport, they usually take a great deal more of them than they leave the producers, and then bribe Congress and courts and State legislatures not to interfere with them.

"And so it goes, and I don't know how to go to work to stop it."

"Wall," replied Mr. Parsons, "you're on the right track anyway, an' you jest want to keep agoin' till you think it all out. What you say about the exchangin' of wealth is sensible. It holds to reason that there oughtn't to be nothin' thrown in the way of folks exchangin' wealth. Them that works creates all the wealth there is, and if they had all the land to begin on, and weren't beat no way in the exchangin' of what they produced, it's mighty clear that ef a fellow didn't produce nothin' er help some way in the exchangin' of what others produced, he wouldn't have anything to eat very long. There ought to be some way discovered so that them that produce the wealth could trade among theirselves without supportin' a lot of fellers that don't do nothin' but stan' around an' look on.

"Ef you an' Rastus, now, could be together you'd figger it out between you in short meter, I'll wager. I tell you, Rastus is smart, and he's got the sand to back it, an' ef anybody ever goes to disturbin' him on his claim, there'll be trouble in camp dead sartin."

At last the day came when Jennie and her husband were to take their departure.

The family arose early and prepared breakfast as usual, but it was with heavy hearts and eyes wet with tears. And when it was eaten, Mr. Parsons went out and hitched the horses to the spring wagon and drove around to the door of the shanty, and helped Ensign to lift in Jennie's trunk. The smaller traveling bags followed. Then came the last kiss and clasping in arms and pledges of constant remembrance and love, over which we willingly draw a veil.

Who is there that has not witnessed similar partings; partings of those whose happiness depended so much on each other's presence, yet who were forced by the cruel necessity of hunting for dollars to tear themselves apart, and each go separate ways with half of the sunshine gone out of their lives?

Will the time never come when men will understand what the Teacher of men meant when He said, "Take no thought for the morrow"? And is it not possible, by being just to each other, to remove that constant, crushing weight of care which comes from the ever-present necessity of taking thought as to what we shall eat, and what we shall drink, and wherewithal we shall be clothed?

I believe it will come; I know that it is entirely possible.

When good-byes had been said, John Parsons drove the young couple to the Landing, where, with tears coursing down his cheeks, he too, bid them good-bye and God speed, and then, having fed his horses, again hitched up and started sadly homeward.

◆

B. B. Redding, Jerome Madden
"RAILROAD LANDS," 1876

> Central Pacific Railroad,
> Southern Pacific Railroad, }
> Land Departments,
> Corner of Fourth and Townsend Streets,
> San Francisco, California, July 1st, 1876

The following statement is made for the information of those who desire to purchase Lands from said Companies:

1st. Congress, to aid in the construction of the above mentioned Railroads, granted all the odd numbered Sections of non-mineral public land, within certain limits, excepting such as were reserved by the United States, and those to which a valid homestead or preemption right had attached prior to such grant, as follows:

To the Central Pacific Railroad (main line), all within twenty miles on each side of its road; to the California and Oregon branch of the C.P.R.R., all within twenty miles on each side of its line, and, where the odd numbered sections within said twenty miles have been taken by preemption, or otherwise, the Company has the right to select other vacant odd numbered sections as indemnity within the twentieth and thirtieth mile on each side of its line; and to the Southern Pacific Railroad, all within twenty miles on each side of its line, with an indemnity grant similar to that of the California and Oregon Railroad.

2d. The Companies have no interest in even numbered sections.

3d. To constitute a valid homestead or preemption claim, within the above exception, the party must have resided on the land prior to the grant to the Railroad, and continuously from that time. He must also, at that time, have been an American citizen (or declared his intentions), over twenty-one years of age, or the head of a family, and have filed his claim in the United States Land Office within the time required by law. If he has not these requisites, or has neglected to file, he will have to buy from the Railroad Company.

4th. All persons who desire to purchase lands from the Railroad Companies should make application to the Land Agents, at the Land Offices of the Companies, in San Francisco, California, either personally or by letter, describing the land by Section, Township and Range, according to legal subdivisions. This application will be filed, and the party allowed three months to complete the purchase, and during this time, the land will not be sold to another without giving the applicant thirty days previous notice. If the purchase is not completed within three months after sale of land shall commence in the locality where the tract is situated, it can be bought by other persons.

5th. An application for land confers no right or privilege on the applicant. It is merely a notice that he wishes to buy. *The first application is not given precedence over those which may be filed later.* Settlers and actual occupants, who in good faith cultivate and improve lands belonging to either of the Companies, will generally be given preference of purchase at the regular price, and they are invited to settle upon and improve the *vacant lands* whether they are applied for or not by other persons. Where there are conflicting claimants who apply to purchase, an adjudication of their respective claims will be made by the Land Agent, upon due notice given to the parties. Applications to purchase lands can be filed in the Land Offices of the Companies at any time after survey by the Government, but no application will be acted upon until three months after the Township plats shall have been filed in the United States Land Office. Blank applications will be furnished to all who desire to purchase. No sales will be made except by legal subdivisions, according to Government surveys. Purchasers will not be limited as to the amount of vacant lands they can buy. It must be borne in mind, however, that 640 acres is the largest tract that can be sold in any one place, the Railroad sections not being contiguous to each other, or *adjoining*.

In filling in the blanks, it is requested that a separate application be made for the lands in each township or, in other words, that lands in two or more Townships shall not be applied for in the same blank.

6th. The Companies sell ordinary agricultural, vineyard and grazing lands, at from $2.50 upwards per acre, according to quality. They will be sold for cash; or in tracts of not less than eighty acres, upon a credit of five years, if desired; that is— twenty per cent. in cash and the remainder payable at any time within five years, with interest at ten per cent. per annum. The interest must be paid yearly in advance, thus:

For example, take 160 acres of land and suppose the price to be $5.00 per acre,
If paid for in full, at time of purchase, the amount would be:
160 acres at $5.00 per acre .... $800.00 U. S. Coin.
If bought on the credit system, the amount
required for the first payment would be:
20 per cent. of $800.00 .... $160. 00
1st year's interest on remainder,
$640.00, at 10 per cent $64.00

Total amount of 1st payment.................. $224.00 U. S. Coin.

The other payments would be $64.00 each year—the annual interest, in advance—and at the end of five years, $640.00—the remainder of the principal. The $640.00 can be paid, and the interest stopped at any time within five years, but no installment of it will be received. No part of any interest paid will be refunded.

Timber and wood land is from $5.00 to $10.00 per acre, according to quality, and payment in full must be made at time of purchase.

7th. Purchasers of Railroad lands have many advantages over those purchasing from the Government. There are no lawyers or witness fees to pay, as is the case in "proving up" at the United States Land Office. Title can be perfected in less time. The land can be bought on credit, and in the interim between buying and final payment, the buyer can reside wherever he pleases; and he can, if he desires, mortgage or sell it.

8th. As the lands are listed by the United States Land Office to the Companies, competent and reliable men are sent to grade them and report the value of each particular piece. The report is examined, and if found correct, a price is established. It is that of unimproved land of the same quality in the immediate vicinity, at the time of the grading. In fixing the value, improvements made on the land are not taken into consideration, and the price is not increased in consequence. There is but one price—that fixed by the Company—and land will be sold at that rate to those entitled in equity to buy, even if a larger sum should be offered by others. The actual settler, therefore, in addition to being accorded the first privilege of purchase, is secured in his improvements.

9th. No deeds are made by the Companies until after the receipt of United States Patent.

B. B. Redding, *Land Agent, C.P.R.R. Co.*
Jerome Madden, *Land Agent, S.P.R.R. Co.*

◆

Frank Norris
"You Can't Break the Railroad"

On a rainy evening, the leading ranchers of the southern San Joaquin Valley come together at Magnus Derrick's home to discuss the railroad's rate setting, the schemes of railroad agent S. Behrman, and the power of the railroad president, the infamous Shelgrim, "a giant figure in the end-of-the-century finance." During the course of the evening, one of the ranchers suggests putting their own candidates on the railroad commission. No one is yet aware, however, that by fighting the railroad using its own underhanded means—influence peddling and bribery—the ranchers will have chosen a path that will have for them an unhappy result: the loss of their own credibility and virtue. In the debate that follows, the ranchers recall how they came to settle on railroad land, land that is not yet legally theirs thanks to the invitations issued by the railroad in their circulars.

When Annixter arrived at the Los Muertos ranch house that same evening, he found a little group already assembled in the dining-room. Magnus Derrick, wearing the frock coat of broadcloth that he had put on for the occasion, stood with his back to the fireplace. Harran sat close at hand, one leg thrown over the arm of his chair. Presley lounged on the sofa, in corduroys and high laced boots, smoking cigarettes. Broderson leaned on his folded arms at one corner of the dining table, and Genslinger, editor and proprietor of the principal newspaper of the county, the "Bonneville Mercury," stood with his hat and driving gloves under his arm, opposite Derrick, a half-emptied glass of whiskey and water in his hand.

As Annixter entered he heard Genslinger observe: "I'll have a leader in the 'Mercury' tomorrow that will interest you people. There's some talk of your ranch lands being graded in value this winter. I suppose you will all buy?"

In an instant the editor's words had riveted upon him the attention of every man in the room. Annixter broke the moment's silence that followed with the remark:

"Well, it's about time they graded these lands of theirs."

The question in issue in Genslinger's remark was of the most vital interest to the ranchers around Bonneville and Guadalajara. Neither Magnus Derrick, Broderson, Annixter, nor Osterman actually owned all the ranches which they worked. As yet, the vast majority of these wheat lands were the property of the P. and S. W. The explanation of this condition of affairs went back to the early history of the Pacific and Southwestern, when, as a bonus for the construction of the road, the national government had granted to the company the odd-numbered sections of land on either side of the proposed line of route for a distance of twenty miles. Indisputably, these sections belonged to the P. and S. W. The even-numbered sections being government property could be and had been taken up by the ranchers, but the railroad sections, or, as they were called, the "alternate sections," would have to be purchased direct from the railroad itself.

But this had not prevented the farmers from "coming in" upon that part of the San Joaquin. Long before this the railroad had thrown open these lands, and, by means of circulars, distributed broadcast throughout the State, had expressly invited settlement thereon. At that time patents had not been issued to the railroad for their odd-numbered sections, but as soon as the land was patented the railroad would grade it in value and offer it for sale, the first occupants having the first chance of purchase. The price of these lands was to be fixed by the price the government put upon its own adjoining lands—about two dollars and a half per acre.

With cultivation and improvement the ranches must inevitably appreciate in value. There was every chance to make fortunes. When the railroad lands about Bonneville had been thrown open, there had been almost a rush in the matter of settlement, and Broderson, Annixter, Derrick, and Osterman, being foremost with their claims, had secured the pick of the country. But the land once settled upon, the P. and S. W. seemed to be in no hurry as to fixing exactly the value of its sections included in the various ranches and offering them for sale. The matter dragged along from year to year, was forgotten for months together, being only brought to mind on such occasions as this, when the rumour spread that the General Office was about to take definite action in the affair.

"As soon as the railroad wants to talk business with me," observed Annixter, "about selling me their interest in Quien Sabe, I'm ready. The land has more than quadrupled in value. I'll bet I could sell it tomorrow for fifteen dollars an acre, and if I buy of the railroad for two and a half an acre, there's boodle in the game."

"For two and a half!" exclaimed Genslinger. "You don't suppose the railroad will let their land go for any such figure as that, do you? Wherever did you get that idea?"

"From the circulars and pamphlets," answered Harran, "that the railroad issued to us when they opened these lands. They are pledged to that. Even the P. and S. W. couldn't break such a pledge as that. You are new in the country, Mr. Genslinger. You don't remember the conditions upon which we took up this land."

"And our improvements," exclaimed Annixter. "Why, Magnus and I have put about five thousand dollars between us into that irrigating ditch already. I guess we are not improving the land just to make it valuable for the railroad people. No matter how much we improve the land, or how much it increases in value, they have got to stick by their agreement on the basis of two-fifty per acre. Here's one case where the P. and S. W. *don't* get everything in sight."

Genslinger frowned, perplexed.

"I *am* new in the country, as Harran says," he answered, "but it seems to me that there's no fairness in that proposition. The presence of the railroad has helped increase the value of your ranches quite as much as your improvements. Why should you get all the benefit of the rise in value and the railroad nothing? The fair way would be to share it between you."

"I don't care anything about that," declared Annixter. "They agreed to charge but two-fifty, and they've got to stick to it."

"Well," murmured Genslinger, "from what I know of the affair, I don't believe the P. and S. W. intends to sell for two-fifty an acre, at all. The managers of the road want the best price they can get for everything in these hard times."

"Times aren't ever very hard for the railroad," hazards old Broderson.

Broderson was the oldest man in the room. He was about sixty-five years of age, venerable, with a white beard, his figure bent earthwards with hard work.

He was a narrow-minded man, painfully conscientious in his statements lest he should be unjust to somebody; a slow thinker, unable to let a subject drop when once he had started upon it. He had no sooner uttered his remark about hard times than he was moved to qualify it.

"Hard times," he repeated, a troubled, perplexed note in his voice; "well, yes—yes. I suppose the road *does* have hard times, maybe. Everybody does—of course. I didn't mean that exactly. I believe in being just and fair to everybody. I mean that we've got to use their lines and pay their charges good years *and* bad years, the P. and S. W. being the only road in the State. That is—well, when I say the only road—no, I won't say the *only* road. Of course there are other roads. There's the D. P. and M. and the San Francisco and North Pacific, that runs up to Ukiah. I got a brother-in-law in Ukiah. That's not much of a wheat country round Ukiah, though they *do* grow *some* wheat there, come to think. But I guess it's too far north. Well, of course there isn't *much.* Perhaps sixty thousand acres in the whole county—if you include barley and oats. I don't know; maybe it's nearer forty thousand. I don't remember very well. That's a good many years ago. I—"

But Annixter, at the end of all patience, turned to Genslinger, cutting short the old man:

"Oh, rot! Of course the railroad will sell at two-fifty," he cried. "We've got the contracts."

"Look to them, then, Mr. Annixter," retorted Genslinger significantly, "look to them. Be sure that you are protected."

Soon after this Genslinger took himself away, and Derrick's Chinaman came in to set the table.

"What do you suppose he meant?" asked Broderson, when Genslinger was gone.

"About this land business?" said Annixter. "Oh, I don't know. Some tom fool idea. Haven't we got their terms printed in black and white in their circulars? There's their pledge."

"Oh, as to pledges," murmured Broderson, "the railroad is not always *too* much hindered by those."

"Where's Osterman?" demanded Annixter, abruptly changing the subject as if it were not worth discussion. "Isn't that goat Osterman coming down here tonight?"

"You telephoned him, didn't you, Presley?" inquired Magnus.

Presley had taken Princess Nathalie upon his knee, stroking her long, sleek hair, and the cat, stupefied with beatitude, had closed her eyes to two fine lines, clawing softly at the corduroy of Presley's trousers with alternate paws.

"Yes, sir," returned Presley. "He said he would be here."

And as he spoke, young Osterman arrived.

He was a young fellow, but singularly inclined to baldness. His ears, very red and large, stuck out at right angles from either side of his head, and his mouth, too, was large—a great horizontal slit beneath his nose. His cheeks were of a brownish red, the cheek bones a little salient. His face was that of a comic actor, a singer of songs, a man never at a loss for an answer, continually striving to make a laugh. But he took no great interest in ranching and left the management of his land to his superintendents and foremen, he, himself, living in Bonneville. He was a poser, a wearer of clothes, forever acting a part, striving to create an impression, to draw attention to himself. He was not without a certain energy, but he devoted it to small ends, to perfecting himself in little accomplishments, continually running after some new thing, incapable of persisting long in any one course.[...]

"Hello, boys and girls. Hello, Governor. Sort of a gathering of the clans to-night. Well, if here isn't that man Annixter. Hello, Buck. What do you know? Kind of dusty out to-night."

At once Annixter began to get red in the face, retiring towards a corner of the room, standing in an awkward position by the case of stuffed birds, shambling and confused, while Mrs. Derrick was present, standing rigidly on both feet, his elbows close to his sides. But he was angry with Osterman, muttering imprecations to himself, horribly vexed that the young fellow should call him "Buck" before Magnus's wife. This goat Osterman! Hadn't he any sense, that fool? Couldn't he ever learn how to behave before a feemale? Calling him "Buck" like that while Mrs. Derrick was there. Why a stableboy would know better; a hired man would have better manners.

All through the dinner that followed Annixter was out of sorts, sulking in his place, refusing to eat by way of vindicating his self-respect, resolving to bring Osterman up with a sharp turn if he called him "Buck" again.

The Chinaman had made a certain kind of plum pudding for dessert, and Annixter, who remembered other dinners at the Derricks', had been saving himself for this, and had meditated upon it all through the meal. No doubt, it would restore all his good humour, and he believed his stomach was so far recovered as to be able to stand it.

But, unfortunately, the pudding was served with a sauce that he abhorred—a thick, gruel-like, colourless mixture, made from plain water and sugar. Before he could interfere, the Chinaman had poured a quantity of it upon his plate.

"Faugh!" exclaimed Annixter. "It makes me sick. Such—such *sloop*. Take it away. I'll have mine straight, if you don't mind."

"That's good for your stomach, Buck," observed young Osterman; "makes it go down kind of sort of slick; don't you see? Sloop, hey? That's a good name."

"Look here, don't you call me Buck. You don't seem to have any sense, and, besides, it *isn't* good for my stomach. I know better. What do *you* know about my stomach, anyhow? Just looking at sloop like that makes me sick."

A little while after this the Chinaman cleared away the dessert and brought in coffee and cigars. The whiskey bottle and the syphon of soda-water reappeared. The men eased themselves in their places, pushing back from the table, lighting their cigars, talking of the beginning of the rains and the prospects of a rise in wheat. Broderson began an elaborate mental calculation, trying to settle in his mind the exact date of his visit to Ukiah, and Osterman did sleight-of-hand tricks with bread pills. But Princess Nathalie, the cat, was uneasy. Annixter was occupying her own particular chair in which she slept every night. She could not go to sleep, but spied upon him continually, watching his every movement with her lambent, yellow eyes, clear as amber.

Then, at length, Magnus, who was at the head of the table, moved in his place, assuming a certain magisterial attitude. "Well, gentlemen," he observed, "I have lost my case against the railroad, the grain-rate case. Ulsteen decided against me, and now I hear rumours to the effect that rates for the hauling of grain are to be advanced."

When Magnus had finished, there was a moment's silence, each member of the group maintaining his attitude of attention and interest. It was Harran who first spoke.

"S. Behrman manipulated the whole affair. There's a big deal of some kind in the air, and if there is, we all know who is back of it; S. Behrman, of course, but who's back of him? It's Shelgrim."

Shelgrim! The name fell squarely in the midst of the conversation, abrupt, grave, sombre, big with suggestion, pregnant with huge associations. No one in the group who was not familiar with it; no one, for that matter, in the county, the State, the whole reach of the West, the entire Union, that did not entertain convictions as to the man who carried it; a giant figure in the end-of-the-century finance, a product of circumstance, an inevitable result of conditions, characteristic, typical, symbolic of ungovernable forces. In the New Movement, the New Finance, the reorganisation of capital, the amalgamation of powers, the consolidation of enormous enterprises—no one individual was more constantly in the eye of the world; no one was more hated, more dreaded, no one more compelling of unwilling tribute to his commanding genius, to the colossal intellect operating the width of an entire continent than the president and owner of the Pacific and Southwestern.

"I don't think, however, he has moved yet," said Magnus.

"The thing for us, then," exclaimed Osterman, "is to stand from under before he does."

"Moved yet!" snorted Annixter. "He's probably moved so long ago that we've never noticed it."

"In any case," hazarded Magnus, "it is scarcely probable that the deal—whatever it is to be—has been consummated. If we act quickly, there may be a chance."

"Act quickly! How?" demanded Annixter. "Good Lord! What can you do? We're cinched already. It all amounts to just this: *You can't buck against the railroad.* We've tried it and tried it, and we are stuck every time. You, yourself, Derrick, have just lost your grain-rate case. S. Behrman did you up. Shelgrim owns the courts. He's got men like Ulsteen in his pocket. He's got the Railroad Commission in his pocket. He's got the Governor of the State in his pocket. He keeps a million-dollar lobby at Sacramento every minute of the time the legislature is in session; he's got his own men on the floor of the United States Senate. He has the whole thing organised like an army corps. What *are* you going to do? He sits in his office in San Francisco and pulls the strings and we've got to dance.

"But—well—but," hazarded Broderson, "but there's the Interstate Commerce Commission. At least on long-haul rates they—"

"Hoh, yes, the Interstate Commerce Commission," shouted Annixter, scornfully, "that's great, ain't it? The greatest Punch and Judy show on earth. It's almost as good as the Railroad Commission. There never was and there never will be a California Railroad Commission not in the pay of the P. and S. W."

"It is to the Railroad Commission, nevertheless," remarked Magnus, "that the people of the State must look for relief. That is our only hope. Once elect Commissioners who would be loyal to the people, and the whole system of excessive rates falls to the ground."

"Well, why not *have* a Railroad Commission of our own, then?" suddenly declared young Osterman.

"Because it can't be done," retorted Annixter. "*You can't buck against the railroad* and if you could you can't organise the farmers in the San Joaquin. We tried it once, and it was enough to turn your stomach. The railroad quietly bought delegates through S. Behrman and did us up."

"Well, that's the game to play," said Osterman decisively, "buy delegates."

"It's the only game that seems to win," admitted Harran gloomily.

"Or ever will win," exclaimed Osterman, a sudden excitement seeming to take possession of him. His face—the face of a comic actor, with its great slit of mouth and stiff, red ears—went abruptly pink.

"Look here," he cried, "this thing is getting desperate. We've fought and fought in the courts and out and we've tried agitation and—and all the rest of it and S. Behrman sacks us every time. Now comes the time when there's a prospect of a big crop; we've had no rain for two years and the land has had a long rest. If there is any rain at all this winter, we'll have a bonanza year, and just at this very moment when we've got our chance—a chance to pay off our mortgages and get clear of debt and make a strike here is Shelgrim making a deal to cinch us and put up rates. And now here's the primaries coming off and a new Railroad Commission going in. That's why Shelgrim chose this time to make his deal. If we wait till Shelgrim pulls it off, we're done for, that's flat. I tell you we're in a fix if we don't keep an eye open. Things are getting desperate. Magnus has just said that the key to the whole thing is the Railroad Commission. Well, why not have a Commission of our own? Never mind how we get it, let's get it. If it's got to be bought, let's buy it and put our own men on it and dictate what the rates will be. Suppose it costs a hundred thousand dollars. Well, we'll get back more than that in cheap rates."

"Mr. Osterman," said Magnus, fixing the voting man with a swift glance, "Mr. Osterman, you are proposing a scheme of bribery, sir."

"I am proposing," repeated Osterman, "a scheme of bribery. Exactly so."

All that the Traffic Will Bear

Wen wealthy railroad tycoon Charles Crocker moved to San Francisco's Nob Hill in the 1870s, he wanted to extend his property across an entire city block. One small property owner, an undertaker named Yung, refused Crocker's offers to buy, so the frustrated railroad magnate surrounded the poor undertaker's property with a wall forty feet high. The "spite fence" took on symbolic importance for San Franciscans as a ridiculous case of capitalist excess.[1] Crocker's apparent indifference to public opinion helped create a climate in which almost every issue touching the Big Four could be spun by an unsympathetic press into an example of capitalist oppression, including—when the time came—the Mussel Slough troubles.

In this highly charged climate of divisive rhetoric, the Mussel Slough Settlers' League published an "Appeal to the People" that sought to play on the public's ready sympathy by using the image of the virtuous yeoman farmer, driven to righteous indignation by the indifference and increasingly familiar excesses of the railroad corporation, a body guided only by the pursuit of profit. In such a climate it really didn't matter to the public how the rates for shipping were set or how the value of railroad land was calculated; nobody ever cares about Goliath's side of the story.

The Mussel Slough novelists often used commonly held images of wealthy capitalists and innocent farmers. Sometimes writers symbolized the gulf between them through describing the lavish foods and expensive clothes and jewelry that made life, they seemed to say, better for the wealthy railroad barons than for poor family farmers. Sometimes writers like William Morrow and C. C. Post showed the gap

---

[1] See Oscar Lewis, *The Big Four: The Story of Huntington, Stanford, Hopkins, and Crocker and the Building of the Central Pacific* (New York: Knopf, 1941), 114–20.

more directly, by creating two-dimensional caricatures of California capitalists. Whatever the method, depicting the differences between the crass railroad owners and the stubborn but admirably virtuous farmers of the San Joaquin formed a familiar context in which the Mussel Slough novelists heightened their narratives' tensions. In the Mussel Slough novels, rumors about raised prices for railroad land and anxiety over uncertain shipping rates inspire farmers to band together to fight their oppressors. Whereas this narrative thread was followed closely by Morrow and Post, Frank Norris employed a more subtle approach, creating characters who in their win-at-all-costs fight against the railroad find themselves adopting the same vile tactics as their enemy. And certainly their motives were not entirely pure ones either.

In this section, prejudice, misunderstanding, intolerance, and greed set the stage for a bloody climax.

Frank Norris
"A Pretty Mess"

Harran Derrick, son of the great opportunist Magnus Derrick—patriarch of the enormous El Rancho De Los Muertos—sets out for the railroad depot to collect his father. After they meet, Magnus is pleased to see that the new plows he has ordered from the east have arrived at the Guadalajara Pacific and Southwestern Railroad depot. But before he can have them offloaded, he encounters the local railroad agent, the odious S. Behrman. Still gloating over the defeat of Derrick's challenge to the railroad's rate structure, Behrman tells Derrick he cannot have his plows: "Freight of this kind coming from the Eastern points into the State must go first to one of our common points and be reshipped from there." [2] Harran thinks the regulation is merely a ploy to make farmers pay higher "short-haul" rates for the additional shipping, a constant sore point with farmers who had little choice but to pay what the railroads asked.

Something very much like the system Norris describes affected the Mussel Slough region. According to Stuart Daggett, several factors governed the rates charged by the railroad, among them distance and the existence of competition.

---

[2] According to J. L. Brown, something very like the incident Norris relates actually occurred in Mussel Slough country and gained local publicity. "The value of good will," says Brown, "was lightly regarded in those days." J. L. Brown, *The Mussel Slough Tragedy* (1958; Lemoore, CA: Kings River Press, 2001), 37–38.

Terminal points were often established near the coast to attract business away from water transportation, which meant that goods from the east might very well be shipped through their final destination to a terminal point, from where they would be sent back to their final destination. This system served the railroad's legitimate interest in efficiency and in keeping long-haul rates low enough to attract transcontinental business.[3]

The morning was fine; there was no cloud in the sky, but as Harran's buggy drew away from the grove of trees about the ranch house, emerging into the open country on either side of the Lower Road, he caught himself looking sharply at the sky and the faint line of hills beyond the Quien Sabe ranch. There was a certain indefinite cast to the landscape that to Harran's eye was not to be mistaken. Rain, the first of the season, was not far off.

"That's good," he muttered, touching the bays with the whip, "we can't get our ploughs to hand any too soon."

These ploughs Magnus Derrick had ordered from an Eastern manufacturer some months before, since he was dissatisfied with the results obtained from the ones he had used hitherto, which were of local make. However, there had been exasperating and unexpected delays in their shipment. Magnus and Harran both had counted upon having the ploughs in their implement barns that very week, but a tracer sent after them had only resulted in locating them, still *en route*, somewhere between The Needles and Bakersfield. Now there was likelihood of rain within the week. Ploughing could be undertaken immediately afterward, so soon as the ground was softened, but there was a fair chance that the ranch would lie idle for want of proper machinery.

It was ten minutes before train time when Harran reached the depot at Guadalajara. The San Francisco papers of the preceding day had arrived on an earlier train. He bought a couple from the station agent and looked them over till a distant and prolonged whistle announced the approach of the down train.

In one of the four passengers that alighted from the train, he recognised his father. He half rose in his seat, whistling shrilly between his teeth, waving his hand, and Magnus Derrick, catching sight of him, came forward quickly.

---

[3] Stuart Daggett, *Chapters on the History of the Southern Pacific* (New York: Augustus M. Kelley, 1966), 275–283.

Magnus—the Governor—was all of six feet tall, and though now well toward his sixtieth year, was as erect as an officer of cavalry. He was broad in proportion, a fine commanding figure, imposing an immediate respect, impressing one with a sense of gravity, of dignity and a certain pride of race. He was smooth-shaven, thin-lipped, with a broad chin, and a prominent hawk-like nose—the characteristic of the family—thin, with a high bridge, such as one sees in the later portraits of the Duke of Wellington. His hair was thick and iron-grey, and had a tendency to curl in a forward direction just in front of his ears. He wore a top-hat of grey, with a wide brim, and a frock coat, and carried a cane with a yellowed ivory head.

As a young man it had been his ambition to represent his native State—North Carolina—in the United States Senate. Calhoun was his "great man," but in two successive campaigns he had been defeated. His career checked in this direction, he had come to California in the fifties. He had known and had been the intimate friend of such men as Terry, Broderick, General Baker, Lick, Alvarado, Emerich, Larkin, and, above all, of the unfortunate and misunderstood Ralston. Once he had been put forward as the Democratic candidate for governor, but failed of election. After this Magnus had definitely abandoned politics and had invested all his money in the Corpus Christi mines. Then he had sold out his interest at a small profit—just in time to miss his chance of becoming a multi-millionaire in the Comstock boom—and was looking for reinvestments in other lines when the news that "wheat had been discovered in California" was passed from mouth to mouth. Practically it amounted to a discovery. Dr. Glenn's first harvest of wheat in Colusa County, quietly undertaken but suddenly realised with dramatic abruptness, gave a new matter for reflection to the thinking men of the New West. California suddenly leaped unheralded into the world's market as a competitor in wheat production. In a few years her output of wheat exceeded the value of her output of gold, and when, later on, the Pacific and Southwestern Railroad threw open to settlers the rich lands of Tulare County—conceded to the corporation by the government as a bonus for the construction of the road—Magnus had been quick to seize the opportunity and had taken up the ten thousand acres of Los Muertos. Wherever he had gone, Magnus had taken his family with him. Lyman had been born at Sacramento during the turmoil and excitement of Derrick's campaign for governor, and Harran at Shingle Springs, in El Dorado County, six years later.

But Magnus was in every sense the "prominent man." In whatever circle he moved he was the chief figure. Instinctively other men looked to him as the leader. He himself was proud of this distinction; he assumed the grand manner very easily and carried it well. As a public speaker he was one of the last of the followers of the old school of orators. He even carried the diction and manner of the rostrum into private life. It was said of him that his most colloquial conversation could be taken down in shorthand and read off as an admirable specimen of pure, well-chosen English. He loved to do things upon a grand scale, to preside, to dominate. In his good humour there was something Jovian. When angry, everybody around him trembled. But he had not the genius for detail, was not patient. The certain grandiose lavishness of his disposition occupied itself more with results than with means. He was always ready to take chances, to hazard everything on the hopes of colossal returns. In the mining days at Placerville there was no more redoubtable poker player in the county. He had been as lucky in his mines as in his gambling, sinking shafts and tunnelling in violation of expert theory and finding "pay" in every case. Without knowing it, he allowed himself to work his ranch much as if he was still working his mine. The old-time spirit of '49, hap-hazard, unscientific, persisted in his mind. Everything was a gamble—who took the greatest chances was most apt to be the greatest winner. The idea of manuring Los Muertos, of husbanding his great resources, he would have scouted as niggardly, Hebraic, ungenerous.

Magnus climbed into the buggy, helping himself with Harran's outstretched hand which he still held. The two were immensely fond of each other, proud of each other. They were constantly together and Magnus kept no secrets from his favourite son.

"Well, boy."

"Well, Governor."

"I am very pleased you came yourself, Harran. I feared that you might be too busy and send Phelps. It was thoughtful."

Harran was about to reply, but at that moment Magnus caught sight of the three flat cars loaded with bright-painted farming machines which still remained on the siding above the station. He laid his hands on the reins and Harran checked the team.

"Harran," observed Magnus, fixing the machinery with a judicial frown, "Harran, those look singularly like our ploughs. Drive over, boy."

The train had by this time gone on its way and Harran brought the team up to the siding.

"Ah, I was right," said the Governor. "'Magnus Derrick, Los Muertos, Bonneville, from Ditson & Co., Rochester.' These are ours, boy."

Harran breathed a sigh of relief.

"At last," he answered, "and just in time, too. We'll have rain before the week is out. I think, now that I am here, I will telephone Phelps to send the wagon right down for these. I started blue-stoning to-day."

Magnus nodded a grave approval.

"That was shrewd, boy. As to the rain, I think you are well informed; we will have an early season. The ploughs have arrived at a happy moment."

"It means money to us, Governor," remarked Harran.

But as he turned the horses to allow his father to get into the buggy again, the two were surprised to hear a thick, throaty voice wishing them good-morning, and turning about were aware of S. Behrman, who had come up while they were examining the ploughs. Harran's eyes flashed on the instant and through his nostrils he drew a sharp, quick breath, while a certain rigour of carriage stiffened the set of Magnus Derrick's shoulders and back. Magnus had not yet got into the buggy, but stood with the team between him and S. Behrman, eyeing him calmly across the horses' backs. S. Behrman came around to the other side of the buggy and faced Magnus.

He was a large, fat man, with a great stomach; his cheek and the upper part of his thick neck ran together to form a great tremulous jowl, shaven and blue-grey in colour; a roll of fat, sprinkled with sparse hair, moist with perspiration, protruded over the back of his collar. He wore a heavy black moustache. On his head was a round-topped hat of stiff brown straw, highly varnished. A light-brown linen vest, stamped with innumerable interlocked horseshoes, covered his protuberant stomach, upon which a heavy watch chain of hollow links rose and fell with his difficult breathing, clinking against the vest buttons of imitation mother-of-pearl.

S. Behrman was the banker of Bonneville. But besides this he was many other things. He was a real estate agent. He bought grain; he dealt in mortgages. He was one of the local political bosses, but more important than all this, he was the representative of the Pacific and Southwestern Railroad in that section of Tulare County. The railroad did little business in that part of the country that S. Behrman did not supervise, from the consignment of a shipment of wheat to the management of a damage suit, or even to the repair and maintenance of the right of way. During the time when the ranchers of the county were fighting the grain-rate case, S. Behrman had been much in evidence in and about the San Francisco court rooms and the lobby of the legislature in Sacramento. He had returned to Bonneville only recently, a decision adverse to the ranchers being foreseen. The position he occupied on the salary list of the Pacific and Southwestern could not readily be defined, for he was neither freight agent, passenger agent, attorney, real-estate broker, nor political servant, though his influence in all these offices was undoubted and enormous. But for all that, the ranchers about Bonneville knew whom to look to as a source of trouble. There was no denying the fact that for Osterman, Broderson, Annixter and Derrick, S. Behrman was the railroad.

"Mr. Derrick, good-morning," he cried as he came up. "Good-morning, Harran. Glad to see you back, Mr. Derrick." He held out a thick hand.

Magnus, head and shoulders above the other, tall, thin, erect, looked down upon S. Behrman, inclining his head, failing to see his extended hand.

"Good-morning, sir," he observed, and waited for S. Behrman's further speech.

"Well, Mr. Derrick," continued S. Behrman, wiping the back of his neck with his handkerchief, "I saw in the city papers yesterday that our case had gone against you."

"I guess it wasn't any great news to *you*," commented Harran, his face scarlet. "I guess you knew which way Ulsteen was going to jump after your very first interview with him. You don't like to be surprised in this sort of thing, S. Behrman."

"Now, you know better than that, Harran," remonstrated S. Behrman blandly. "I know what you mean to imply, but I ain't going to let it make me get mad. I wanted to say to your Governor—I wanted to say to you, Mr. Derrick—as one man to another—letting alone for the minute that we were on opposite sides of the case—that I'm sorry you didn't win. Your side made a good fight, but it was in a mistaken cause. That's the whole trouble. Why, you could have figured out before you ever went into the case that such rates are confiscation of property. You must allow us—must allow the railroad—a fair interest on the investment. You don't want us to go into the receiver's hands, do you now, Mr. Derrick?"

"The Board of Railroad Commissioners was bought," remarked Magnus sharply, a keen, brisk flash glinting in his eye.

"It was part of the game," put in Harran, "for the Railroad Commission to cut rates to a ridiculous figure, far below a *reasonable* figure, just so that it *would* be confiscation. Whether Ulsteen is a tool of yours or not, he had to put the rates back to what they were originally."

"If you enforced those rates, Mr. Harran," returned S. Behrman calmly, "we wouldn't be able to earn sufficient money to meet operating expenses or fixed charges, to say nothing of a surplus left over to pay dividends—"

"Tell me when the P. and S. W. ever paid dividends."

"The lowest rates," continued S. Behrman, "that the legislature can establish must be such as will secure us a fair interest on our investment."

"Well, what's your standard? Come, let's hear it. Who is to say what's a fair rate? The railroad has its own notions of fairness sometimes."

"The laws of the State," returned S. Behrman, "fix the rate of interest at seven per cent. That's a good enough standard for us. There is no reason, Mr. Harran, why a dollar invested in a railroad should not earn as much as a dollar represented by a promissory note—seven per cent. By applying your schedule of rates we would not earn a cent; we would be bankrupt."

"Interest on your investment!" cried Harran, furious. "It's fine to talk about fair interest. *I* know and *you* know that the total earnings of the P. and S. W.—their main, branch and leased lines for last year— was between nineteen and twenty millions of dollars. Do you mean to say that twenty million dollars is seven per cent. of the original cost of the road?"

S. Behrman spread out his hands, smiling.

"That was the gross, not the net figure—and how can you tell what was the original cost of the road?"

"Ah, that's just it," shouted Harran, emphasising each word with a blow of his fist upon his knee, his eyes sparkling, "you take cursed good care that we don't know anything about the original cost of the road. But we know you are bonded for treble your value; and we know this: that the road *could* have been built for fifty-four thousand dollars per mile and that you *say* it cost you eighty-seven thousand. It makes a difference, S. Behrman, on which of these two figures you are basing your seven per cent."

"That all may show obstinacy, Harran," observed S. Behrman vaguely, "but it don't show common sense."

"We are threshing out old straw, I believe, gentlemen," remarked Magnus. "The question was thoroughly sifted in the courts."

"Quite right," assented S. Behrman. "The best way is that the railroad and the farmer understand each other and get along peaceably. We are both dependent on each other. Your ploughs, I believe, Mr. Derrick." S. Behrman nodded toward the flat cars.

"They are consigned to me," admitted Magnus.

"It looks a trifle like rain," observed S. Behrman, easing his neck and jowl in his limp collar. "I suppose you will want to begin ploughing next week."

"Possibly," said Magnus.

"I'll see that your ploughs are hurried through for you then, Mr. Derrick. We will route them by fast freight for you and it won't cost you anything extra."

"What do you mean?" demanded Harran. "The ploughs are here. We have nothing more to do with the railroad. I am going to have my wagons down here this afternoon."

"I am sorry," answered S. Behrman, "but the cars are going north, not, as you thought, coming *from* the north. They have not been to San Francisco yet."

Magnus made a slight movement of the head as one who remembers a fact hitherto forgotten. But Harran was as yet unenlightened.

"To San Francisco!" he answered, "we want them here—what are you talking about?"

"Well, you know, of course, the regulations," answered S. Behrman. "Freight of this kind coming from the Eastern points into the State must go first to one of our common points and be reshipped from there."

Harran did remember now, but never before had the matter so struck home. He leaned back in his seat in dumb amazement for the instant. Even Magnus had turned a little pale. Then, abruptly, Harran broke out violent and raging.

"What next? My God, why don't you break into our houses at night? Why don't you steal the watch out of my pocket, steal the horses out of the harness, hold us up with a shot-gun; yes, 'stand and deliver; your money or your life.' Here we bring our ploughs from the East over your lines, but you're not content with your long-haul rate between Eastern points and Bonneville. You want to get us under your ruinous short-haul rate between Bonneville and San Francisco, *and return.* Think of it! Here's a load of stuff for Bonneville that can't stop at Bonneville, where it is consigned, but has got to go up to San

Francisco first *by way of* Bonneville, at forty cents per ton and then be reshipped from San Francisco back to Bonneville again at *fifty-one* cents per ton, the short-haul rate. And we have to pay it all or go without. Here are the ploughs right here, in sight of the land they have got to be used on, the season just ready for them, and we can't touch them. Oh," he exclaimed in deep disgust, "isn't it a pretty mess! Isn't it a farce! the whole dirty business!"

S. Behrman listened to him unmoved, his little eyes blinking under his fat forehead, the gold chain of hollow links clicking against the pearl buttons of his waistcoat as he breathed.

"It don't do any good to let loose like that, Harran," he said at length. "I am willing to do what I can for you. I'll hurry the ploughs through, but I can't change the freight regulation of the road."

"What's your blackmail for this?" vociferated Harran. " How much do you want to let us go? How much have we got to pay you to be *allowed* to use our own ploughs—what's your figure? Come, spit it out."

"I see you are trying to make me angry, Harran," returned S. Behrman, "but you won't succeed. Better give up trying, my boy. As I said, the best way is to have the railroad and the farmer get along amicably. It is the only way we can do business. Well, s'long, Governor, I must trot along. S'long, Harran." He took himself off.

Frank Norris
"Every Lump of Dirt"

Buck Annixter wants to get things settled. So he visits the land office of the Pacific and Southwestern Railroad, where he finds annoying, small-minded bureaucrat Cyrus Blakelee Ruggles in charge but unwilling to take Annixter's money, meant as a down payment on the railroad sections contained within his Quien Sabe Rancho borders. Annixter, speaking for himself and his fellow farmers, tells Ruggles, "We want to own our land, want to feel we can do what we blame please with it." It is a cry for independence and an assertion of confidence and self-sufficiency.

In the centre of the best business block of the street was a three-story building of rough brown stone, set off with plate glass windows and gold-lettered signs. One of these latter read, "Pacific and Southwestern Railroad, Freight and Passenger Office," while another, much smaller, beneath the windows of the second story, bore the inscription, "P. and S. W. Land Office."

Annixter hitched his horse to the iron post in front of this building and tramped up to the second floor, letting himself into an office where a couple of clerks and bookkeepers sat at work behind a high wire screen. One of these latter recognised him and came forward.

"Hello," said Annixter abruptly, scowling the while, "Is your boss in? Is Ruggles in?"

The bookkeeper led Annixter to the private office in an adjoining room, ushering him through a door, on the frosted glass of which was painted the name, "Cyrus Blakelee Ruggles." Inside, a man in a frock coat, shoestring necktie, and Stetson hat sat writing at a roller-top desk. Over this desk was a vast map of the railroad holdings in the country about Bonneville and Guadalajara, the alternate sections belonging to the Corporation accurately plotted.

Ruggles was cordial in his welcome of Annixter. He had a way of fiddling with his pencil continually while he talked, scribbling vague lines and fragments of words and names on stray bits of paper, and no sooner had Annixter sat down than he had begun to write, in full-bellied script, *Ann Ann* all over his blotting pad.

"I want to see about those lands of mine—I mean of yours—of the railroad's," Annixter commenced at once. "I want to know when I can buy. I'm sick of fooling along like this."

"Well, Mr. Annixter," observed Ruggles, writing a great *L* before the *Ann,* and finishing it off with a flourishing *d.* "The lands"—he crossed out one of the *n*'s and noted the effect with a hasty glance— "the lands are practically yours. You have an option on them indefinitely, and, as it is, you don't have to pay the taxes."

"Rot your option! I want to own them," Annixter declared. "What have you people got to gain by putting off selling them to us. Here this thing has dragged along for over eight years. When I came in on Quien Sabe, the understanding was that the lands—your alternate sections—were to be conveyed to me within a few months."

"The land had not been patented to us then," answered Ruggles.

"Well, it has been now, I guess," retorted Annixter.

"I'm sure I couldn't tell you, Mr. Annixter."

Annixter crossed his legs weariedly.

"Oh, what's the good of lying, Ruggles? You know better than to talk that way to me."

Ruggles's face flushed on the instant, but he checked his answer and laughed instead.

"Oh, if you know so much about it—" he observed.

"Well, when are you going to sell to me?"

"I'm only acting for the General Office, Mr. Annixter," returned Ruggles. "Whenever the Directors are ready to take that matter up, I'll be only too glad to put it through for you."

"As if you didn't know. Look here, you're not talking to old Broderson. Wake up, Ruggles. What's all this talk in Genslinger's rag about the grading of the value of our lands this winter and an advance in the price?"

Ruggles spread out his hands with a deprecatory gesture.

"I don't own the 'Mercury,'" he said.

"Well, your company does."

"If it does, I don't know anything about it."

"Oh, rot! As if you and Genslinger and S. Behrman didn't run the whole show down here. Come on, let's have it, Ruggles. What does S. Behrman pay Genslinger for inserting that three-inch ad. of the P. and S. W. in his paper? Ten thousand a year, hey?"

"Oh, why not a hundred thousand and be done with it?" returned the other, willing to take it as a joke.

Instead of replying, Annixter drew his check-book from his inside pocket.

"Let me take that fountain pen of yours," he said. Holding the book on his knee he wrote out a check, tore it carefully from the stub, and laid it on the desk in front of Ruggles.

"What's this?" asked Ruggles.

"Three-fourths payment for the sections of railroad land included in my ranch, based on a valuation of two dollars and a half per acre. You can have the balance in sixty-day notes."

Ruggles shook his head, drawing hastily back from the check as though it carried contamination.

"I can't touch it," he declared. "I've no authority to sell to you yet."

"I don't understand you people," exclaimed Annixter. "I offered to buy of you the same way four years ago and you sang the same song. Why, it isn't business. You lose the interest on your money. Seven per cent of that capital for four years—you can figure it out. It's big money."

"Well, then, I don't see why you're so keen on parting with it. You can get seven per cent. the same as us."

"I want to own my own land," returned Annixter. "I want to feel that every lump of dirt inside my fence is my personal property. Why, the very house I live in now—the ranch house—stands on railroad ground."

"But, you've an option—"

"I tell you I don't want your cursed option. I want ownership; and it's the same with Magnus Derrick and old Broderson and Osterman and all the ranchers of the county. We want to own our land, want to feel we can do as we blank please with it. Suppose I should want to sell Quien Sabe. I can't sell it as a whole till I've bought of you. I can't give anybody a clear title. The land has doubled in value ten times over again since I came in on it and improved it. It's worth easily twenty an acre now. But I can't take advantage of that rise in value so long as you won't sell, so long as I don't own it. You're blocking me."

"But, according to you, the railroad can't take advantage of the rise in any case. According to you, you can sell for twenty dollars, but *we* can only get two and a half."

"Who made it worth twenty?" cried Annixter. "I've improved it up to that figure. Genslinger seems to have that idea in his nut, too. Do you people think you can hold that land, untaxed, for speculative purposes until it goes up to thirty dollars and then sell out to some one else—sell it over our heads? You and Genslinger weren't in office when those contracts were drawn. You ask your boss, you ask S. Behrman, *he* knows. The General Office is pledged to sell to us in preference to any one else, for two and a half."

"Well," observed Ruggles decidedly, tapping the end of his pencil on his desk and leaning forward to emphasise his words, "we're not selling *now*. That's said and signed, Mr. Annixter."

"Why not? Come, spit it out. What's the bunco game this time?"

"Because we're not ready. Here's your check."

"You won't take it?"

"No."

"I'll make it a cash payment, money down—the whole of it—payable to Cyrus Blakelee Ruggles, for the P. and S. W."

"No."

"Third and last time."

"No."

"Oh, go to the devil!"

"I don't like your tone, Mr. Annixter," returned Ruggles, flushing angrily.

"I don't give a curse whether you like it or not," retorted Annixter, rising and thrusting the check into his pocket, "but never you mind, Mr. Ruggles, you and S. Behrman and Genslinger and Shelgrim and the whole gang of thieves of you—you'll wake this State of California up some of these days by going just one little bit *too* far, and there'll be an election of Railroad Commissioners of, by, and for the people, that'll get a twist of you, my bunco-steering friend—you and your backers and cappers and swindlers and thimble-riggers, and *smash* you, lock, stock, and barrel. That's my tip to you and be damned to you, Mr. Cyrus Blackleg Ruggles."

Annixter stormed out of the room, slamming the door behind him, and Ruggles, trembling with anger, turned to his desk and to the blotting pad written all over with the words *Lands, Twenty dollars, Two and a half, Option,* and, over and over again, with great swelling curves and flourishes, *Railroad, Railroad, Railroad.*

But as Annixter passed into the outside office, on the other side of the wire partition he noted the figure of a man at the counter in conversation with one of the clerks. There was something familiar to Annixter's eye about the man's heavy built frame, his great shoulders and massive back, and as he spoke to the clerk in a tremendous, rumbling voice, Annixter promptly recognised Dyke.

There was a meeting. Annixter liked Dyke, as did every one else in and about Bonneville. He paused now to shake hands with the discharged engineer and to ask about his little daughter, Sidney, to whom he knew Dyke was devotedly attached.

"Smartest little tad in Tulare County," asserted Dyke. "She's getting prettier every day, Mr. Annixter. *There's* a little tad that was just born to be a lady. Can recite the whole of 'Snow Bound' without ever stopping. You don't believe that, maybe, hey? Well, it's true. She'll be just old enough to enter the Seminary up at Marysville next winter, and if my hop business pays two per cent. on the investment, there's where she's going to go."

"How's it coming on?" inquired Annixter.

"The hop ranch? Prime. I've about got the land in shape, and I've engaged a foreman who knows all about hops. I've been in luck. Everybody will go into the business next year when they see hops go to a dollar, and they'll overstock the market and bust the price. But I'm going to get the cream of it now. I say two per cent. Why, Lord love you, it will pay a good deal more than that. It's got to. It's cost more than I figured to start the thing, so, perhaps, I may have to borrow somewheres; but then on such a sure game as this—and I do want to make something out of that little tad of mine."

"Through here?" inquired Annixter, making ready to move off.

"In just a minute," answered Dyke. "Wait for me and I'll walk down the street with you."

Annixter grumbled that he was in a hurry, but waited, nevertheless, while Dyke again approached the clerk.

"I shall want some empty cars of you people this fall," he explained. "I'm a hop-raiser now, and I just want to make sure what your rates on hops are. I've been told, but I want to make sure. Savvy?"

There was a long delay while the clerk consulted the tariff schedules, and Annixter fretted impatiently. Dyke, growing uneasy, leaned heavily on his elbows, watching the clerk anxiously. If the tariff was exorbitant, he saw his plans brought to naught, his money jeopardised, the little tad, Sidney, deprived of her education. He began to blame himself that he had not long before determined definitely what the railroad would charge for moving his hops. He told himself he was not much of a business man; that he managed carelessly.

"Two cents," suddenly announced the clerk with a certain surly indifference.

"Two cents a pound?"

"Yes, two cents a pound—that's in car-load lots, of course. I won't give you that rate on smaller consignments."

"Yes, car-load lots, of course…two cents. Well, all right."

He turned away with a great sigh of relief.

"He sure did have me scared for a minute," he said to Annixter, as the two went down to the street, "fiddling and fussing so long. Two cents is all right, though. Seems fair to me. That fiddling of his was all put on. I know 'em, these railroad heelers. He knew I was a discharged employee first off, and he played the game just to make me seem small because I had to ask favours of him. I don't suppose the General Office tips its slavees off to act like swine, but there's the feeling through the whole herd of them. 'Ye got to come to us. We let ye live only so long as we choose, and what are ye going to do about it? If ye don't like it, git out.'"

◆

Anonymous
"SUBSIDY: A GOAT ISLAND BALLAD"
FROM THE SAN FRANCISCO *CALIFORNIA MAILBAG*, 1872

I

There is a corporation within this Golden State,
Which owns a line of railroads for conveying men and freight
To the Mormon town of Ogden, at an elevated rate,
And which began in a very small way *via* the Dutch Flat swindle,
    but by perseverance and bonds, including subsidies,
    became both strong and great,
For this Railroad Corporation is the deuce in subsidies.

2

Now this mighty Corporation had placed its terminus
At Sacramento City, after no small bit of fuss,
Whereat the San Franciscans raved and Oaklanders did cuss,
And tried their best to have a change, so that we of the Bay
    might have all the benefits, profits, and advantages
    come flowing into us,
Of this Railroad Corporation and its heap of subsidies.

3

First, San Francisco said 'twould give all down on Mission Bay,
If the Corporation would but make its terminus that way,
Some sixty acres more or less of finest kind of clay,
Which could be brought to the surface by a dredge with a
    ten-foot stroke or covered over with nice long piles if they
    wished to build a quay,
For this Railroad Corporation from its many subsidies.

4

The Railroad took the handsome gift, but said 'twould wait a
    while
Before it filled the marsh-land in or drove a single pile,
And then it went to Oakland, and with clever word and smile,
Agreed to make the terminus at that place if the city would
    donate all its waterfront and never expect the cars to stop
    within a mile,
For this Railroad Corporation is the deuce on subsidies.

5

Next the Corporation bought the old Vallejo route,
And then, before the people could mistrust what 'twas about,
It gobbled all the other roads, and then expressed a doubt
Concerning the permanent location of this remarkable
    terminus, which was as unreliable as a Spanish land title or
    an old black cat with a bad rheumatic gout,
For this Railroad Corporation wanted other subsidies.

6

And then this city rose from sleep, and in a hearty way,
Exclaimed, "If you'll come here we'll build a bridge across
    the Bay,
We'll raise the funds, you'll have a bridge and not a cent to pay!"
But the Corporation wrote a letter half a yard long, which,
    being interpreted, implied that the Corporation was on
    another lay;
For this Railroad Corporation has its eye on subsidies.

7

Then the People grew excited, and raised a hue and cry
Of "Anti-Subsidy," and vowed they never more would try
To help the Corporation, but would break its power by
A lot of incorruptible and undefiled Legislators, who had been
    elected for the express purpose of bestowing a black eye
On this Railroad Corporation which is fond of subsidies.

8

But when the Legislature met, the simple People found
That the Corporation's agents had been slyly prowling round,
Till the Legislators one and all had changed their stamping
    ground,
And voted as the railroad wished on every question, and sent
    Sargent to the Senate with the understanding that he
    should help Jim Nye and his *confreres* to expound
How this Railroad Corporation should have other subsidies.

9

And now that Stanford owns the railroads and the boats,
One half the State and more than half the Legislative votes,
For Frisco or for Oakland he doesn't care two goats,

And has decided to retire to a secluded isle of the sea sometimes
    called Yerba Buena, but more familiarly known as the
    Island of the Goats,
With his terminus, his railroad, and his lots of subsidies.

10

Which little rhyming narrative just shows us that, Whereas,
The Corporation's clever and the Public is an ass—
Resolved, the first must always win, the other go to grass;
Which happy consummation every one who has noted the
    brilliant efforts of a San Francisco community to make a
    commercial idiot of itself hopes soon may come to pass,
As also hopes the Railroad with its wealth of subsidies.

C. C. Post
"Conspirators"

Just as some of the Mussel Slough novelists stereotyped the God-fearing yeoman farmers of the San Joaquin, they also stereotyped the evil capitalists who ran the railroad. In an extraordinary chapter, C. C. Post portrays railroad royalty as greedy, corrupt men, here complaining about the settlers' pleas for relief while they themselves plan the outcome of a congressional election to suit the railroad's own interests. "To the confusion of the people" seems a most fitting toast, a sentiment at odds with the people's interest in an uncorrupted democracy.

A close carriage drawn by a splendidly matched pair of bay horses rolled up California street, in the city of San Francisco, and on Nob Hill stopped in front of a palatial residence, the home of a man who, not very many years since, was the possessor of but little if any money or property, but who is now a railroad king and the possessor of millions.

As the horses were brought to a stop, a liveried servant climbed down from his perch, opened the door of the carriage, and a heavy, dark-complexioned man in the prime of life descended and approached the mansion.

As he reached the broad marble steps, the door opened, and four boy pages in dark livery ranged themselves on either side of the steps, returning to the hall to await orders only after the heavy man, their master, had passed on in advance.

Once inside, the heavy man turned to the right and entered a large room, the furniture of which was of rosewood and mahogany, and of European manufacture. The most costly of Axminster carpets was upon the floor, and the heaviest of damask and finest of lace draped the windows. Costly pictures were upon the walls, marble statuettes adorned the mantels and the corners of the room, while solid silver chandeliers of many hundred pounds weight depended from the ceiling.

From this room the heavy man passed through an archway with massive sliding doors to another room of similar size and ornamentation, and from this to a smaller one furnished as a library.

Magnificently carved cases of rosewood held artistically bound and beautifully illustrated works of the best authors in fiction, in history and travel, but none of these were of much interest to their possessor, who, without pausing, passed onward, and at the left entered another room supplied with a small table, a desk, a sofa, and a few chairs—the private room of the railroad king and holder of the title deed to the mansion.

Seating himself at the desk, he drew a key from his pocket and, unlocking one of the drawers, took therefrom a bundle of papers, which he ran over carefully, noting down an item or two from each. After an hour spent in this manner, he desisted from his work, replaced the papers, locked the drawer, and, turning half round in his chair, touched a button in the wall. Almost immediately a servant in livery appeared and stood waiting for orders.

"Bring me a lunch,—some fruit or something, and a bottle of wine."

Again the servant bowed and retired. A few moments later he re-entered with a tray, on which was a bit of cold chicken, some grapes, apricots, peaches, a bottle of wine and some glasses. These he deposited on the table, which he wheeled around in front of his master's chair, and was about to retire, when the railroad king again spoke:

"Tell Barnes to come here."

The servant bowed and disappeared. The heavy man poured himself a glass of wine, set it beside the tray, and then devoted himself to his lunch.

He was still eating when the door opened, and a man in middle life, well dressed, and with a look which indicated both persistence and cunning, entered.

"Peters said you wished to see me," he said, bowing slightly.

"Yes," replied the heavy man, "I want you to see the merchants and business men of the city and give them to understand that we don't want any of their interference with our business, and that we shall find a way to make it unpleasant for them if they do."

Barnes, who was a kind of private detective to the railroad king, and accustomed to all kinds of work requiring cheek and impudence, did not change his expression or move a muscle while receiving this order, but remained entirely passive while the other was speaking and for a few seconds after he had ceased. Then, with a movement as if turning to go, he said, in a tone which was intended to indicate only a desire to fully understand his orders:

"Anything you want especially emphasized?"

"Yes," replied the other, taking up his wine glass and setting it down again with force; "yes," he repeated, "there is. I want you to make them understand that we can take care of our own affairs, without any assistance or advice from them, and that if they have any sympathy with the outlaws who are claiming homestead rights on the land which Congress gave to us, they had better keep it to themselves, unless they know of some better way of shipping goods than over our lines of road."

"All right. I only wanted to know just what you wanted done, and how far I was to go in the matter."

"You can go far enough to make them understand that we are not in the habit of arresting grangers for the pleasure of seeing them bailed out of jail by the business men of San Francisco, and we don't propose to form any such habits at this time. Hello! is that you? Well, come in," he said, suddenly changing his tone, and addressing a man about his own age but much less given to flesh than himself, who appeared at the door and stood as if waiting for an invitation to enter. Then again addressing himself to Barnes, he said:

"You can go now. You have got your orders, and understand what you are to do."

As Barnes passed out the other entered, shook hands cordially with the heavy man, and, seating himself in a chair which the latter set for him, reached over and helped himself to a glass of wine, saying, as he did so:

"Just got back on last train. Called at the office ten minutes after you left; found our noble partner there, and as he wanted to talk over matters, we thought we'd come over to your house. They told me you were in your private room, and I took the liberty of coming unannounced."

"That's right," replied the heavy man, "glad you came. Was anxious to see you. Where's he now?"

"He'll be along in a few moments. Some old fellow from down below, some homesteader I guess, was trying to talk him into giving up our claim to his land, and as I didn't care to listen to the old fellow's lingo about how hard he had worked to improve his claim, and how tough it was to be turned out of house and home without anything to start on again, I came on ahead and left him to follow as soon as he could get rid of his visitor."

"That's it," replied the heavy man. "They are everlastingly whining about being turned out of their homes. Why don't they go somewhere else and begin again? They ought to know by this time that they can't fight a rich corporation, such as we are."

The thinner man laughed. It was not what one might call a hearty laugh. Neither was it exactly forced. The person of the party emitting it shook just a little, as much at least as a person with that amount of flesh could be expected to do. Evidently the thinner man saw something mirth-provoking in the suggestions of the other, that these men whose lands they were seeking to possess themselves of, should go elsewhere in the State and preëmpt again; and he looked at his companion with a kind of quizzical expression, as if he would have said:

"Suppose you suggest some place in the State where these men can find land open for preëmption that we do not claim, and perhaps they will go there."

The other evidently understood the look, for he winced a little beneath it, and then said, in a petulant kind of way:

"Well, let 'em stay where they are, then, and work for a share of the crop. All the more reason why they should, if they can't find any land to preëmpt anywhere else in the State. Anyhow," he continued, in a more determined tone, "if they are going to whine, I propose to give them something worth whining about. I was just ordering Barnes, as you came in, to notify the business men that they had better keep their fingers out of our pie if they don't want to get them burnt."

"Anything new?" asked the thinner man, with a sudden show of interest.

"Nothing special; only, if we conclude to have any of those pretended settlers arrested again, and let 'em lie in jail awhile, until they come to their senses, we don't want anybody coming forward with offers to go their bail."

The thinner man laughed again, the same quiet kind of laugh as before.

"Well, governor," he said, "I guess you can manage that without any assistance, and I am willing to leave it to you as long as you do it properly. It has to be done, of course, for the land we must have, but I own that I prefer buying congressmen and senators to driving those poor devils out of their homes."

"Oh, yes, that's all very nice," replied the other, "but what is the use of buying congressmen and senators, if we are not to reap the benefit of the purchase? It isn't the senators and congressmen that we bought, either. They did the selling. The thing bought was the land, and it isn't our fault if the men that are on the land have got themselves into such shape that they go with it; and, besides, if we are going to be squeamish about taking what we have bought, we might better have kept our purchase money."

The thinner man smiled. Then he leaned back in his chair, stretched out his legs, ran both hands deep into his pants pockets, and gazed up at the ceiling.

"All right, governor," he said. " I'm not going to moralize about the right of congressmen or courts to sell the land or the men that work it. We went into this thing to win, and of course we are going to see it through. If the people have no more sense or spirit than to sit still and let us gobble up the country, they are only fit for slaves, and slaves they shall be. If we can keep them quiet a few years more, until we get our plans all laid and in operation, get possession of the water transportation as thoroughly as we have of the railroad facilities, their whining won't count for much; and you can depend on me standing by you until the thing is done. I was only saying that I like better the work of paying congress and the courts to let us take what we want, than I do the work of turning those poor devils out of their homes, after congress and the courts have given us permission to do so. Now a congressman or a judge is well fed and generally well satisfied with himself and the world at large, and so is not given to unpleasant reminiscences or predilections, while at the same time they are generally sufficiently ready to turn an honest penny to make them anxious to make themselves agreeable to anyone who is known to have a little matter that he is willing to pay for having attended to—at least that has been my experience. All of which helps to make the work of getting their consent to our little schemes very pleasant; at least a good deal more pleasant than listening to the complaints of the poor wretches of grangers whose homes have been disposed of without their consent, and who, when we have driven them off, bag and baggage, with their wives and young ones, will begin again somewhere else, with the certainty that the same thing will be done to them again as soon as they get enough together to make it an object for anybody to do it."

"That's it," replied the heavy man. "If we don't do it, somebody else will; and, besides, we have paid for the privilege, and so have the best right to make the first assessment. And while we are about it we may as well make it large enough so no one else will be tempted to trouble them for awhile at least. But here he comes. Come in," he called, in response to a rap on the door, and a gentleman entered, nodded familiarly to the heavy man and his companion, and, drawing a chair up to the table, sat down.

Nodding sideways towards the thinner man, he said: "He came in just after you left, governor, and as we knew you would want to hear how things were looking at the Capital, we concluded to come up and let him make his report to us here."

"That's right. Glad you came," replied the heavy man. I am anxious to hear just what shape affairs are in at Washington, and what the outlook is. It is of the utmost importance that our friends there stand by us now. Do you think," he added, addressing the thinner man, "that we can depend on enough votes in the House and Senate to pull us through?"

"I don't see why we should fail," replied the thinner man. "The president of the Senate has kindly permitted the use of the room directly back of his desk for our private lobby, so that we can watch matters and have a consultation with our friends at any moment. I think everything is all right there now, but if need be we can fix a man or two at the last moment.

"In the House, matters have not progressed quite so far, but there is time enough yet. Congressmen are not becoming any more virtuous or hard to approach as the years pass, that I can see; but the contrary. There's a difference, to be sure, but it's a difference of price. When we first began we had to satisfy only a few of the party leaders, and the rest followed; but of late they have all dropped to our racket, and either kick out and refuse to vote with us on any terms, or they demand to be paid for their votes the same as the leaders, which makes it rather expensive getting what we want. Still it's a good investment."

"How much will it take, according to your estimates?" asked the heavy man.

"How much? Oh, well, that's hard to say exactly. You can judge about as well as I. Congressmen this year range all the way from five thousand dollars up to fifty thousand, and senators proportionately higher, and we must have a majority of both houses.

"Of course we can count on getting some votes on the plea of the public good, and the necessity for more railroads to open up the country and to provide competition. Then there is a certain number of members who are afraid to vote with us, but who can be persuaded that they need a vacation about the time the bill comes to a vote, and can be got rid of for the day for the cost of a trip home or to New York, with provision for a good time after they get there. Then a certain other number can be sent off on committees of investigation, and the number who must be paid directly be greatly reduced in that way. I should say it would cost about half a million to get what we want."

"Half a million," echoed the heavy man with a sigh. "Congressmen at five to fifty thousand dollars—what is the country coming to?"

As neither of his companions ventured a prediction, the heavy man continued: "When we commenced business here on the coast we could get all the help we wanted from members of Congress by placing a few thousand dollars of our stock in the hands of the right men. And down South, before the war, they say able-bodied niggers used to sell for a thousand dollars apiece, the best of 'em." And the heavy man lay back in his chair and looked grum and disgusted.

"You don't look at the thing in the right light," returned the thinner man, laughing. "A thousand dollars apiece for niggers is high, is way up, compared to what we pay for white men. At a half million dollars for the lot, there are already enough squatters on the land we are after to bring the price to five hundred dollars for a whole family, with several million acres of land thrown in, enough for several pretty good sized plantations, I should say."

"I wish you wouldn't always put things in that disagreeable kind of a way," remarked the third man. "It is but a few years since we fought to set the negroes free in this country, and I don't like to hear about making slaves of white men. It don't sound well."

"Oh, well, just as you like. It's only a choice of terms," replied the thinner man, good-naturedly. "By the way, you say 'we fought;' I don't remember ever to have heard the number of your regiment and company? What State did you enlist from?"

"Come, come," interrupted the heavy man. "What's the use of your sparring each other? If none of us went to war ourselves, we did all we could to induce others to go, and so helped sustain the government. As governor of the State during that time, I did everything I could in support of the administration. It was conceded at the time that to my efforts was due the fact that the Pacific coast remained true to the Union. We both understand your way of putting things, of course, and it's all right with us; but it wouldn't do to let outsiders hear you talk that way. They might think you were in earnest."

"Never you fear for that, governor. I am not going to give the thing away. Why, you ought to hear me expound the matter to members of congress. I actually get eloquent sometimes, I do believe, dwelling on the advantages which our enterprise will be to the country; opening up its resources and laying bare its great natural wealth to the energy and enterprise of the people. Why, I'll contract to keep any congressman or senator who votes the way we want him to, in arguments to prove himself a patriot and statesman. I do that regularly with lots of our fellows, besides writing whole columns of matter for the newspapers, setting forth the desirability of the thing from a commercial standpoint. Maybe you didn't know that that great speech of Thompson's in the House last week was written by me. Well, it was. That is, I furnished the figures and outlined the argument. Thompson put the thing into shape a little; rounded off the periods so they would sound well, and then shot it off to the country. It made a big noise, too, I tell you. The associated press reported it, and all the big dailies had it next morning with double headlines."

"I hope Thompson succeeded in convincing the rest of the members of the House that our enterprise has been a great benefit," remarked the last comer.

"I should say so. Why, benefit is no word for it. Considering the fact that we invested exactly eleven thousand five hundred dollars in this thing to start on, and now own half the coast, with a prospect of gobbling up the other half, I should say it had been a benefit, with a big B."

"Oh, come, now, I'm tired of your nonsense; let's talk business. Give me the names of the men whom you have seen and the price they can be had at, and anything else of importance, so we can decide what to do at once. I suppose, though, we will have to pay them their price, whatever it is, but we must get it down as low as possible, for we may have to fight the thing in the courts, if not in the departments, after we get the bill through. And election is coming on, and we have to take care of our friends, or some of 'em may get left, and it's cheaper and safer to help those to a reelection whom we know to be friendly, than it is to trust to new men who may not be of our way of thinking."

"That's true," returned the other. "It is always harder to approach a man the first time than the second or third. Your new man may be either afraid to deal, or what is quite as likely, afraid of selling too cheap, not being posted on the price of votes. Or he may possibly have too exalted an opinion of the position of Congressman and lawmaker to make it safe to approach him with a business proposition. Such men are not common in Congress now-a-days, but occasionally one gets there by accident, and we have to be cautious and feel our way. And it all costs. Wine is higher in Washington than it is in California; and a champagne supper, about as good a thing to bring men together and get acquainted and friendly as any, will spoil a thousand dollar note.

"How about the third House?" asked the last man in.

"The Lobby? Oh, well, we have to use the lobby, of course. It is generally safer to deal through a third party. Gives one a chance to swear he did not authorize anything of the kind, you know. The trouble of it is one can't always tell how much the go-between is beating him. I expect them to keep a good big per cent. of what passes through their fingers, of course. One can't expect them to act from disinterested motives entirely, but it isn't exactly pleasant to learn, after the deal is closed, that some fellow to whom you paid ten or twenty thousand dollars to do certain things with, has kept the whole of it and trusted to luck to prevent your finding it out. However, I flatter myself that such things don't occur very often. Anyway, one must take the bitter with the sweet in life."

"I suppose that's so," replied the heavy man, "but I hope you don't allow them to beat you out of such sums often. But come, get out your memorandum, and let's get down to business at once. I want to know what the whole thing is going to cost us."

The three men drew close about the table, the tray with the bottle and glasses being shoved to one side. The thinner man produced a small morocco-covered memorandum book with a gold clasp, in which were written the initials of certain lobbyists, members of Congress and the Senate of the United States. Opposite to these initials were the amounts in pencil which he had either formally contracted to pay for the service which he desired at their hands, or which he believed would be required to induce them to comply with the wishes of the corporation which he represented.

The three conspirators spent a half hour in examining these. Then followed a discussion of who among the candidates for congress should be aided and who defeated, not only upon the coast, but in other States and portions of the Union, after which the two men last introduced arose to go. As they did so, the heavy man poured out three glasses of wine. Passing one to each of his companions, he raised the other to his lips.

"Let us drink to the success of our enterprise," he said.

"And to the confusion of the people," added the thinner man.

The third man scowled slightly, and glanced about him with the least sign of nervousness, as if he feared that the reckless language of the other might reach ears for which it was not intended; but he drank his wine and said nothing.

The heavy man emptied his glass at a gulp, refilled and again emptied it. "To the confusion of the people," he said, repeating the words of the other.

Then following his guests to the door, he bowed them out into the hall, and calling a page, bade him attend them to a carriage in waiting, and returned to his private room.

William C. Morrow
"The Dictates of Their Natures"

John Graham has been unsuccessful locating money stolen two decades before from his father and buried somewhere in Mussel Slough country. As imagined in W. C. Morrow's Blood-Money, *Graham, a perfect stereotype of the hardworking Jeffersonian farmer, would also become "one of the many unfortunate persons who had fallen into the clutches of a powerful monopoly," controlled by the capitalists in charge of the railroad.*

The following dialogue between John Graham and his beloved Nellie casts each in a familiar role. John—a small-scale Central Valley farmer—is the defender of the people, defender of the right "of all men to acquire property and enjoy life." True to his beliefs, he has refused a lucrative job offer from his fiancée Nellie's capitalist "friends," fearing they mean to corrupt him. Nellie, her head turned by the lavish lifestyle of her rich companions, argues that they are "good, charitable, honest men." But to John, they are little more than robbers "following the dictates of their natures," a notion that holds little promise for the reform-minded.

Nellie was no longer the Nellie that John had known. She no longer talked over his plans with him, nor gave him bright words of encouragement through the trials that had beset him, and that still rendered his future dark. On the contrary, she added to his sorrows with her upbraidings and complaints. The poison had entered her life. Dark shadows had crept in, and driven out the sunshine and the bright hopefulness.

She was discontented with her humble lot, and longed to be in reality one of those who go to make up that society of California whose standing is on a basis of money. No rupture had taken place between her and John, but it was sure to come. A gulf had been created between them. John, with his patient, charitable disposition, had often tried to convince her of the hollowness of the life she longed for; but even at that late day he had never suspected the true motives that led to Nellie's temporary adoption by her new friends. She had never ceased reproaching him for refusing the situation that had been offered him, and that she had urged him to accept with all her winning eloquence. But he would not, and that was the end of it.

Nor was that all. He had warmly espoused the cause of the Mussel Slough settlers, which had taken a more serious turn during the past few years. Nellie's sympathies were not with them.

"Why, John," she once said petulantly, "those people are not worth getting into trouble for. You ought to hear Judge Harriott and those great men who sometimes go to his house talk about those poor fools in Mussel Slough They make all manner of fun of them. Judge Harriott—you know he is a manager or something—said that it is really amusing to see those ignorant creatures in Mussel Slough trying to fight the railroad company, which can tie them all in a bundle, and throw them into the fire. What do you trouble yourself about them for, John?"

"Nellie," John replied earnestly, "those people in Mussel Slough have been shamefully wronged, and I am in a position similar to theirs. Do you suppose we will be such cowards as to sit down and see our homes taken from us, even if the power that is attempting the outrage is rich enough to buy the courts, the legislature, and the congressional committees that assisted to rob the people of these lands? Why, Nellie, it would be difficult for a disinterested spectator to believe that such things are done in a country where every man is supposed to be free. If we quietly submit to these wrongs, what, in the name of God, is to become of us?"

"But, John, you don't understand. The men you speak of in that harsh way are good, charitable, honest men; and they have done so much for the country!"

"Because it paid them to do it, Nellie."

"It is not right to talk in that way, John."

"Nellie, Nellie! have they so far poisoned your mind that you are blind to the truth? You think they are good men; yet how could good men make promises and offer inducements to poor people, and then, when these poor people have rendered a piece of property immensely valuable, they are called upon to give it up, or pay in money what they have paid already a hundred times over in sufferings that you can't imagine?"

"They have been very kind to me, John; and surely they don't expect me to be of any service to them?"

"How do you know, Nellie? Don't you know that placing people under obligations is one of the regular departments of their business, as well as employing lobbyists, lawyers, and political managers who corrupt conventions and buy the votes of needy and unscrupulous men? Don't you know why I refused to accept the situation they offered me?"

"No: I know only that it would have been a great thing for you, and that some day you would be a rich man."

John paced the floor in considerable agitation, and thus expostulated:

"Nellie, there was a motive in that offer. Do you imagine for a moment that they care anything for me, or would give me a crust of bread if I were starving? No, Nellie! They naturally reasoned that the situation would, if I accepted it, have put a gag in my mouth. Why, Nellie, see how successfully they have practiced that very ruse right here in our section! There are a great many men here who sympathize with the railroad company and curse the poor settlers. How did it come about? Through some favor that the railroad company granted. I admit, Nellie, that it is a very difficult matter for a man to withstand many of the temptations that are offered; but, Nellie, what is money when manhood is gone? Here we are, a mere handful of men, opposed to the strongest power in the country—the power of money; the power that lies behind the law and courts; the power whose sole object is the accumulation of greater wealth and greater power; a power that is determined, with the aid of the machinery of the law, to crush out all semblance of opposition, and that directs its most powerful shafts against those who are least able to withstand them.

"I say we are a mere handful of men, because the time has not yet come when wrongs have become so great and so general that a larger and more united band of the oppressed feel the crushing weight of the heel that grinds them; but that we are few is no reason that we should be cowards. We have God and right on our side, Nellie. We have on our side the prayers of the widow and the cries of the children for bread. We have on our side right against might, justice against infamous wrongs, honesty against theft, industry against robbery, hunger against a feast; and before God, Nellie, we will fight for our rights to the bitter end; and other people, seeing our brave little band standing up and defiantly opposing a power that is great enough to buy a nation, will flock to our standard, and maintain their rights as secured by the Constitution of the United States—the right of all men to acquire property and enjoy life. If no stand is ever made against these outrages practiced by the rich on the poor, what will become of this country? Even now, Nellie, money is the great power in this country; and with a single stroke of the pen, a few rich men can stop every railroad and factory in the country, and send millions of people out upon the highways clamoring for bread."

"Then why don't they do it?"

"Because they dare not. Because hungry, red-handed violence would take them by the throat, and make them disgorge the fortunes they have made out of the miseries of poor men! Because the sun would rise some morning and discover them dangling between heaven and earth, with a rope around their necks!"

John was pale with excitement, and Nellie quaked under the ferocity that appeared in his face. Nevertheless, she said:

"John, Judge Harriott says that the corporations are very lenient that they don't send to the penitentiary men who talk like that."

John was calmer in a moment.

"I know it, Nellie. I know they laugh at us in our weakness, and have great fun at our writhings under the misfortunes that are thrust upon us. But the day is coming, Nellie, when these wrongs will be righted. I hope it will not be through blood, though I fear that blood will be spilled. I fear that it must be spilled before the people are sufficiently aroused to the danger that assails them—the danger of cold, cruel, grasping money. There is good ground for hope that the people will soon be awakened. We are not all who suffer. There are the thousands of corporation laborers who are compelled to renounce their manhood; there are those who have angered the corporations, and who are hounded out of the country; there are those who must pay as a tribute to the corporations all they can earn by hard labor; there are the merchants who are bound under contracts to ship all their goods by rail, to the end that ocean transportation may be driven from the seacoast of California; there are the outspoken newspapers from which the corporations compel merchants to withhold advertising patronage; there are the great masses of voters who are cheated and cajoled into voting for men whom their respective parties nominate in the interest of the corporations. Why, Nellie, there is hardly a man, woman, or child in all this country who does not feel, directly or indirectly, the weight of this curse. A reaction is bound to come. People must, in simple self-protection, organize to defeat this monster."

"It seems to me, John," said Nellie, somewhat overawed, "that if the corporations are driving people to such an extremity, the rich men would, for the sake of their own interests, change their policy."

"Nellie, that which makes a man a robber will cause him to continue a thief. These rich men are following the dictates of their natures. Furthermore, they are so inflated with power that they no longer deem it necessary to be conciliatory and just. What have they to fear? Surely not the government, which their money can control; and surely not the people, for the people are not organized; and besides, they are cowardly. But mark my words, Nellie, the time is coming when the people will rise up in their majesty, and crush this power that is stronger than the law. It may be through blood, but I hope not. Still, history shows that such wrongs are righted only through blood, or through some local catastrophe that may be sufficient to arouse the whole people."

Nellie sat stubborn and offended. She could not believe that John was right, but attributed his remarks to the influence of the men with whom he had associated so much recently. She knew not, poor, simple Nellie, that she was among those who had been marked for the slaughter.

"Nellie," continued John, "I would not be a servant for the railroad company for all the money it would pay me. Don't you remember that shameful case the other day, when poor Simpson's young widow sued the railroad company for damages? Her husband was a brakeman, and he was killed by reason of a defect in the brake-wheel. Well, the railroad company had a great crowd of railroad men as witnesses, who all swore that Simpson came to his death through his own carelessness, although the brake-wheel itself showed that it was fatally defective. Those witnesses perjured themselves—as they always do in such cases—to retain their positions. One man, who had the courage and honor to tell the truth, was soon afterwards discharged; and you know that as a result of his testimony he couldn't find employment on any railroad in this country, and was finally compelled to cross the Rocky Mountains. In spite of all that testimony, the jury brought in a verdict for the widow; and it is such things as these that give us hope in the people. Did you ever reflect upon what that verdict meant? It meant this: We know that these witnesses swore untruths, and the law of every country declares that we shall make due allowance for the testimony of the servants of corporations, for the reason that corporations have great power, and can injure a servant who testifies against them. We do not blame these witnesses, but we pity them from the bottom of our hearts. We pity rather than blame any condition to which humanity can be brought, in which manhood and honor are sold for the bread that keeps the wolf from the door; but we do blame—and this verdict bears us testimony—the power that is so abused in that it enslaves the soul of a man, and blackmails his conscience with threats of hunger."

"But, John, I have heard these gentlemen say that many things are done wrong in their name without their knowledge or consent. How can you blame them for that?"

"When a knowledge of these wrongs comes to them, do they discharge the servants who committed them? By no means! These are notorious facts, Nellie. We do not blame the servants so much, because the system that controls them compels them to do wrong; and having become once ensnared, they cannot shake off the yoke."

Frank Norris
"The Toilers"

After Presley composes his socialist poem "The Toilers," he seeks out his friend, the mystic shepherd Vanamee, who approvingly tells Presley that his inspiration has come "from the People." Better, he advises, to bypass the literary periodicals with their small, bookish readership and give the poem back "to the People." This advice Presley takes, using the poem as a tiny salvo aimed at the capitalist class on behalf of the common people of the southern San Joaquin, characters like the socialist saloonkeeper Carahar and the one-time railroad engineer Dyke. The character of Presley is partly based on Edwin Markham, whose famous poem "The Man with the Hoe" is the model for "The Toilers." Unfortunately, Norris never offers readers the text of Presley's poem.

Presley's room in the ranch house of Los Muertos was in the second story of the building. It was a corner room; one of its windows facing the south, the other the east. Its appointments were of the simplest. In one angle was the small white painted iron bed, covered with a white counterpane. The walls were hung with a white paper figured with knots of pale green leaves, very gay and bright. There was a straw matting on the floor. White muslin half-curtains hung in the windows, upon the sills of which certain plants bearing pink waxen flowers of which Presley did not know the name, grew in oblong green boxes. The walls were unadorned, save by two pictures, one a reproduction of the "Reading from Homer," the other a charcoal drawing of the Mission of San Juan de Guadalajara, which Presley had made himself. By the east window stood the plainest of deal tables, innocent of any cloth or covering, such as might have been used in a kitchen. It was Presley's work table, and was invariably littered with papers, half-finished manuscripts, drafts of poems, notebooks, pens, half-smoked cigarettes, and the like. Near at hand, upon a shelf, were his hooks. There were but two chairs in the room—the straight-backed wooden chair, that stood in front of the table, angular, upright, and in which it was impossible to take one's ease, and the long comfortable wicker steamer chair, stretching its length in front of the south window. Presley was immensely fond of this room. It amused and interested him to maintain its air of rigorous simplicity and freshness. He abhorred cluttered bric-a-brac and meaningless *objets d'art*. Once in so often he submitted his room to a vigorous inspection; setting it to rights, removing everything but the essentials, the few ornaments which, in a way, were part of his life.

His writing had by this time undergone a complete change. The notes for his great Song of the West, the epic poem he once had hoped to write, he had flung aside, together with all the abortive attempts at its beginning. Also he had torn up a great quantity of "fugitive" verses, preserving only a certain half-finished poem, that he called "The Toilers." This poem was a comment upon the social fabric, and had been inspired by the sight of a painting he had seen in Cedarquist's art gallery. He had written all but the last verse.

On the day that he had overheard the conversation between Dyke and Caraher, in the latter's saloon, which had acquainted him with the monstrous injustice of the increased tariff, Presley had returned to Los Muertos, white and trembling, roused to a pitch of exaltation, the like of which he had never known in all his life. His wrath was little short of even Caraher's. He too "saw red"; a mighty spirit of revolt heaved tumultuous within him. It did not seem possible that this outrage could go on much longer. The oppression was incredible; the plain story of it set down in truthful statement of fact would not be believed by the outside world.

He went up to his little room and paced the floor with clenched fists and burning face, till at last, the repression of his contending thoughts all but suffocated him, and he flung himself before his table and began to write. For a time, his pen seemed to travel of itself; words came to him without searching, shaping themselves into phrases,—the phrases building themselves up to great, forcible sentences, full of eloquence, of fire, of passion. As his prose grew more exalted, it passed easily into the domain of poetry. Soon the cadence of his paragraphs settled to an ordered beat and rhythm, and in the end Presley had thrust aside his journal and was once more writing verse.

He picked up his incomplete poem of "The Toilers," read it hastily a couple of times to catch its swing, then the Idea of the last verse— the Idea for which he so long had sought in vain—abruptly springing to his brain, wrote it off without so much as replenishing his pen with ink. He added still another verse, bringing the poem to a definite close, resuming its entire conception, and ending with a single majestic thought, simple, noble, dignified, absolutely convincing.

Presley laid down his pen and leaned back in his chair, with the certainty that for one moment he had touched untrod heights. His hands were cold, his head on fire, his heart leaping tumultuous in his breast.

Now at last, he had achieved. He saw why he had never grasped the inspiration for his vast, vague, *impersonal* Song of the West. At the time when he sought for it, his convictions had not been aroused; he had not then cared for the People. His sympathies had not been touched. Small wonder that he had missed it. Now he was of the People; he had been stirred to his lowest depths. His earnestness was almost frenzy. He *believed,* and so to him all things were possible at once.

Then the artist in him reasserted itself. He became more interested in his poem, as such, than in the cause that had inspired it. He went over it again, retouching it carefully, changing a word here and there, and improving its rhythm. For the moment, he forgot the People, forgot his rage, his agitation of the previous hour, he remembered only that he had written a great poem.

Then doubt intruded. After all, was it so great? Did not its sublimity overpass a little the bounds of the ridiculous? Had he seen true? Had he failed again? He re-read the poem carefully; and it seemed all at once to lose force.

By now, Presley could not tell whether what he had written was true poetry or doggerel. He distrusted profoundly his own judgment. He must have the opinion of some one else, some one competent to judge. He could not wait; to-morrow would not do. He must know to a certainty before he could rest that night.

He made a careful copy of what he had written, and putting on his hat and laced boots, went downstairs and out upon the lawn, crossing over to the stables. He found Phelps there, washing down the buckboard.

"Do you know where Vanamee is to-day?" he asked the latter. Phelps put his chin in the air.

"Ask me something easy," he responded. "He might be at Guadalajara, or he might be up at Osterman's, or he might be a hundred miles away from either place. I know where he ought to be, Mr. Presley, but that ain't saying where the crazy gesabe is. He *ought* to be range-riding over east of Four, at the head waters of Mission Creek."

"I'll try for him there, at all events," answered Presley. "If you see Harran when he comes in, tell him I may not be back in time for supper."

Presley found the pony in the corral, cinched the saddle upon him, and went off over the Lower Road, going eastward at a brisk canter.

At Hooven's he called a "How do you do" to Minna, whom he saw lying in a slat hammock under the mammoth live oak, her foot in bandages; and then galloped on over the bridge across the irrigating ditch, wondering vaguely what would become of such a pretty girl as Minna, and if in the end she would marry the Portuguese foreman in charge of the ditching-gang. He told himself that he hoped she would, and that speedily. There was no lack of comment as to Minna Hooven about the ranches. Certainly she was a good girl, but she was seen at all hours here and there about Bonneville and Guadalajara, skylarking with the Portuguese farm hands of Quien Sabe and Los Muertos. She was very pretty; the men made fools of themselves over her. Presley hoped they would not end by making a fool of her.

Just beyond the irrigating ditch, Presley left the Lower Road, and following a trail that branched off southeasterly from this point, held on across the Fourth Division of the ranch, keeping the Mission Creek on his left. A few miles farther on, he went through a gate in a barbed wire fence, and at once engaged himself in a system of little arroyos and low rolling hills, that steadily lifted and increased in size as he proceeded. This higher ground was the advance guard of the Sierra foothills, and served as the stock range for Los Muertos. The hills were huge rolling hummocks of bare ground, covered only by wild oats. At long intervals were isolated live oaks. In the cañons and arroyos, the chaparral and manzanita grew in dark olive-green thickets.

The ground was honey-combed with gopher-holes, and the gophers themselves were everywhere. Occasionally a jack rabbit bounded across the open, from one growth of chaparral to another, taking long leaps, his ears erect. High overhead, a hawk or two swung at anchor, and once, with a startling rush of wings, a covey of quail flushed from the brush at the side of the trail.

On the hillsides, in thinly scattered groups were the cattle, grazing deliberately, working slowly toward the water-holes for their evening drink, the horses keeping to themselves, the colts nuzzling at their mothers' bellies, whisking their tails, stamping their unshod feet. But once in a remoter field, solitary, magnificent, enormous, the short hair curling tight upon his forehead, his small red eyes twinkling, his vast neck heavy with muscles, Presley came upon the monarch, the king, the great Durham bull, maintaining his lonely state, unapproachable, austere.

Presley found the one-time shepherd by a water-hole, in a far distant corner of the range. He had made his simple camp for the night. His blue-grey army blanket lay spread under a live oak, his horse grazed near at hand. He himself sat on his heels before a little fire of dead manzanita roots, cooking his coffee and bacon. Never had Presley conceived so keen an impression of loneliness as his crouching figure presented. The bald, bare landscape widened about him to infinity. Vanamee was a spot in it all, a tiny dot, a single atom of human organisation, floating endlessly on the ocean of an illimitable nature.

The two friends ate together, and Vanamee, having snared a brace of quails, dressed and then roasted them on a sharpened stick. After eating, they drank great refreshing draughts from the water-hole. Then, at length, Presley having lit his cigarette, and Vanamee his pipe, the former said:

"Vanamee, I have been writing again."

Vanamee turned his lean ascetic face toward him, his black eyes fixed attentively.

"I know," he said, "your journal."

"No, this is a poem. You remember, I told you about it once. 'The Toilers,' I called it."

"Oh, verse! Well, I am glad you have gone back to it. It is your natural vehicle."

"You remember the poem?" asked Presley. "It was unfinished."

"Yes, I remember it. There was better promise in it than anything you ever wrote. Now, I suppose, you have finished it."

Without reply, Presley brought it from out the breast pocket of his shooting coat. The moment seemed propitious. The stillness of the vast, bare hills was profound. The sun was setting in a cloudless brazier of red light; a golden dust pervaded all the landscape. Presley read his poem aloud. When he had finished, his friend looked at him.

"What have you been doing lately?" he demanded. Presley, wondering, told of his various comings and goings.

"I don't mean that," returned the other. "Something has happened to you, something has aroused you. I am right, am I not? Yes, I thought so. In this poem of yours, you have not been trying to make a sounding piece of literature. You wrote it under tremendous stress. Its very imperfections show that. It is better than a mere rhyme. It is an Utterance—a Message. It is Truth. You have come back to the primal heart of things, and you have seen clearly. Yes, it is a great poem."

"Thank you," exclaimed Presley fervidly. "I had begun to mistrust myself."

"Now," observed Vanamee, "I presume you will rush it into print. To have formulated a great thought, simply to have accomplished, is not enough."

"I think I am sincere," objected Presley. "If it is good it will do good to others. You said yourself it was a Message. If it has any value, I do not think it would be right to keep it back from even a very small and most indifferent public."

"Don't publish it in the magazines at all events," Vanamee answered. "Your inspiration has come *from* the People. Then let it go straight *to* the People—not the literary readers of the monthly periodicals, the rich, who would only be indirectly interested. If you must publish it, let it be in the daily press. Don't interrupt. I know what you will say. It will be that the daily press is common, is vulgar, is undignified; and I tell you that such a poem as this of yours, called as it is, 'The Toilers,' must be read *by* the Toilers. It *must be* common; it must be vulgarised. You must not stand upon your dignity with the People, if you are to reach them."

"That is true, I suppose," Presley admitted, "but I can't get rid of the idea that it would be throwing my poem away. The great magazine gives me such—a—background; gives me such weight."

"Gives *you* such weight, gives *you* such background. Is it *yourself* you think of? You helper of the helpless. Is that your sincerity? You must sink yourself; must forget yourself and your own desire of fame, have admitted success. It is *your* poem, *your* message, that must prevail,—not *you*, who wrote it. You preach a doctrine of abnegation, of self-obliteration, and you sign your name to your words as high on the tablets as you can reach, so that all the world may see, not the poem, but the poet. Presley, there are many like you. The social reformer writes a book on the iniquity of the possession of land, and out of the proceeds, hues a corner lot. The economist who laments the hardships of the poor, allows himself to grow rich upon the sale of his book."

But Presley would hear no further.

"No," he cried, "I know I am sincere, and to prove it to you, I will publish my poem, as you say, in the daily press, and I will accept no money for it."

◆

Edwin Markham
"THE MAN WITH THE HOE"
FROM THE SAN FRANCISCO *EXAMINER*, 1899

Written after seeing Millet's world-famous painting.
"God made man in His own image,
In the image of God made He him."
—Genesis

Bowed by the weight of centuries he leans
Upon his hoe and gazes on the ground,
The emptiness of ages in his face,
And on his back the burden of the world.
Who made him dead to rapture and despair,
A thing that grieves not and that never hopes,
Stolid and stunned, a brother to the ox?
Who loosened and let down this brutal jaw?
Whose was the hand that slanted back this brow?
Whose breath blew out the light within this brain?

Is this the Thing the Lord God made and gave
To have dominion over sea and land;

To trace the stars and search the heavens for power;
To feel the passion of Eternity?
Is this the Dream He dreamed who shaped the suns
And pillared the blue firmament with light?
Down all the stretch of Hell to its last gulf
There is no shape more terrible than this—
More tongued with censure of the world's blind greed—
More filled with signs and portents for the soul—
More fraught with menace to the universe.

What gulfs between him and the seraphim!
Slave of the wheel of labor, what to him
Are Plato and the swing of Pleiades?
What the long reaches of the peaks of song,
The rift of dawn, the reddening of the rose?
Through this dread shape the suffering ages look;
Time's tragedy is in that aching stoop;
Through this dread shape humanity betrayed,
Plundered, profaned and disinherited,
Cries protest to the Judges of the World,
A protest that is also prophecy.

O masters, lords and rulers in all lands,
Is this the handiwork you give to God,
This monstrous thing distorted and soul-quenched?
How will you ever straighten up this shape;
Touch it again with immortality;
Give back the upward looking and the light;
Rebuild in it the music and the dream;
Make right the immemorial infamies,
Perfidious wrongs, immedicable woes?

O masters, lords and rulers in all lands,
How will the Future reckon with this Man?
How answer his brute question in that hour
When whirlwinds of rebellion shake the world?
How will it be with kingdoms and with kings—
With those who shaped him to the thing he is—
When this dumb Terror shall reply to God,
After the silence of the centuries?

Frank Norris
"Dead Sure of a Bonanza"

*Ex-engineer Dyke is "dead sure of a bonanza" in his new hops business.
But when he visits the land office of the Pacific and Southwest Railroad and
double-checks the rate for shipping his crop, he finds an unexpected increase.
When he confronts S. Behrman, asking about the reason for the increase, he
gets a familiar response from the railroad toady.*

"I'll be wanting some cars of you people before the summer is
out," observed Dyke to the clerk as he folded up and put away
the order that the other had handed him. He remembered perfectly
well that he had arranged the matter of transporting his crop some
months before, but his role of proprietor amused him and he liked to
busy himself again and again with the details of his undertaking.

"I suppose," he added, "you'll be able to give 'em to me. There'll
be a big wheat crop to move this year and I don't want to be caught
in any car famine."

"Oh, you'll get your cars," murmured the other.

"I'll be the means of bringing business your way," Dyke went on;
"I've done so well with my hops that there are a lot of others going
into the business next season. Suppose," he continued, struck with an
idea, "suppose we went into some sort of pool, a sort of shippers'
organisation, could you give us special rates, cheaper rates—say a
cent and a half?"

The other looked up.

"A cent and a half! Say *four* cents and a half and maybe I'll talk
business with you."

"Four cents and a half," returned Dyke, "I don't see it. Why, the
regular rate is only two cents."

"No, it isn't," answered the clerk, looking him gravely in the eye,
"it's five cents."

"Well, there's where you are wrong, m'son," Dyke retorted, genially.
"You look it up. You'll find the freight on hops from Bonneville to
'Frisco is two cents a pound for car load lots. You told me that your-
self last fall."

"That was last fall," observed the clerk. There was a silence. Dyke
shot a glance of suspicion at the other. Then, reassured, he remarked:

"You look it up. You'll see I'm right."

S. Behrman came forward and shook hands politely with the ex-engineer.

"Anything I can do for you, Mr. Dyke?"

Dyke explained. When he had done speaking, the clerk turned to S. Behrman and observed, respectfully:

"Our regular rate on hops is five cents."

"Yes," answered S. Behrman, pausing to reflect; "yes, Mr. Dyke, that's right—five cents."

The clerk brought forward a folder of yellow paper and handed it to Dyke. It was inscribed at the top "Tariff Schedule No. 8," and underneath these words, in brackets, was a smaller inscription, *"Supersedes No. 7 of Aug. 1."*

"See for yourself," said S. Behrman. He indicated an item under the head of "Miscellany."

"The following rates for carriage of hops in car load lots," read Dyke, "take effect June 1, and will remain in force until superseded by a later tariff. Those quoted beyond Stockton are subject to changes in traffic arrangements with carriers by water from that point."

In the list that was printed below, Dyke saw that the rate for hops between Bonneville or Guadalajara and San Francisco was five cents.

For a moment Dyke was confused. Then swiftly the matter became clear in his mind. The Railroad had raised the freight on hops from two cents to five.

All his calculations as to a profit on his little investment he had based on a freight rate of two cents a pound. He was under contract to deliver his crop. He could not draw back. The new rate ate up every cent of his gains. He stood there ruined.

"Why, what do you mean?" he burst out. "You promised me a rate of two cents and I went ahead with my business with that understanding. What do you mean?"

S. Behrman and the clerk watched him from the other side of the counter.

"The rate is five cents," declared the clerk doggedly.

"Well, that ruins me," shouted Dyke. "Do you understand? I won't make fifty cents. *Make!* Why, I will *owe*,—I'll be—be—That ruins me, do you understand?"

The other raised a shoulder.

"We don't force you to ship. You can do as you like. The rate is five cents."

"Well—but—damn you, I'm under contract to deliver. What am I going to do? Why, you told me—you promised me a two-cent rate."

"I don't remember it," said the clerk. "I don't know anything about that. But I know this; I know that hops have gone up. I know the German crop was a failure and that the crop in New York wasn't worth the hauling. Hops have gone up to nearly a dollar. You don't suppose we don't know that, do you, Mr. Dyke?"

"What's the price of hops got to do with you?"

"It's got *this* to do with us," returned the other with a sudden aggressiveness, "that the freight rate has gone up to meet the price. We're not doing business for our health. My orders are to raise your rate to five cents, and I think you are getting off easy."

Dyke stared in blank astonishment. For the moment, the audacity of the affair was what most appealed to him. He forgot its personal application.

"Good Lord," he murmured, "good Lord! What will you people do next? Look here. What's your basis of applying freight rates, any-how?" he suddenly vociferated with furious sarcasm. "What's your rule? What are you guided by?"

But at the words, S. Behrman, who had kept silent during the heat of the discussion, leaned abruptly forward. For the only time in his knowledge, Dyke saw his face inflamed with anger and with the enmity and contempt of all this farming element with whom he was contending.

"Yes, what's your rule? What's your basis?" demanded Dyke, turning swiftly to him.

S. Behrman emphasised each word of his reply with a tap of one forefinger on the counter before him:

"All—the—traffic—will—bear."

C. C. Post
"The First Hot Flush of Righteous Anger"

With the irrigation ditches beginning to function, Erastus Hemmingway and his wife, Lucy, feel sure enough in their prospects to expand their orchard and plant rosebushes, a symbol of better times. But when rumors that the railroad lands will not come as cheaply as the farmers expected reach Hemmingway, he starts to worry. As the Mussel Slough region greens—and "new and pretty cottages" replace the worn-out huts originally built by the settlers—the rail-road finally names its price, evoking from the settlers "the first hot flush of righteous anger." C. C. Post names as the principle source of this misery Leland Stanford, a self-centered nabob who even as an elected official behaved more like a feudal lord than a servant of the people.

M eantime Erastus and Lucy worked on.
The size of orchard and vineyard was increased by the plant-ing of other trees and vines. Rose-bushes were set out at the corners of the porch and beneath the windows, and evergreens and flowering shrubs in the front yard.

The main irrigating ditch having been completed the year before, the work of carrying the water wherever needed, by means of small side ditches, was comparatively easy and rapid, so that some pretty broad fields of grain and grass were beginning to stretch away on every side of their cottage.

But now came a terrible rumor.

It was told doubtingly at first, as something that could hardly be possible—that the Pacific Railroad Company laid claim to the lands about the Slough, and would compel payment of their present market value, all improvements included, or evict the homesteaders from possession.

The settlers quite generally laughed at the tale, as being started by someone for the purpose of giving them a fright.

"What!" they said, "the railroad company claim our lands! Why, the land was absolutely valueless, thought not to be worth paying taxes on, until we irrigated it and built houses and put out orchards and vineyards.

"Besides, the land grant by Congress was made to a company whose charter fixed the line of their road more than a hundred miles away, on the other side of a range of mountains; and even this grant the company has forfeited long ago, the time in which the road was to be built in order to obtain the land having expired two years since, and the road is not built yet."

It seemed absurd for anybody to talk about a railroad company having a claim to their lands, when they had redeemed them from the desert, and were almost ready to prove up on them under the home-stead and pre-emption laws.

Yet there were those who were less easily disarmed of fear.

They knew that in Iowa a railroad company had dispossessed settlers who had actually proved up and received deeds to their homes from government.

There were those among them, too, who had suffered from the overflow of hydraulic mines, others from the Suscol Ranch, and yet others who had suffered from the encroachments of corporations in other states and other portions of this state, and these were prepared to believe that nothing was too preposterous for the railroad company to claim, if its officers thought there was the remotest chance of enforcing it, either by fair means or foul.

When Erastus Hemmingway heard the rumor his heart sunk, for he had seen too much of the heartlessness and greed of corporations not to fear the worst, and he at once took steps to ascertain the truth.

He wrote to the headquarters of the company, repeating what he had heard, and asking if there was any truth in the statement that the company professed to have any claim to the land in the vicinity of the Slough.

In reply he received a letter and also a circular.

The letter was signed by Leland Stanford, president of the railroad company, and was to the effect that the company hoped to be allowed the original grant of lands made by Congress in aid of the road, but the boundaries of the grant had not been determined, and probably would not be for some time.

Meanwhile, the letter went on to say, the settlers could be assured that in no case should they be the losers, as, if it should eventually be determined that the land which they occupied was within the limits of the grant to the road, the company pledged itself to transfer it to the occupants on payment of the government price, and attention was called to the accompanying circular, copies of which, the letter said, were being issued and distributed all over the state for the purpose of inducing people to take up land at the Slough. This circular also contained a pledge that if found to be within the grant of Congress to the road, the company would transfer the land to whoever had improved it, immediately on payment of the government price.

This letter, taken in connection with the circulars, which were scattered freely among the settlers, if it did not remove all feeling of fear from the minds of Erastus and a few others, did serve to allay the general alarm, which was before on the increase, and improvements went on as usual.

The circulars of the company sent to other portions of the state had the desired effect, and very soon other families began to come in in considerable numbers, all taking up claims and relying upon the printed pledges of the company that in no case should the land cost them more than the price asked by government for wild land.

So time sped on.

And now those who came first to the Slough began to reap abundantly of the fruit of their labor and perseverance.

The work of turning a veritable desert into a garden had been accomplished. It had been done, too, without capital, and by men who were forced to support themselves and their families while the transformation was being made.

Orchards and vineyards were loaded with fruit. Olives and apples, peaches, plums, apricots, pears, pineapples, lemons, pomegranates, nectarines—all the semi-tropical fruits, and some which grow nowhere else outside of the tropics themselves, were to be found in full bearing upon the irrigated lands of the settlers at Mussel Slough.

Green fields grew broader and greener. Little flocks and herds of cattle and sheep were to be seen feeding on the rich vegetation which came with the water that overspread the land from the system of irrigating ditches; and as the result of all this, new and pretty cottages were taking the place of the wretched huts in which nearly all had been forced to live during the first years of their residence; and it was in the midst of this prosperity, when want had been banished by years of patient, persevering toil, and they were rejoicing over troubles past, and the thought that for the rest of their days they could take life easy, that the stroke came which turned all their joy into mourning, and changed the current of their blood from the peaceful flow of quiet, happy hearts to a seething flood in hearts made hot with fear and hatred.

This was no rumor from an unknown source that reached their ears, awaking doubt in some and ridicule in others. It was not the faint murmuring of a distant storm that might never reach them, but the sudden rush of the whirlwind; the flash of the lightning, the falling of the thunderbolt from a sunny sky. It came as a notice from the railroad company to each settler, informing him that he was a trespasser on the lands of the company, and must immediately vacate unless he was prepared to pay the value of the lands occupied by him, which had been carefully appraised, so the notice read, by competent judges, whose estimate of the value of each quarter-section accompanied the notice.

This appraisement ranged from ten to thirty-five dollars per acre; that of Erastus Hemmingway being thirty dollars per acre, or a total of four thousand eight hundred dollars, which he was asked to pay to the railroad company for the land he had redeemed from the desert; or failing therein was ordered to at once vacate the premises.

The excitement which the receipt of these notices caused can be imagined.

Threats of vengeance upon the officers of the company were both loud and frequent, and had they been present, there is no question as to what their fate would have been. Death in some form would unquestionably have been meted out to them.

But they were careful not to be present.

They had deliberately laid, and were now executing, a plan to rob these people of their homes, and they were too cunning to come within reach of their victims while the first hot flush of righteous anger was upon them.

With the power which their immense wealth, the gift of Congress, gave them, they did not fear the courts or the state authorities.

They already controlled these, and were prepared to bribe or threaten, as they deemed most likely to accomplish their ends, any official who stood in the way of their plans for wholesale robbery.

The leaders in the plot stood high in social and political circles.

Stanford, the president of the company, had been Governor of the State, and it was while filling this exalted position that he first began to lay plans for the subjugation of the people, and in Huntington and Crocker he had able partners and unscrupulous allies.

The settlers had small means of making the outrage upon their rights known, and their cause was, indeed, desperate, and it is small wonder, when in every dwelling at the Slough were women whose eyes were red with weeping, that there should be men whose lips uttered curses, and whose muscles twitched with eagerness to lay hand upon the authors of their woe.

Frank Norris
"League First, Principles Afterward"

Buck Annixter's new barn is finished and becomes the site of an eventful community celebration, "a very whirlwind of gayety." During the festivities, Annixter not only coolly faces down the fearsome party-crasher Delaney (Norris' fanciful version of Walter Crow, one of the historical Mussel Slough belligerents), but he also receives a special message, one co-signed by the hateful S. Behrman on behalf of the Pacific and Southwestern Railroad and its corporate executive, Shelgrim. Annixter's reaction—and those of his rancher companions—is immediate.

"Message for you, sir. Will you sign?"

He held the book to Annixter, who signed the receipt, wondering.

The boy departed, leaving a thick envelope of yellow paper in Annixter's hands, the address typewritten, the word "Urgent" written in blue pencil in one corner.

Annixter tore it open. The envelope contained other sealed envelopes, some eight or ten of them, addressed to Magnus Derrick, Osterman, Broderson, Garnett, Keast, Gethings, Chattern, Dabney, and to Annixter himself.

Still puzzled, Annixter distributed the envelopes, muttering to himself:

"What's up now?"

The incident had attracted attention. A comparative quiet followed, the guests following the letters with their eyes as they were passed around the table. They fancied that Annixter had arranged a surprise.

Magnus Derrick, who sat next to Annixter, was the first to receive his letter. With a word of excuse he opened it.

"Read it, read it, Governor," shouted a half-dozen voices. "No secrets, you know. Everything above board here to-night."

Magnus cast a glance at the contents of the letter, then rose to his feet and read:

Magnus Derrick,
    Bonneville, Tulare Co., Cal.

Dear Sir:

By regrade of October 1st, the value of the railroad land you occupy, included in your ranch of Los Muertos, has been fixed at $27.00 per acre. The land is now for sale at that price to any one.

Yours, etc.,
CYRUS BLAKELEE RUGGLES,
Land Agent, P. and S. W. R. R.
S. BEHRMAN,
Local Agent, P. and S. W. R. R.

In the midst of the profound silence that followed, Osterman was heard to exclaim grimly:

"That's a pretty good one. Tell us another."

But for a long moment this was the only remark.

The silence widened, broken only by the sound of torn paper as Annixter, Osterman, old Broderson, Garnett, Keast, Gethings, Chattern, and Dabney opened and read their letters. They were all to the same effect, almost word for word like the Governor's. Only the figures and the proper names varied. In some cases the price per acre was twenty-two dollars. In Annixter's case it was thirty.

"And—and the company promised to sell to me, to—to all of us," gasped old Broderson, "at *two dollars and a half* an acre."

It was not alone the ranchers immediately around Bonneville who would be plundered by this move on the part of the Railroad. The "alternate section" system applied throughout all the San Joaquin. By striking at the Bonneville ranchers a terrible precedent was established. Of the crowd of guests in the harness room alone, nearly every man was affected, every man menaced with ruin. All of a million acres was suddenly involved.

Then suddenly the tempest burst. A dozen men were on their feet in an instant, their teeth set, their fists clenched, their faces purple with rage. Oaths, curses, maledictions exploded like the firing of successive mines. Voices quivered with wrath, hands flung upward, the fingers hooked, prehensile, trembled with anger. The sense of wrongs, the injustices, the oppression, extortion, and pillage of twenty years suddenly culminated and found voice in a raucous howl of execration. For a second there was nothing articulate in that cry of savage exasperation, nothing even intelligent. It was the human animal hounded to its corner, exploited, harried to its last stand, at bay, ferocious, terrible, turning at last with bared teeth and upraised claws to meet the death grapple. It was the hideous squealing of the tormented brute, its back to the wall, defending its lair, its mate and its whelps, ready to bite, to rend, to trample, to batter out the life of The Enemy in a primeval, bestial welter of blood and fury.

The roar subsided to intermittent clamour, in the pauses of which the sounds of music and dancing made themselves audible once more.

"S. Behrman again," vociferated Harran Derrick.

"Chose his moment well," muttered Annixter. "Hits his hardest when we're all rounded up having a good time."

"Gentlemen, this is ruin."

"What's to be done now?"

"*Fight!* My God! do you think we are going to stand this? Do you think we *can*?"

The uproar swelled again. The clearer the assembly of ranchers understood the significance of this move on the part of the Railroad, the more terrible it appeared, the more flagrant, the more intolerable. Was it possible, was it within the bounds of imagination that this tyranny should be contemplated? But they knew—past years had driven home the lesson—the implacable, iron monster with whom they had to deal, and again and again the sense of outrage and oppression lashed them to their feet, their mouths wide with curses, their fists clenched tight, their throats hoarse with shouting.

"Fight! How fight? What *are* you going to do?"

"If there's a law in this land—"

"If there is, it is in Shelgrim's pocket. Who owns the courts in California? Ain't it Shelgrim?"

"God damn him."

"Well, how long are you going to stand it? How long before you'll settle up accounts with six inches of plugged gas-pipe?"

"And our contracts, the solemn pledges of the corporation to sell to us first of all—"

"And now the land is for sale to anybody."

"Why, it is a question of my home. Am I to be turned out? Why, I have put eight thousand dollars into improving this land."

"And I six thousand, and now that I have, the Railroad grabs it."

"And the system of irrigating ditches that Derrick and I have been laying out. There's thousands of dollars in that!"

"I'll fight this out till I've spent every cent of my money."

"Where? In the courts that the company owns?"

"Think I am going to give in to this? Think I am to get off my land? By God, gentlemen, law or no law, railroad or no railroad, I—will—not."

"Nor I."

"Nor I."

"Nor I."

"This is the last. Legal means first; if those fail—the shotgun."

"They can kill me. They can shoot me down, but I'll die—die fighting for my home—before I'll give in to this."

At length Annixter made himself heard:

"All out of the room but the ranch owners," he shouted. "Hooven, Caraher, Dyke, you'll have to clear out. This is a family affair. Presley, you and your friend can remain."

Reluctantly the others filed through the door. There remained in the harness room—besides Vanamee and Presley—Magnus Derrick, Annixter, old Broderson, Harran, Garnett from the Ruby rancho, Keast from the ranch of the same name, Gethings of the San Pablo, Chattern of the Bonanza, about a score of others, ranchers from various parts of the county, and, last of all, Dabney, ignored, silent, to whom nobody spoke and who, as yet, had not uttered a word.

But the men who had been asked to leave the harness room spread the news throughout the barn. It was repeated from lip to lip. One by one the guests dropped out of the dance. Groups were formed. By swift degrees the gayety lapsed away. The Virginia reel broke up. The musicians ceased playing, and in the place of the noisy, effervescent revelry of the previous half hour, a subdued murmur filled all the barn, a mingling of whispers, lowered voices, the coming and going of light footsteps, the uneasy shifting of positions, while from behind the closed doors of the harness room came a prolonged, sullen hum of anger and strenuous debate. The dance came to an abrupt end. The guests, unwilling to go as yet, stunned, distressed, stood clumsily about, their eyes vague, their hands swinging at their sides, looking stupidly into each others' faces. A sense of impending calamity, oppressive, foreboding, gloomy, passed through the air overhead in the night, a long shiver of anguish and of terror, mysterious, despairing.

In the harness room, however, the excitement continued unchecked. One rancher after another delivered himself of a torrent of furious words. There was no order, merely the frenzied outcry of blind fury. One spirit alone was common to all—resistance at whatever cost and to whatever lengths.

Suddenly Osterman leaped to his feet, his bald head gleaming in the lamp-light, his red ears distended, a flood of words filling his great, horizontal slit of a mouth, his comic actor's face flaming. Like the hero of a melodrama, he took stage with a great sweeping gesture.

"Organisation," he shouted, "that must be our watchword. The curse of the ranchers is that they fritter away their strength. Now, we must stand together, now, *now.* Here's the crisis, here's the moment. Shall we meet it? *I call for the League.* Not next week, not tomorrow, not in the morning, but now, now, now, this very moment, before we go out of that door. Every one of us here to join it, to form the beginnings of a vast organisation, banded together to death, if needs be, for the protection of our rights and homes. Are you ready? Is it now or never? I call for the League."

Instantly there was a shout. With an actor's instinct, Osterman had spoken at the precise psychological moment. He carried the others off their feet, glib, dexterous, voluble. Just what was meant by the League the others did not know, but it was something, a vague engine, a machine with which to fight. Osterman had not done speaking before the room rang with outcries, the crowd of men shouting, for what they did not know.

"The League! The League!"

"Now, to-night, this moment; sign our names before we leave."

"He's right. Organisation! The League!"

"We have a committee at work already," Osterman vociferated. "I am a member, and also Mr. Broderson, Mr. Annixter, and Mr. Harran Derrick. What our aims are we will explain to you later. Let this committee be the nucleus of the League—temporarily, at least. Trust us. We are working for you and with you. Let this committee be merged into the larger committee of the League, and for President of the League"—he paused the fraction of a second—"for President there can be but one name mentioned, one man to whom we all must look as leader—Magnus Derrick."

The Governor's name was received with a storm of cheers. The harness room reëchoed with shouts of:

"Derrick! Derrick!"

"Magnus for President!"

"Derrick, our natural leader."

"Derrick, Derrick, Derrick for President."

Magnus rose to his feet. He made no gesture. Erect as a cavalry officer, tall, thin, commanding, he dominated the crowd in an instant. There was a moment's hush.

"Gentlemen," he said, "if organisation is a good word, moderation is a better one. The matter is too grave for haste. I would suggest that we each and severally return to our respective homes for the night, sleep over what has happened, and convene again to-morrow, when we are calmer and can approach this affair in a more judicious mood. As for the honour with which you would inform me, I must affirm that that, too, is a matter for grave deliberation. This League is but a name as yet. To accept control of an organisation whose principles are not yet fixed is a heavy responsibility. I shrink from it—"

But he was allowed to proceed no farther. A storm of protest developed. There were shouts of:

"No, no. The League to-night and Derrick for President."

"We have been moderate too long."

"The League first, principles afterward."

"We can't wait," declared Osterman. "Many of us cannot attend a meeting to-morrow. Our business affairs would prevent it. Now we are all together. I propose a temporary chairman and secretary be named and a ballot be taken. But first the League. Let us draw up a set of resolutions to stand together, for the defence of our homes, to death, if needs be, and each man present affix his signature thereto."

He subsided amidst vigorous applause. The next quarter of an hour was a vague confusion, every one talking at once, conversations going on in low tones in various corners of the room. Ink, pens, and a sheaf of foolscap were brought from the ranch house. A set of resolutions was draughted, having the force of a pledge, organising the League of Defence. Annixter was the first to sign. Others followed, only a few holding back, refusing to join till they had thought the matter over. The roll grew; the paper circulated about the table; each signature was welcomed by a salvo of cheers. At length, it reached Harran Derrick, who signed amid tremendous uproar. He released the pen only to shake a score of hands.

"Now, Magnus Derrick."

"Gentlemen," began the Governor, once more rising, "I beg of you to allow me further consideration. Gentlemen—"

He was interrupted by renewed shouting.

"No, no, now or never. Sign, join the League."

"Don't leave us. We look to you to help."

But presently the excited throng that turned their faces towards the Governor were aware of a new face at his elbow. The door of the harness room had been left unbolted and Mrs. Derrick, unable to endure the breathtaking suspense of waiting outside, had gathered up all her courage and had come into the room. Trembling, she clung to Magnus's arm, her pretty light-brown hair in disarray, her large young girl's eyes wide with terror and distrust. What was about to happen she did not understand, but these men were clamouring for Magnus to pledge himself to something, to some terrible course of action, some ruthless, unscrupulous battle to the death with the iron-hearted monster of steel and steam. Nerved with a coward's intrepidity, she, who so easily obliterated herself, had found her way into the midst of this frantic crowd, into this hot, close room, reeking of alcohol and tobacco smoke, into this atmosphere surcharged with hatred and curses. She seized her husband's arm imploring, distraught with terror.

"No, no," she murmured; "no, don't sign."

She was the feather caught in the whirlwind. *En masse,* the crowd surged toward the erect figure of the Governor, the pen in one hand, his wife's fingers in the other, the roll of signatures before him. The clamour was deafening; the excitement culminated brusquely. Half a hundred hands stretched toward him; thirty voices, at top pitch, implored, expostulated, urged, almost commanded. The reverberation of the shouting was as the plunge of a cataract.

It was the uprising of The People; the thunder of the outbreak of revolt; the mob demanding to be led, aroused at last, imperious, resistless, overwhelming. It was the blind fury of insurrection, the brute, many-tongued, red-eyed, bellowing for guidance, baring its teeth, unsheathing its claws, imposing its will with the abrupt, resistless pressure of the relaxed piston, inexorable, knowing no pity.

"No, no," implored Annie Derrick. "No, Magnus, don't sign."

"He *must,*" declared Harran, shouting in her ear to make himself heard, "he must. Don't you understand?"

Again the crowd surged forward, roaring. Mrs. Derrick was swept back, pushed to one side. Her husband no longer belonged to her. She paid the penalty for being the wife of a great man. The world, like a colossal iron wedge, crushed itself between. She was thrust to the wall. The throng of men, stamping, surrounded Magnus; she could no longer see him, but, terror-struck, she listened. There was a moment's lull, then a vast thunder of savage jubilation. Magnus had signed.

Harran found his mother leaning against the wall, her hands shut over her ears; her eyes, dilated with fear, brimming with tears. He led her from the harness room to the outer room, where Mrs. Tree and Hilma took charge of her, and then, impatient, refusing to answer the hundreds of anxious questions that assailed him, hurried back to the harness room.

Already the balloting was in progress, Osterman acting as temporary chairman. On the very first ballot he was made secretary of the League *pro tem.*, and Magnus unanimously chosen for its President. An executive committee was formed, which was to meet the next day at the Los Muertos ranch house.

It was half-past one o'clock. In the barn outside the greater number of the guests had departed. Long since the musicians had disappeared. There only remained the families of the ranch owners involved in the meeting in the harness room. These huddled in isolated groups in corners of the garish, echoing barn, the women in their wraps, the young men with their coat collars turned up against the draughts that once more made themselves felt.

For a long half hour the loud hum of eager conversation continued to issue from behind the door of the harness room. Then, at length, there was a prolonged scraping of chairs. The session was over. The men came out in groups, searching for their families.

At once the homeward movement began. Every one was worn out. Some of the ranchers' daughters had gone to sleep against their mothers' shoulders.

Billy, the stableman, and his assistant were awakened, and the teams were hitched up. The stable yard was full of a maze of swinging lanterns and buggy lamps. The horses fretted, champing the bits; the carry-alls creaked with the straining of leather and springs as they received their loads. At every instant one heard the rattle of wheels, as vehicle after vehicle disappeared in the night.

A fine, drizzling rain was falling, and the lamps began to show dim in a vague haze of orange light.

Magnus Derrick was the last to go. At the doorway of the barn he found Annixter, the roll of names—which it had been decided he was to keep in his safe for the moment—under his arm. Silently the two shook hands. Magnus departed. The grind of the wheels of his carry-all grated sharply on the gravel of the driveway in front of the ranch house, then, with a hollow roll across a little plank bridge, gained the roadway. For a moment the beat of the horses' hoofs made itself heard on the roadway. It ceased. Suddenly there was a great silence.

Annixter, in the doorway of the great barn, stood looking about him for a moment, alone, thoughtful. The barn was empty. That astonishing evening had come to an end. The whirl of things and people, the crowd of dancers, Delaney, the gun fight, Hilma Tree, her eyes fixed on him in mute confession, the rabble in the harness room, the news of the regrade, the fierce outburst of wrath, the hasty organising of the League, all went spinning confusedly through his recollection. But he was exhausted. Time enough in the morning to think it all over. By now it was raining sharply. He put the roll of names into his inside pocket, threw a sack over his head and shoulders, and went down to the ranch house.

But in the harness room, lighted by the glittering lanterns and flaring lamps, in the midst of overturned chairs, spilled liquor, cigar stumps, and broken glasses, Vanamee and Presley still remained talking, talking. At length, they rose, and came out upon the floor of the barn and stood for a moment looking about them.

Billy, the stableman, was going the rounds of the walls, putting out light after light. By degrees, the vast interior was growing dim. Upon the roof overhead the rain drummed incessantly, the eaves dripping. The floor was littered with pine needles, bits of orange peel, ends and fragments of torn organdies and muslins and bits of tissue paper from the "Phrygian Bonnets" and "Liberty Caps." The buckskin mare in the stall, dozing on three legs, changed position with a long sigh. The sweat stiffening the hair upon her back and loins, as it dried, gave off a penetrating, ammoniacal odour that mingled with the stale perfume of sachet and wilted flowers.

Presley and Vanamee stood looking at the deserted barn. There was a long silence. Then Presley said:

"Well…what do you think of it all?"

"I think," answered Vanamee slowly, "I think that there was a dance in Brussels the night before Waterloo."

Settlers' Committee
"AN APPEAL TO THE PEOPLE," PAMPHLET
VISALIA: DELTA PRINTING ESTABLISHMENT, 1880

The Struggle
of the
Mussel Slough Settlers
for their homes!
An Appeal to the People
History of the land troubles in Tulare and Fresno Counties.
The grasping greed of the railroad monopoly.
By the Settlers' Committee

To the Candid Men and Women
of the World

The Mussel Slough Settlers of Tulare and Fresno counties, in the State of California, herewith submit to the candid world a plain and unvarnished statement of the history, of the land grant made to the Railroad, the section of the officers of the Government thereupon, and the rights and equities under which we claim the lands along the line of what is called the Goshen branch of the Southern Pacific Railroad, over which the contests arose that resulted in the lamentable occurrence of the 11th of May, when seven men lost their lives.

This address is issued solely to inform the public mind as to the facts surrounding this contest. All good people sympathize with the right. Generous impulses and a desire that justice shall prevail are with them universal. Among them jealousy of railroad corporations does not exist simply because they *are* corporations, but because it is known to all men that they too often take advantage of their great power to annoy and oppress individuals. Our opponent is one of the most powerful corporations in the land. Whether or not it is oppressive, exacting, rapacious and heartless, we desire shall be a verdict which each shall render for himself after reading what is here submitted. And in rendering this verdict, the reader will also render another verdict, and that is, as to whether or not the hundreds of poor men who, with their families, have settled upon these lands, are mere "squatters" upon the lands and trespassers upon the rights of the Railroad Company.

The first thing to consider in arriving at a just conclusion of the controversy is, has the Railroad Company any right to these lands? Did it ever have a grant to lands along this line of road? And if it did, has it complied with the conditions of the grant? —or has it forfeited them by con-compliance? If it *did* have a grant along that line, and if it complied with the conditions of the grant, then no one will deny its right to the land and the duty of the settlers to purchase it from the Company upon such terms and under such representations as were made to them by the Company as inducements for their settlement.

But, on the other hand, if it can be shown from the highest authority that no grant has ever made along this line of road, and that, if made, it was not completed as required by Act of Congress, and is not now completed, and that the time when it was required to be completed has long since expired, then this candid mind to which we appeal will at once come to its conclusion upon the issue.

But aside from this question so vital as to the right of the Railroad to a foot of land along this line of road, the settlers have yet another right which springs from and is based upon circulars issued by authority of the Railroad Company, upon the good faith of which hundreds of men went upon the lands. These circulars set forth definite prices per acre at which the different qualities of land would be sold, ranging from $2.50 to $10, none higher than $10, and most of it at $2.50 to $5 per acre.

These are the issues of this great contest, and are the ones upon which we ask the opinion of all good men.

One of the Nineteen
"THE MUSSEL SLOUGH DIFFICULTY"
FROM THE SAN FRANCISCO *ARGONAUT,* 1881

[On the twenty-eighth of last month a committee of the "Settlers' Land League" of the Mussel Slough District, issued a letter, (reproduced in the *Examiner* of this city,) setting forth some of the principles of the league, and animadverting in strong terms against the action of "Nineteen Settlers," who had written a letter to the Visalia *Delta* in extenuation of the railroad position in its dispute with the Leaguers. In the course of the article, the nineteen settlers not in sympathy with the league were spoken of as follows: "In choosing the side of an oppressive monopoly that has made itself obnoxious all over the Pacific Coast, these few neighbors stand toward our cause in the same position that the Tories of the Revolution occupied toward our forefathers who wrested the liberty we now enjoy from the English Crown. If they are at any time severely criticised by our friends, as the Tories were and are, they have none to blame but themselves." In reply to the long article from which the above extract is taken, "One of the Nineteen" has sent us the following letter:]

EDITOR ARGONAUT: I read in the daily *Examiner* of April 1st a communication from the Settlers' Land League of the Mussel Slough District, wherein its members attack what it terms the nineteen settlers. This attack is of a very serious character. As I am "one of the nineteen," I propose to pay my respects to the aforesaid league by making a brief statement of facts. In so doing, I will draw a parallel case to that of the league, and endeavor to so reveal its true inwardness as to fully expose its actions and its intentions.

Let us suppose that myself and others from this place go over into Kern County, and feloniously occupy the land of Carr and Haggin, because they are a "big monopoly." The title to their lands is not any better than that to the land of the railroad company, so we would dispute the title, and would then organize ourselves into a "Settlers' Land League." We would say "Settlers," because that sounds big, because that embraces the honest tiller of the soil, the hardy and courageous pioneer that has braved the dangers and hardships of the early settlements of the Far West; because it commands the respect of all mankind. Under a big name we would be the better able to commit the grossest wrongs with impunity. So, after organizing we would begin to agitate the question of title to the lands in question. We would begin by proclaiming to the public that "this gigantic land monopoly has no shadow of title to those lands," and that "the land is subject to homestead and preëmption." We would then invite our neighbors and our friends to come and squat on those lands with us;

and we would then proceed to make a grand fight for the same. In arguing the case, we would say: "This monopoly has gobbled up this land under the Desert Land Act, and has held it by fraud and perjury. This land is not desert land, as is claimed, but is good agricultural and grazing land. We will file a protest against the issue of patents in the Department of the Interior, and we will also contest the title in the courts, and keep the case there for an indefinite term of years; thereby we shall have the use and profits of the land for a long time, whether we eventually steal it or not. Upon the whole, we will have a pretty good thing, paying no taxes, paying no rents, paying nothing—monarch of all we survey."

Now, this is precisely what these leaguers have done. Nay, they have done a great deal more: they have entered on the railroad land with a full knowledge that it was railroad land. They were told so, time and again, by the officers in the land office at Visalia. They did not go on those lands through a mistake, but have gone on for speculation, determined, if they can not whip the railroad company out of the land, to have the use of it for eight or ten years free of rent and taxes. In a large number of cases this land has changed hands from one to three, and even four times. A great many claims sold for from five hundred to a thousand dollars. In very many instances men have moved the buildings off their own land on to railroad land. Others again would sell their homes and move on to railroad land. This railroad land has been the principal stock in trade in the Mussel Slough country. And the league and the railroad land together have been the source of a great deal of trouble and bad feeling in this part of the country.

I will here relate how a leaguer and the league served one of the "nineteen" before alluded to. The man had made the preliminary arrangements to buy a piece of railroad land, and was occupying and cultivating the same. When the owner was away from home, one of those honest and innocent leaguers moved his house and other outfit on to the man's land. When the man returned, and attempted to remonstrate with the leaguer against such proceedings, he had the satisfaction of being told that the land in question was not railroad land, that the railroad company had no shadow of title to it, and that he (the leaguer) was going to hold the land as Government land. A little while afterward the league had the impudence to ask the man to donate ten or twenty dollars to fight the railroad company. I mention this particular case, as it represents a great many similar cases that have occurred in this Mussel Slough country, and to show to the public that this land question is like all other questions—and has two sides to it.

There is another land difficulty on record here, that occurred previous to the railroad land difficulties. In this, some of the same people now belonging to the league experimented before they "tackled" the railroad company. That was on the Sutherland ranch. Mr. Sutherland had at that time about ten thousand acres of swamp and overflowed land, situated between Kings River and Mussel Slough, all enclosed with a good fence. He had reclaimed the same by building dams and levees. After the water left the land it became very attractive. There were a few "smart Alicks" here then, as well as now. They began to agitate the question whether or not the land was really swamp land, and the more they talked the matter up the more they would think it was not swamp land. So, while Mr. Sutherland was living in Stockton, they "went for it," and it was not long till they had built huts and shanties all over the land, and were plowing and seeding in earnest. They did then what they are doing now; they stayed with it till they were moved off by the sheriff, and some of them were not satisfied even then, but went back on the land the second time. A term in jail for several of them ended that land trouble.

Now, these are all stubborn facts, which I can substantiate by a hundred witnesses. The great trouble with these leaguers seems to be that the most of them belong to a class that have got a kind of mania for fighting "land monopolies." A great many of them have been at it ever since they came into the country. They have been at it all over the State before they came here, and are at it now. It is a singular fact that ever so many of these leaguers, when they came here, settled on some of the best land in the country, and acquired a good title to the same. But they were still not satisfied; something was wanting; they could not rest; they had to have a land fight—"that's what's the matter!" Some of them sold their land at a big figure to raise money to fight the railroad company. Others acted more wisely; they kept their land, but moved their buildings on to railroad land, and now they are happy.

A few hints in regard to the military department of the league will not be out of place here. They admit that they marched out on the street at Hanford, eighty strong; and they also admit that they applied to the State for arms. Now the idea of asking for arms from the State to fight the Government of the United States, is decidedly the cheekiest thing of the age. But they fail to say anything about marching the streets at the dead hour of night, calling peaceable citizens out of their midnight slumbers, and ordering them to leave the country. They also fail to say anything about marching through the country after dark, dragging innocent women and children from their houses and applying the torch to their property. All these things seem to be an innocent and peaceable pastime for these men. At the trial of the convicted leaguers, the league witnesses all swore that it might have been Indians that burned Perry Phillips's house. That is about as "thin" as things generally get. I don't think that there is one man, woman, or child of any size in all the Mussel Slough country but fully believes that the league burned Perry Phillips's house. All their talk about their organization being for peaceable purposes is the merest bosh. They have said, time and time again, in a braggadocio kind of way, that the railroad company could not bring officers and men enough to dispossess them of their lands; that they had plenty of Winchester rifles and breech-loading shotguns, and that no man should live that would buy those lands from the railroad company. They seem to deny the fact that they hurrahed and applauded Kearney when he made his speech here. I was there, and if there was a man that applauded or hurrahed outside of the league and their claqueurs, I did not see him. When Kearney told them to stay with their land, that he would come to their assistance with forty thousand men from San Francisco, and would "murder the red-eyed monsters," members of the league hurrahed as if they would split their throats.

As to the league going out on the 11th of last May, forty or fifty in number, and a good many of them well armed, as peacemakers: they went out there just for what they said they were going out for. They told several responsible men, that they met on their way out, that they were going out to stop the marshal from dispossessing any more men, and were going to make him leave the country, and they carried it out to the letter. It was very clearly proved at the trial that they rode up to the marshal and his party with pistols drawn, and told them to surrender. But Walter Crow would not surrender worth a cent. A brave man hardly ever surrenders to outlaws. Now the leaguers try to make it appear that Walter Crow murdered those five or six men. The idea of one man murdering six men, when there were ten or twelve men shooting at him, is certainly very hard to believe. But Walter Crow did just what any other brave man would have done under like circumstances; and if ever there was a cold-blooded murder, the killing of Crow was one. If they had killed him in the fight, it would not have looked so bad; but the evidence is very strong that they killed him in ambush, an hour or two after the fight.

"One of the Nineteen"
Hanford, April 15, 1881

May Merrill Miller
"He that Hath Lands"

Edwin Blansford learns that the railroad land he and Amelie have settled on has been graded at $37.60 an acre, a cost far in excess of what they had expected to pay. Already a leader in the Sierra Ditch Company, Edwin takes an active role as the settlers of the region form their league, a secret organization whose members have signed a pledge "to stay together and to act only according to legal means." Yet some of the organization's members threaten to break that pledge, as Colonel Becker, once a Confederate officer, takes charge and advocates more forceful resistance. Colonel Becker is reminiscent of one-time Confederate officer Major T. J. McQuiddey, an actual Mussel Slough landowner and a leader of the Settlers' League, an organization steeped in the mythos of the family farmer.

It was a cold night in November when Ralph Walker came over to see Edwin, Harry Gordon with him. The valley fog was lying thick as it had that first fall on the slough. Harry Gordon's fair hair was curling crisply, his cheeks red, as he stood with Ralph unwrapping their mufflers in the warm sitting-room. Amelie noticed Harry's fingers were shaking as he unwound his own. How young Harry looked!—no older than Duncan—only tonight there was something strange about him—new lines down to his mouth, grown up and terrible. And Ralph, bleak and silent.

"Well, it's started, Mr. Blansford," Harry said shortly, "the El Dorado Pacific. About five o'clock tonight a man named Hodges came by my house with another who said he was the El Dorado Pacific's land agent. Parker, his name was. He read me some kind of a paper as if I didn't have any rights at all. I told them I was ready to pay for my land although I could not pay ten times over again for my house I had built myself and the ditch I had dug and all, but they paid me no notice. Then they just began to move things out, furniture, beds, everything. They carried out the stove with the fire in it. You never saw such a pile; they weren't careful at all, chairs upside down, tables scratched, everything just stacked right in the middle of the road.

"It was hard on my wife. You know how she's been about her furniture. But with our new house built I was hoping she would be all right now. She has been too, almost like she used to be. But when this happened Janet just went sort of flighty. We haven't been able to help her. When the men left she ran out in the road to her furniture and she took off her white apron for a dust-cloth and she just kept crying and dusting, dusting, dusting....We couldn't do a thing with her. Dark came on, so we had to leave the things in the road. A band of cattle going by tonight could trample down all that isn't already broken. Janet's still there, Rhoda with her. We can't get Janet to come in. She just stays out in the road, trying to dust in the dark...."

Harry threw out his hands helplessly. Once more he looked young and bewildered and Amelie wanted to rush to him as she might her own brother, but she sat still, tears in her eyes. You can't treat him as a boy, not when he's come out here all the way from the East and he's trying to prove himself out in this country.

"Harry and Janet are staying with us tonight," Ralph answered Amelie's invitation. "At least they will if we can get Janet to come in....They will be right at home with us as they were before—until we do something about it...."

"I'll see you about it tomorrow, Ralph." Edwin stopped Ralph with that warning look Amelie knew meant: "Let's not talk about it in front of the women."

"Until we do something about it"—what could they do?

"Until we do something about it"—he had been so certain that something would be done.

A few days later Edwin came home from town with an express box from San Francisco in the back of the buggy.

"It's something for the Lodge," Edwin explained. Amelie thought it odd that he had not left the package in town.

That night Edwin asked Amelie for a needle and shears and a spool of black thread.

"What on earth for?" she asked in surprise, for Edwin never attempted any mending.

"I want to sew some harness," Edwin answered.

"But this thread is too light, Edwin—Zeke has some heavy waxed linen thread in the harness shed."

"I'll take this anyway." Edwin put it in his pocket and took up a lantern.

Something in his face made Amelie cease her questioning. Edwin stayed out in the barn a long time.

Later Edwin had to go to an Oracle Lodge meeting—a committee meeting he said, although it wasn't a regular Lodge night.

"Go to bed, Amelie—and don't wait up for me."

Amelie lay awake a long time, looking from her bed toward the window. She could scarcely tell windowpane from wall—it was a moonless night and very dark.

The next day, in Frank Bailey's store, Amelie was surprised to learn the railroad tenants whom the El Dorado Pacific's agent, Parker, had put into Harry Gordon's new house had been as quietly put out in the dead of last night, quite firmly but peaceably by a band of masked men wearing long black cloaks. The hired tenants had taken the morning train out of town. You could tell by looking at them they weren't farmers who really intended to settle—they didn't even pretend to have a plow or wagon or anything, only a roll of blankets apiece. A pair of tramps the El Dorado Pacific had hired to squat for them. The town was well rid of them.

Amelie did not like the way Frank Bailey looked at her as he handed her her parcels. She adjusted her veil and walked out.

On the way home Amelie stopped in to see Janet. She seemed quite cheerful as she told Harry and Ralph where to set the lyre-based tables and the blocked front desk back in her new parlor, her dustcloth in her hand. But every once in a while she would stop and stand still and look about her vacantly as if she were trying to remember something. Then she would go on directing the furniture-moving as if nothing had happened.

"You can see she isn't as well as she was before all this happened," Rhoda whispered to Amelie, "but at least we think we can get her to leave off her dusting part of the time and go to bed of nights."

When Amelie asked Edwin about Harry and Janet being put back in their house, he answered slowly, his face flushing a little: "I can't say anything to you, Amelie. It's for the best. If you do not know, you will be able to say you know nothing."

That was what Father had said, long ago, when the horses began to be tethered under the maples on dark nights. Amelie had believed in rebellion then; now she was not so sure. She was beginning to fear it. This rebellion was something furtive. She wished for none of it. But when you are married to a man, he is the one who makes that choice. First your father, then your husband. And you are supposed to say nothing.

But Amelie would not keep silent.

"Oh, Edwin," she cried, "I thought you believed in the law."

"I do, Amelie," he answered vehemently, "I'm going to San Francisco again next week, our test case on Tim Connery's land comes up there before the United States Circuit Court, and we will carry it right on to the Supreme Court if need be. And if the law goes against us we'll abide by it. But it's the El Dorado Pacific that's not willing to wait for the law. When they want a test case they throw a man who has set-tled the land in good faith and is willing to pay the price it was adver-tised for right out into the road. I suppose maybe they had to do that to get one test case, but the El Dorado Pacific's not going to stop at one. Matthews is boasting already about all the folks the company's going to dispossess.

Then he added slowly, painfully, "I've thought about this thing a lot, Amelie....It's easy enough to decide in your mind what's right...but that morning when I saw poor little Janet Gordon out in the road with her furniture stacked up like kindling...and her still out there in the road with cattle going by...people going by...with her white apron trying to dust...my God, Amelie, it's different when it's someone you know—your neighbors...."

When Amelie's son Dennis was born, he was a quiet baby. Amelie decided sometimes it was almost as if he knew how worried all of them were, as if he understood there was not much time to think of babies when you did not know whether the roof over your head were your own or not. And then she feared sometimes that this child did not look as sturdy as the rest, but that was foolish. She had so many more things to eat now, and this child had a bed so much more com-fortable and warm than the others had in the pine-box house. Surely these would compensate for the bad effects of all the worry she was feeling.

But if Amelie did not have much time for the new baby and Edwin was seldom home, Larry, left at home alone now that Isobel was in school, was enthusiastic, hanging over Denny's crib, always asking when his new brother would be old enough to play with him.

After Denny was born Amelie did not seem to get her strength back as she should. Perhaps it was the new house; it was so much larger than the pine cabin had been, and although it was bare and echoing with its uncarpeted floors, and there was, as yet, little furniture to dust, the floors had to be kept clean.

So Amelie scrubbed floors and longed for her pretty dishes, her books, the lamp with the blue bowl, the red carpet, and the carved rosewood parlor set of love-seat and chairs. The house remained an almost empty shell. Amelie agreed with Edwin she wouldn't want her nice love-seat and chairs and that lovely red carpet stacked out in the road in the dust to be torn and broken.

The neighbors as well as Amelie were growing tense and worried. No one knew when his turn would come next. Dan Fleming's brother-in-law, Wade Norris, and Bess and their children had been put out on the road, and Ralph Walker's cousin, Henry Brooks, who had bought the west half of Ralph's eighty, and on dark nights had as quietly been put back.

The day Orrin Moore was dispossessed, he and Arne came over to tell Edwin. Amelie could not bear to look at Orrin, but she could not shut out Orrin's words falling upon her ears with mortal mildness. "I'm not a young fool any more, Ed. When I was sixteen I ran away from home thinking I could find gold in the Calaveras in a week or two. Well, I didn't find it in '49; I don't expect it now. I know most of us aren't going to see anything in the bottom of the pan but dirt without any pay in it, but I've stopped panning and sluicing for luck, only for my share of ditch-water and land I'm willing to pay fair for."

Arne's voice, harsh as Amelie had never heard it, rasped in interruption: "Pay for it—that's yust it, not once but ten times, and your family too....I tell it to you, it is yust too much to see a woman and childrens dumped out on the road like as if they were animals—yust animals...."

Arne was not facing the east this morning. He was standing with his back to the mountains. "I had thought," he said bitterly, "the Lord was rewarding us for our trouble when we finished our ditches, that He was on our side. But it was only because we dug the ditches and the Indians did not. He does not care who digs them, only who is the smartest yet. The El Dorado Pacific is the smartest of all and Tim is right—it's Law and Landlords and the Devil you have to look out for. The Lord yust don't care if we sow the crops, or if others reap them....I hear it is my own place is next on the list," he added after a moment. "They tell me a man named Ellis wants it."

"Oh, Arne," Amelie cried, "if it does happen, bring Sigrid and the children here."

"Thank you, Mrs. Blansford, but is it strange we should want to sleep in our own house and not yust give it to another?" He smiled as Amelie had never seen Arne smile before.

One morning Amelie went out to the barn, where Edwin was hitching up his horse to the buggy. Amelie looked around to be sure no one was near, and going closer, whispered: "Edwin, I wouldn't talk to you in front of the children, but you've just got to stop. It isn't the right way."

He did not pretend not to understand. Everyone knew by now that Orrin and Stella and the Moore tribe of twins had been put back in their own house the last moonless night.

Amelie saw Edwin looking down at her face, which was drawn and haggard now every time she looked at herself in the mirror.

"I simply can't stand it, Edwin. I get so worried about you, and besides—I think it's wrong."

Edwin bent down from the buggy seat and kissed her as she stood between the wheels.

"I know, Amelie, and it isn't any use anyway...I heard yesterday the Vosburgs were put out at Highwillow and a man with a wife and children put in. That's different from hired scalawags. Now the El Dorado Pacific's got out new circulars and they're offering to pay the railroad fare of any family coming down into the valley to settle. That means decent folks who don't know about our trouble coming in to locate in good faith as we did. They wouldn't be the kind of folks to put out in the road and the El Dorado Pacific's smart enough to know it. This thing's got to be settled by law, but we've got to do something to stop them moving these families in—and it's got to be done open and aboveboard. The El Dorado Pacific's got money, lawyers—everything. Us neighbors getting together with our test case isn't going to be more than a drop in the bucket to what the El Dorado Pacific and their lawyers can think of. Yes," he sighed, as he took up the whip, "it will take more than a bunch of Sandlappers to stand out against the El Dorado Pacific."

One day in October Edwin came in the house looking happier than he had for months. He held a long narrow paper dodger in his hands.

"How's this, Amelie?" he asked proudly as he showed it to her.

MASS MEETING
SETTLERS ATTENTION!

Alta!   Nueva Esperanza!   Highwillow!

And all farmers in Tulare and Fresno counties within ten miles of the El Dorado Pacific railroad!

Since several decent self-respecting settlers of our communities have recently been ejected from the land and houses which they regard as their homes, such ejectments taking place by the order of the El Dorado Pacific R.R. Co., it has been decided to hold a mass meeting in Jameson's Warehouse in Nueva Esperanza at 8 o'clock, Tuesday evening, October 8, 1878, for the purpose of forming an organization to effect our legal rights and to take such measures as may peaceably and lawfully be determined on to protect our homes.

Reverend Gilmer will deliver the invocation.

Judge Terry will address the meeting.

All law-abiding citizens are urged to attend! None other are welcome!

By order of the Committee

The night of the mass meeting Edwin and Amelie were early, but the warehouse was already lighted with tallow candles set on tins nailed against the walls, so that when Amelie entered the long gloomy rectangular cavern through the great door slid open by the railroad siding, she glimpsed dimly high dusty rafters crossed in a succession of pointed arches.

At the other end of the warehouse stood a new platform, while between it and the rear of the room where Amelie stood were row after row of planks set up for benches. The Oracle Lodge parlor would be lost in this vastness—there just could not be enough people in the San Joaquin Valley, let alone Nueva Esperanza, to fill these benches.

But they came. From Nueva Esperanza, the farms near by, the neighbors Amelie knew, but more from the new little towns of Highwillow and Alta, from what was left of Kings Crossing, from across the county line in Fresno County—from every mile along the El Dorado Pacific tracks where the Sandlappers new and old had settled, they came to this meeting. Every time Amelie looked around she found the rows of benches were filling until finally she saw nothing but staring candlelighted faces all the way back to the door.

When Judge Terry and the Reverend Mr. Gilmer and Attorney Neblett and Colonel Becker—the last the president of the New Prospect Ditch Company—took seats on the platform, Amelie whispered to Edwin beside her: "I should think you'd be up there too, Edwin."

And he answered, whispering: "No, Amelie, the more folks we can get into this thing the better. The way to get things done is to lay low yourself. They're going to call on me later—that's the best way to have it happen."

After the invocation Chairman Attorney Neblett announced: "I'm going to call on Colonel Becker now to explain the purpose of this meeting."

Colonel Becker had been an officer in the Confederate army and before that a legislator in his native state of Tennessee. When he spoke, it was with the bellowing of a patriarch, although he must be only nearing fifty. Amelie almost tumbled off the bench at the first sound of that rumble of words, drawling a little, heavy with legislative eloquence, but always ending with unmistakable military crispness.

"My good friends, we are met here as good citizens, but citizens, I may add, with a weighty problem to consider. I need not tell my good neighbors of the Sierra Ditch Company or my own nearer neighbors of the New Prospect Ditch Company, at what cost we have improved these lands we look upon as our own."

Amelie saw Edwin stiffen at this: the New Prospect Ditch Company had copied the Sierra Ditch Company's headgates, had been able to get loans from the Nueva Esperanza bank, and had hired men for much of the ditch-digging the first Sandlappers had done themselves.

"Now a controversy has arisen, my friends. The El Dorado Pacific Company has not only put our neighbors out upon the road, but has, through their agent, threatened to dispossess others if they will not pay the vulture price demanded. This, my good citizens, without even being certain the El Dorado Pacific owns a foot of the land they are trying to sell. Talk about Ireland"—the colonel's fist pounded on the table as his voice echoed back from the dimness of faces and tallow candles, while across the aisle Tim Connery's smile was growing wider in delight "talk about Ireland being oppressed by landlords— they have many, many landlords, while we have only one. The El Dorado Pacific is that landlord, and it is unjust. Not willing to wait until this case is decided legally, they cast their helpless victims— women and children and babes—out into the road without warning. Gentlemen! I call upon you to protect your homes!"

Tim Connery called back: "By God and you're right, colonel!"

The colonel, astonished, put down the glass of water he was pouring and scowled down at the interruption. Tim's red head slumped a little at the pulling of Mary's hand at his elbow.

"But by peaceful means. By legal means!" the colonel continued. "There has been no violence among the Irish Land Leagues and we must have none. But we must protect ourselves. I have a proposal here that we form a Land League of our own—the name of the San Joaquin Grand Land League has been proposed for the main league, the branches to be named for the towns they represent, and a constitution and by-laws have been prepared for adoption. I read you from the constitution:

"'The sole purpose of the San Joaquin Grand Land League shall be to unite for the purpose of hiring counsel to present our case through the courts of the United States, the United States Supreme Court if necessary, and to employ all peaceful and legal means to remain upon our lands until the controversy with the El Dorado Pacific Railroad Company is legally settled.'

"But, gentlemen, in order to employ lawyers, and since our business must not be known to those who would gain advantage thereby, the League must be a secret organization. Therefore an invitation will be given at the close of this meeting to take our oath and such as desire to do so will remain to join our League."

After Judge Terry expressed the point of view that he could not see why such an organization would not be legal, Edwin was called upon.

Amelie was surprised Edwin wasn't embarrassed—but of course his wasn't a speech—he was just thinking of what he wanted to say.

"Folks, you all know how our ditches were dug—pick and shovel and crows and beans and catfish—you all know what the El Dorado Pacific promised us and how those promises have been broken. A bunch of us on the Sierra Ditch Company got worried and wanted title, so we've already started to go to law. But we can't keep on forever alone—lawyers cost money—and we're willing for you folks to have all the benefit of the suit we've started that comes up in the Circuit Court next week if you will help us present it to the higher court. And that's why we're here. We want you to come in with us and carry this case right through to Washington."

There was enormous applause and Amelie thought the whole proposition was decided. She settled against Edwin when he sat down, with a sigh of relief.

But a questioning voice rose behind her. "This is all right for you folks on odd-numbered sections where the land is in controversy, but how about us even-numbered fellows? We're buying our land from the railroad land agents too, only they bought it from the stockmen and have clear title because it was homestead land originally. I sympathize with you folks on the odd-numbered sections, but I don't know whether I want to join your League or not. My land's been graded and I'm ready to pay for it."

"I'd like to ask this gentleman a question." Edwin rose. "Do you mind telling us what your land was graded per acre?"

"No, I don't—five dollars an acre."

"Mine was thirty-seven dollars and sixty cents," Edwin said, and sat down.

Several men jumped to their feet; the one standing in the row in front of Tim Connery was recognized by Attorney Neblett.

"I'm Frank Emory, settled lately near Alta on even land. I'm ready to buy mine, but I think it's an outrage the way you odds have been treated. I'm in favor of us evens holding a meeting ourselves and maybe we can help you out—even if we don't join your League.... How about it, Evens?"

At least half the hall applauded. It was heartening, but Amelie knew Edwin was disappointed. He had hoped the others would join.

Amelie was happy, however, as she drove home with Mary Connery. Amelie could scarcely credit, even now, the great knot of men who had crowded around the platform at the end of the mass meeting—they looked like a military company as they marched to the schoolhouse for their secret session.

"Oh, something will come of this, Mary," Amelie said jubilantly.

Mary was a wan bundle in her shawl on the seat beside Amelie in the new buggy. "Sure and I hope you're right," she said, "or Tim will make something happen. Tim's that kind," she sighed. "And he's for taking too much now," she added; "he's for saying he drank barley tea so long he'll drink what he likes now and whenever."

That night Edwin made a fire in the kitchen stove, late as it was. In a few moments the house was filled with the stench of burning cloth.

"You're burning something, Edwin?"

"Yes, Amelie—we signed a pledge in the League to stay together and to act only according to legal means—and none of us to act at all without orders of a meeting and anything important must go through the Grand League, the branches all being represented. It's all secret, Amelie, but I can tell you that much.

"I can sleep tonight," he said. "They've appointed me to keep on seeing the San Francisco lawyers. Just think, Amelie, I may even go back east clear to Washington."

The winter after the warehouse meeting there was peace. There were no more settlers dispossessed and Amelie began to wonder if the San Joaquin Grand Land League and the Nueva Esperanza Branch League, which took so much of Edwin's time, were, after all, just meetings of another Lodge. Surely now that the League was so well organized, over three hundred in the Grand League all told, with all its branches, the El Dorado Pacific Company would see the light.

But if there were no more evictions, no adjustment was made in the prices set by the grader or any attention paid to the League's requests for a meeting of arbitration with the El Dorado Pacific's officials. Edwin's land was not yet paid for—or Tim's—or Arne's—or any of the three hundred who had settled on the odd-numbered sections.

But Amelie could not think of it always. When winter came she had to make the house more habitable. Edwin bought a new heating stove with comfortable foot-rails for the sitting-room, and Amelie a rag carpet from Stella Moore's mother, who had set up a loom. With rocking-chairs and the new lamp Edwin had brought home from San

Francisco—a huge wicked affair with a big white glass shade, the whole letting up and down on Britannica sliding chains from the ceiling— the sitting-room was so cozy Amelie rebelled at the rest of the cold almost empty rooms and asked Edwin one day: "Don't you think we could send for the parlor set, Edwin?"

When she saw the sick look on his face she knew she had been wrong. Edwin never talked much about the lawsuits any more—the Land League was really secret.

"We can't send for it yet, Amelie," was all he said.

One day when Amelie drove into town with Edwin, she saw a new cabin being built directly across the road from Tim Connery's place.

"Why, who's going to live there?" she cried in surprise. "I always thought Uncle Amos Jordan said he wouldn't sell that eighty."

"He hasn't," Edwin replied grimly, "but he let these two men who are building this cabin rent it for a year without inquiring much about them. He's sorry now, but it's too late. One of them is named Ellis, the other, Cole. Cole claims he's bought Tim Connery's place from the El Dorado Pacific and Ellis says he's bought Arne's. It may be just talk, for they haven't any writs and can't take possession yet, but they say they're going to later on."

"Have they families?"

"I don't know about Ellis, but Cole has—only," Edwin pulled out the whip and snapped the horse smartly as if he never wanted to see the cabin or the men building it again, "Cole says he's going to wait to bring his wife here until he moves into Tim's house—Cole likes Tim's house better, he says, than this cabin he's building now."

"I wish he were a little farther away," Edwin added later, a half-mile down the road.

"Who, Edwin?"

"Cole. I don't know how things are going to come out with him perched right across from Tim's place—his eyes on Tim's crops, boasting they're really his."

At first Edwin's near neighbors of the Sierra Ditch Company and those of the other companies assented to his persuasion that only the courts could remedy their difficulties. The Land League raised assessment after assessment for the lawyers—for costs of drawing and presenting to Congress a petition to restore railroad land to homestead entry, for costs of separate lawsuits—but after each one that was lost and Edwin returned home defeated, Amelie sensed that the faith of the settlers was wavering; she could mark it in the faces of most of the men when they came to visit Edwin.

Twelve cases now against the settlers lost in the lower courts.

"What's the use, Blansford?" Amelie heard Colonel Becker complain one morning, tapping his cane in an irritated staccato on the porch. Amelie thought Edwin was a little chagrined the colonel was elected president of the combined Leagues, but Edwin said the League wanted him to look after the lawsuits and he would be away too often to be chairman.

"Erringer and Loring from San Francisco both say this last point they are bringing up now couldn't be covered in the other suits," Edwin replied. "We've got this one now to the United States Circuit Court, we just can't leave it there. It would be foolish not to try. If it goes against us, let us take it to the United States Supreme Court and settle it once and for all."

"But our people have spent so much money already, they haven't had the ditches long enough, they have had to begin from the beginning, most of them trying to build houses and barns now instead of the shanties and sheds they have been using."

"Yes, I know," Edwin's voice was weary. The Sierra Ditch Company had been organized first of all. Amelie knew Edwin did not appreciate being told of their hardships by another. The Sierra Ditch Company had been glad enough to have neighbors, but, after all, things had been easier for the New Prospect Company, being able to copy the Sierra's headgates and borrow money and hire men.

"How much will this lawsuit cost?" the colonel was asking.

"A thousand dollars. We'll have to get a Washington lawyer. Max can't leave everything to go, or the San Francisco lawyers either. You told me yourself the League has three hundred members now. They can raise that much according to their acreage."

"I suppose so," the colonel answered. "We're not just a handful now as you folks in the Sierra Ditch Company were before all these other settlers came. The El Dorado Pacific has seen to that, paying folks' railway fare to get here, offering land just last fall at two-fifty an acre. Most of the new settlers around here have joined the League by now, and there's more to join if the delegations from Highwillow and Alta Rio mean what they said. We'll have close to six hundred members if they all sign.

Six hundred. Amelie could scarcely believe it even now with Nueva Esperanza a new town. Somehow she had thought the first handful of block cabins would be the first and the last tipped out on the plain.

When the colonel had gone, Edwin came in and sat down at the dining-room table.

"There's so many new people here now, Amelie," he sighed. "Arne and Ralph and Tim and I used to know them all. We can't any more, but the colonel does. He gets around. He keeps saying action is what we have to have, but action never sees land questions long. I'm afraid of what could happen when I'm gone. But Erringer says we have a sure chance with this last case. When it's settled in our favor, we can have peace. I've always thought we could never turn the land back to the Government—for, after all, the railroad did build this part of the road, even if they did change the route of the first grant—but surely the Supreme Court will not hold that the El Dorado Pacific can go back on their printed contract, their advertisements for the land, not when we settled here in good faith."

Edwin was gone to Washington six months. Amelie learned to hire men for the plowing, the seeding. She paid them, she fired them when they were drunk. She ordered grease for the windmill when she took the eggs into town. She bought blue-stone for the wheat the same day she bought a pattern of plaid twill for a dress for Lucy. On Sundays she took the children to Sunday school and often stayed to church. She liked the Reverend Mr. Gilmer and Mrs. Gilmer, they reminded her of Uncle Andrew and Aunt Cordelia. Edwin had got a buggy just before he left, on time, he said, good crops could not pay for everything. Amelie enjoyed having the buggy and the new bay mare, going into town when Roger and Lucy and Isobel were at school, with Larry and Denny beside her, the robe tucked around both of them.

Nueva Esperanza was quite a town now. Two blocks of stores, and a bank and a second hotel. Amelie was always amazed, no matter how often she drove back and forth along their own familiar road, that where this had been the single one in the beginning, now it was multiplied in all directions by other settlers and other ditch companies, still looking upon the Sierra Ditch Company as a parent, yet with individual strengths of their own.

Amelie stopped today at Mary Connery's. Whenever Amelie saw her, Amelie thought of that first time, when Mary had come out of her cabin to greet her shyly by the gate, the first day Amelie rode with Edwin to see the ditch. Even now Mary was usually shy and quiet, but today she came out to the buggy and talked quickly and fast. She always began with a compliment first; it was brief today.

"How fine your big boy looks, how tall he is getting!" Amelie smiled as Larry squirmed beside her. "And did you be getting a letter from your husband in town perhaps?" Mary asked, her eyes meeting Amelie's in an anxious, squint. "He is through with the law surely and all is well?"

"No, I didn't hear from Edwin," Amelie answered, Mary Connery's concern echoing within herself. "And I should. He said he would send me a telegram when it was decided."

"You can't depend on them things," sniffed Mary. "Listen, Mrs. Blansford"—she looked back at the house—"please tell your husband to tell the law to hurry. Tim isn't going to be satisfied much longer. He has tried to pay for the land, the price he said he would pay—I don't know what he said to the railroad's land agent when he wouldn't take Tim's money, but some of the men brought Tim home and told him to be careful. He could do nothing by himself, they said. And he grumbled at them: 'Oh yes, there is plenty I can do,' and they told him he must take care what he said. Tim was never one for taking heed."

Then she stepped between the circles of the buggy wheels, her hands gripping the bars of the top's supports, her face lifted to Amelie in trusting appeal. "Oh, I tell you, Mrs. Blansford, I'm that afraid of what might happen....He sits every night and says his father brought him to this country from oppressed Ireland, but talk of the landlords there, not one of them can compare to the El Dorado Pacific, and he says he did not bring his children into the world to serve under another landlord in America—and I'm that worried. He just sits and sits when he is home, saying the same of it over and over. Please tell your husband to hurry the law. Tim's getting impatient."

It was a few nights later that Edwin came walking into the sitting-room. Amelie looked up from her chair and could not move. He had not written. He had not telegraphed.

He took off his hat and laid it down. His brow was beaded with damp. It was such a warm night. "No need to ask him," she thought after one look at his face.

She went to him now and laid her hand on his sleeve. But she knew he did not notice it. He was looking past her, as if he did not see her or the walls of the room. She was glad the children were in bed.

"I came back," he said slowly as if he himself could not believe it, as if he were just learning to speak the words he was saying. "The case was on the docket of the United States Supreme Court; it's hard to get a case on the calendar, there are so many. But I was glad in a way—I knew it would give the lawyer more time to get our case ready. I kept telling the Washington lawyer, Elliston, who was recommended to us, all that I could about it, and he always said: 'Now, don't worry, Mr. Blansford, it will be presented in due form.'

"I kept telling myself he was right, I ought not to be so anxious, only I couldn't seem to help it with all the neighbors depending on me and having such a time to raise that thousand-dollar fee. But I finally stopped worrying, glad to put it all on someone else's shoulders who really knew what to do.

"I went early the day our case was set. I was glad to be there at last. The courtroom is right in the Capitol, Amelie—a half-circle facing the east—not such a large room, but grand somehow. You feel small in it. I noticed everyone stood still in the doorway a moment before they went in; I did too. And even when folks were waiting they didn't talk out loud, though nobody told them not to. There is a great bar of justice there with dark pillars behind it, and a clock with a gold eagle above it, as if time and law must always keep together. And grand as it was, it seemed as if that room were meant for plain people, with sheaves of wheat set across the long arch above the court where the pleas are heard. Those nine men in robes, I felt they would do the right thing, even if we were farmers disputing a great company, whatever the law would allow. I enjoyed just being there, knowing our case was to have consideration.

"When I looked around for Elliston among the lawyers right before the bench, he wasn't there. Not at all. But there were still a few minutes. He would be there. But the court opened. I was glad there were motions and the setting of cases on the calendar—it took up a little time. I kept looking at the door. No sign of him. Our case was called and Elliston didn't come. Not at all, not at all. The Chief justice himself asked about him. The Court had to dismiss the case for lack of counsel....Oh, Amelie—to have it all ready, everyone depending upon you—to have waited so long, and now the justices ready to listen...

"I don't know how I got down those steps and into the horse-car and out again or if I rode in one at all—I don't remember....Just cabs...horse-cars...walking...his hotel, his office....He wasn't there. I stayed two weeks longer. I saw the police, lawyers—we could not find him. No one knew where he had gone."

Amelie had no words for Edwin as he sat down in the chair, his legs sprawled out in front of him. She stood above him, she would have put her arms about him, but still he looked away and not at her.

"I don't know if the El Dorado Pacific bought Elliston out or not. I don't know. I can't say. I can't prove it. But I'm sure they must have done so, else why did he run away? But I know what the settlers will say. They will say it was the law. They will say the law is no use—but it was not the law, only one man who failed us. They won't see that. And they will blame me. I thought he was a good lawyer. Max inquired about him, so did Mr. Loring in San Francisco—he was the one who sent me to Elliston. I trusted him. Now nothing at all has been really settled. Things will stand as they are, with the last suits against us in the Circuit Court if they are not appealed. It would take another year and more money—and all the while folks moved out onto the road. I know the boys won't send me again. I'm afraid they won't wait."

He sat there a long time. Like Letitia the time Ulysses was drowned, Edwin's face turned to stone even as hers had done. This is the real death—to see hope going.

Amelie knew she must not comfort him yet.

Finally he looked at her, his face working. "Why, you've been here all the time, haven't you, Amelie?"

"Yes, all the time."

She could go to him now.

"Yes," she laughed, her voice shaking, "I'm getting to be quite a rancher. You'll be surprised to see the hay. We have a good crop...."

"Come here, Amelie."

And she knew that if he were lost to her sometimes, it was not for always.

That summer there was but little talk of the harvest although it was a fair one. Edwin said most of the men had borrowed from the bank and paid so many assessments for lawyers' fees none of them would have much left over. And the first Sandlappers, Edwin's and Amelie's nearest neighbors, both the men and their wives, were becoming impatient. The wives wanted new houses for their increasing families and the husbands said they would build no houses for the El Dorado Pacific. And there you were.

One noon Tim Connery came over shouting before he reached the door. It was too early in the day for Tim to have gone into town. Anger alone was fusing the words together.

"And what will your fine Land League do about this?" Tim banged at the dining-room door where Amelie and Edwin and the children were having their dinner.

"About what, Tim? Come in."

"It's for being that Cole—he has been telling and telling the boys about writing his letters for my place and how it belonged to him and even his fine partner Ellis admitted the El Dorado Pacific didn't answer them letters; but they did today. Cole was for showing it to me himself. My God, Ed, if I'd a gun I'd have shot him."

"Hush...."

Suddenly Tim drew a chair to the table beside the astonished Larry and, with his own freckled face bleak, and for the moment young as Larry's, looked at Amelie and Edwin hopelessly.

Then he began to speak again, faster still. "Sure and the El Dorado Pacific sent Cole a check for two hundred and forty dollars—rent for my place...damages for him not getting possession...paying *him* rent for my place."

His voice broke as he ran his fingers through his red hair and looked about him as if he had come to his neighbors' table from a far desolate place they had never seen and could never know.

Then he stared at Edwin, crying out:

"What's the use of your law, Ed? It's turned against us. You're for knowing the El Dorado Pacific wouldn't be paying him rent unless they thought they could take it from me. But I'll not be for seeing any landlord...."

He stood up, his body moving from side to side.

"Of course not, Tim—of course not...."

Edwin got up from the table and led Tim out gently, Tim finally walking away with slow steps.

When Edwin came back in the house he said: "Amelie, I'm sick of this. I think the El Dorado Pacific doesn't want trouble now, they're trying to hush Cole up by paying him that rent, but it's given him an advantage and he knows it. He's a born trouble-maker. Things can't go on like this forever without something popping. We've just got to do something. I told the colonel the other day that I would like to go up to see the president of the El Dorado Pacific face to face. I'm going to get a League meeting called and propose it. Up in his office and seeing things there as he must, to Asbury we're just names written across odd sections on his railroad land map—but if I go to him and tell him how things are, what it means to Orrin and Arne and Tim and all the rest living on beans and crows and catfish for five years to build the ditches and now having to pay for them twenty times over, it may do some good....I'll tell him all about it anyway. Maybe we can get him to come down here.

"I want you to come along with me," he added after a minute. "You need to get away. You've been looking right peaked lately. You can visit your aunt in San Francisco and my folks when I go to Sacramento. For we're not going to stop with Asbury and the El Dorado Pacific—I'm going to see the Governor too. We're going to ask him to preside if we can get the El Dorado Pacific to arbitrate."

"Oh, I couldn't, the El Dorado Pacific might dispossess us while we're gone and put the children out on the road."

"They would do it while we were here if they were a mind to. We'll get someone to stay here with the children. Please come, Amelie, I want you to go with me."

And she, remembering the time she could not go to the coast with him, said she would go.

At least the El Dorado Pacific never hurt anybody—all they did was to pile all your things out in the road and settle some new people in your house.

Ambrose Bierce
"POEM ON RAILROAD CONTROL"
FROM THE SAN FRANCISCO *WASP*, 1885

"We want a man the Railroad can't control!"
The humor tickled every little soul;
Assenting giggles ran through all the land
And idiots approved what rascals planned.
You've had your joke, you have your man, and lo!

The man's a trifle meaner than the *mot*.
Blind fools! with clay and spittle I anoint
Your understandings and reveal the point
Of your poor jest; and if the wit is just
Yourselves are welcome to its backward thrust.
If Stanford's independent of the sway
Of Crocker and of Huntington, not they,
But he himself, has riveted the chains
Upon your limbs, your hearts, your souls, your brains;
His the superior strong hand that cracks
The master's whip above your bleeding backs,
Or, by fatigue made merciful, forbears
To strike, and picks your pocket unawares.
Your humor, friends (indulge me in that view)
Is builded rather better than you knew.

◆

Frank Norris
"Fairness to the Corporation is Fairness to the Farmer"

The committee formed to place a pro-farmer candidate on the state railroad commission has secured the position for Lyman Derrick, Magnus' son, whom everyone hopes will succeed in cutting the grain shipping rates. Despite their great confidence in Lyman, he warns that too deep a cut will bring an injunction, tying up any rate change in the courts. Lyman's pleasure at playing politics overshadows his sympathy for the farmers, but surprisingly, Magnus doesn't seem to care. He's aiming at the big score: a repudiation of the Jeffersonian principles that made public land available to farmers. Magnus is not interested in rates, he's interested in land, an attitude that best becomes Norris' representative of the speculator who looks to take every advantage of land policies.

I t was Harran who first suggested that his brother, Lyman, be put forward as the candidate for this district. At once the proposition had a great success. Lyman seemed made for the place. While allied by every tie of blood to the ranching interests, he had never been identified with them. He was city-bred. The Railroad would not be over-suspicious of him. He was a good lawyer, a good business man, keen, clear-headed, far-sighted, had already some practical knowledge of politics, having served a term as assistant district attorney, and even at the present moment occupying the position of sheriff's attorney. More than all, he was the son of Magnus Derrick; he could be relied upon, could be trusted implicitly to remain loyal to the ranchers' cause.

The campaign for Railroad Commissioner had been very interesting. At the very outset Magnus's committee found itself involved in corrupt politics. The primaries had to be captured at all costs and by any means, and when the convention assembled it was found necessary to buy outright the votes of certain delegates. The campaign fund raised by contributions from Magnus, Annixter, Broderson, and Osterman was drawn upon to the extent of five thousand dollars.

Only the committee knew of this corruption. The League, ignoring ways and means, supposed as a matter of course that the campaign was honorably conducted.

For a whole week after the consummation of this part of the deal, Magnus had kept to his house, refusing to be seen, alleging that he was ill, which was not far from the truth. The shame of the business, the loathing of what he had done, were to him things unspeakable. He could no longer look Harran in the face. He began a course of deception with his wife. More than once, he had resolved to break with the whole affair, resigning his position, allowing the others to proceed without him. But now it was too late. He was pledged. He had joined the League. He was its chief, and his defection might mean its disintegration at the very time when it needed all its strength to fight the land cases. More than a mere deal in bad politics was involved. There was the land grab. His withdrawal from an unholy cause would mean the weakening, perhaps the collapse, of another cause that he believed to be righteous as truth itself. He was hopelessly caught in the mesh. Wrong seemed indissolubly knitted into the texture of Right. He was blinded, dizzied, overwhelmed, caught in the current of events, and hurried along he knew not where. He resigned himself.

In the end, and after much ostentatious opposition on the part of the railroad heelers, Lyman was nominated and subsequently elected.

When this consummation was reached, Magnus, Osterman, Broderson, and Annixter stared at each other. Their wildest hopes had not dared to fix themselves upon so easy a victory as this. It was not believable that the corporation would allow itself to be fooled so easily, would rush open-eyed into the trap. How had it happened?

Osterman, however, threw his hat into the air with wild whoops of delight. Old Broderson permitted himself a feeble cheer. Even Magnus beamed satisfaction. The other members of the League, present at the time, shook hands all around and spoke of opening a few bottles on the strength of the occasion. Annixter alone was recalcitrant.

"It's too easy," he declared. "No, I'm not satisfied. Where's Shelgrim in all this? Why don't he show his hand, damn his soul? The thing is yellow, I tell you. There's a big fish in these waters somewheres. I don't know his name, and I don't know his game, but he's moving round off and on, just out of sight. If you think you've netted him, I *don't*, that's all I've got to say."

But he was jeered down as a croaker. There was the Commission. He couldn't get around that, could he? There was Darrell and Lyman Derrick, both pledged to the ranches. Good Lord, he was never satisfied. He'd be obstinate till the very last gun was fired. Why, if he got drowned in a river he'd float up-stream just to be contrary.

In the course of time, the new board was seated. For the first few months of its term, it was occupied in clearing up the business left over by the old board and in the completion of the railway map. But now, the decks were cleared. It was about to address itself to the consideration of a revision of the tariff for the carriage of grain between the San Joaquin Valley and tidewater.

Both Lyman and Darrell were pledged to an average ten per cent. cut of the grain rates throughout the entire State.

The typewriter returned with the letters for Lyman to sign, and he put away the map and took up his morning's routine of business, wondering, the while, what would become of his practice during the time he was involved in the business of the Ranchers' Railroad Commission.

But towards noon, at the moment when Lyman was drawing off a glass of mineral water from the siphon that stood at his elbow, there was an interruption. Some one rapped vigorously upon the door, which was immediately after opened, and Magnus and Harran came in, followed by Presley.

"Hello, hello!" cried Lyman, jumping up, extending his hands, "why, here's a surprise. I didn't expect you all till to-night. Come in, come in and sit down. Have a glass of sizz-water, Governor."

The others explained that they had come up from Bonneville the night before, as the Executive Committee of the League had received a despatch from the lawyers it had retained to fight the Railroad, that the judge of the court in San Francisco, where the test cases were being tried, might be expected to hand down his decision the next day.

Very soon after the announcement of the new grading of the ranchers' lands, the corporation had offered, through S. Behrman, to lease the disputed lands to the ranchers at a nominal figure. The offer had been angrily rejected, and the Railroad had put up the lands for sale at Ruggles's office in Bonneville. At the exorbitant price named, buyers promptly appeared—dummy buyers, beyond shadow of doubt, acting either for the Railroad or for S. Behrman—men hitherto unknown in the county, men without property, without money, adventurers, heelers. Prominent among them, and bidding for the railroad's holdings included on Annixter's ranch, was Delaney.

The farce of deeding the corporation's sections to these fictitious purchasers was solemnly gone through with at Ruggles's office, the Railroad guaranteeing them possession. The League refused to allow the supposed buyers to come upon the land, and the Railroad, faithful to its pledge in the matter of guaranteeing its dummies possession, at once began suits in ejectment in the district court in Visalia, the county seat.

It was the preliminary skirmish, the reconnaissance in force, the combatants feeling each other's strength, willing to proceed with caution, postponing the actual death-grip for a while till each had strengthened its position and organised its forces.

During the time the cases were on trial at Visalia, S. Behrman was much in evidence in and about the courts. The trial itself, after tedious preliminaries, was brief. The ranchers lost. The test cases were immediately carried up to the United States Circuit Court in San Francisco. At the moment the decision of this court was pending.

"Why, this is news," exclaimed Lyman, in response to the Governor's announcement; "I did not expect them to be so prompt. I was in court only last week and there seemed to be no end of business ahead. I suppose you are very anxious?"

Magnus nodded. He had seated himself in one of Lyman's deep chairs, his grey top-hat, with its wide brim, on the floor beside him. His coat of black broadcloth that had been tightly packed in his valise, was yet wrinkled and creased; his trousers were strapped under his high boots. As he spoke, he stroked the bridge of his hawklike nose with his bent forefinger.

Leaning back in his chair, he watched his two sons with secret delight. To his eye, both were perfect specimens of their class, intelligent, well-looking, resourceful. He was intensely proud of them. He was never happier, never more nearly jovial, never more erect, more military, more alert, and buoyant than when in the company of his two sons. He honestly believed that no finer examples of young manhood existed throughout the entire nation.

"I think we should win in this court," Harran observed, watching the bubbles break in his glass. "The investigation has been much more complete than in the Visalia trial. Our case this time is too good. It has made too much talk. The court would not dare render a decision for the Railroad. Why, there's the agreement in black and white—and the circulars the Railroad issued. How *can* one get around those?"

"Well, well, we shall know in a few hours now," remarked Magnus.

"Oh," exclaimed Lyman, surprised, "it is for this morning, then. Why aren't you at the court?"

"It seemed undignified, boy," answered the Governor. "We shall know soon enough."

"Good God!" exclaimed Harran abruptly, "when I think of what is involved. Why, Lyman, it's our home, the ranch house itself, nearly all Los Muertos, practically our whole fortune, and just now when there is promise of an enormous crop of wheat. And it is not only us. There are over half a million acres of the San Joaquin involved. In some cases of the smaller ranches, it is the confiscation of the whole of the rancher's land. If this thing goes through, it will absolutely beggar nearly a hundred men. Broderson wouldn't have a thousand acres to his name. Why, it's monstrous."

"But the corporations offered to lease these lands," remarked Lyman. "Are any of the ranchers taking up that offer—or are any of them buying outright?"

"Buying! At the new figure!" exclaimed Harran, "at twenty and thirty an acre! Why, there's not one in ten that can. They are land-poor. And as for leasing—leasing land they virtually own—no, there's precious few are doing that, thank God! That would be acknowledging the railroad's ownership right away—forfeiting their rights for good. None of the *Leaguers* are doing it, I know. That would be the rankest treachery."

He paused for a moment, drinking the rest of the mineral water, then interrupting Lyman, who was about to speak to Presley, drawing him into the conversation through politeness, said: "Matters are just romping right along to a crisis these days. It's a make or break for the wheat growers of the State now, no mistake. Here are the land cases and the new grain tariff drawing to a head at about the same time. If we win our land cases, there's your new freight rates to be applied, and then all is beer and skittles. Won't the San Joaquin go wild if we pull it off, and I believe we will."

"How we wheat growers are exploited and trapped and deceived at every turn," observed Magnus sadly. "The courts, the capitalists, the railroads, each of them in turn hoodwinks us into some new and wonderful scheme, only to betray us in the end. Well," he added, turning to Lyman, "one thing at least we can depend on. We will cut their grain rates for them, eh, Lyman?"

Lyman crossed his legs and settled himself in his office chair.

"I have wanted to have a talk with you about that, sir," he said. "Yes, we will cut the rates—an average 10 per cent. cut throughout the State, as we are pledged. But I am going to warn you, Governor, and you, Harran; don't expect too much at first. The man who, even after twenty years' training in the operation of railroads, can draw an equitable, smoothly working schedule of freight rates between shipping point and common point, is capable of governing the United States. What with main lines, and leased lines, and points of transfer, and the laws governing common carriers, and the rulings of the Inter-State Commerce Commission, the whole matter has become so confused that Vanderbilt himself couldn't straighten it out. And how can it be expected that railroad commissions who are chosen—well, let's be frank—as ours was, for instance, from out a number of men who don't know the difference between a switching charge and a differential rate, are going to regulate the whole business in six months' time? Cut rates; yes, any fool can do that; any fool can write one dollar instead of two, but if you cut too low by a fraction of one per cent and if the railroad can get out an injunction, tie you up and show that your new rate prevents the road being operated at a profit, how are you any better off?"

"Your conscientiousness does you credit, Lyman," said the Governor. "I respect you for it, my son. I know you will be fair to the railroad. That is all we want. Fairness to the corporation is fairness to the farmer, and we won't expect you to readjust the whole matter out of hand. Take your time. We can afford to wait."

"And suppose the next commission is a railroad board, and reverses all our figures?"

The one-time mining king, the most redoubtable poker player of Calaveras County, permitted himself a momentary twinkle of his eyes.

"By then it will be too late. We will, all of us, have made our fortunes by then."

The remark left Presley astonished out of all measure. He never could accustom himself to these strange lapses in the Governor's character. Magnus was by nature a public man, judicious, deliberate, standing firm for principle, yet upon rare occasion, by some such remark as this, he would betray the presence of a subnature of recklessness, inconsistent, all at variance with his creeds and tenets.

At the very bottom, when all was said and done, Magnus remained the Forty-niner. Deep down in his heart the spirit of the Adventurer yet persisted. "We will all of us have made fortunes by then." That was it precisely. "After us the deluge." For all his public spirit, for all his championship of justice and truth, his respect for law, Magnus remained the gambler, willing to play for colossal stakes, to hazard a fortune on the chance of winning a million. It was the true California spirit that found expression through him, the spirit of the West, unwilling to occupy itself with details, refusing to wait, to be patient, to achieve by legitimate plodding; the miner's instinct of wealth acquired in a single night prevailed, in spite of all. It was in this frame of mind that Magnus and the multitude of other ranchers of whom he was a type, farmed their ranches. They had no love for their land. They were not attached to the soil. They worked their ranches as a quarter of a century before they had worked their mines. To husband the resources of their marvellous San Joaquin, they considered niggardly, petty, Hebraic. To get all there was out of the land, to squeeze it dry, to exhaust it, seemed their policy. When, at last, the land worn out, would refuse to yield, they would invest their money in something else; by then, they would all have made fortunes. They did not care. "After us the deluge."

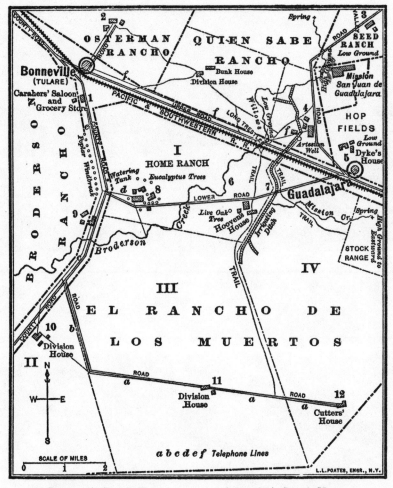

2. Osterman's Ranch House.   8. Derrick's Ranch House.
4. Annixter's Ranch House.   9. Broderson's Ranch House.

"Map of Country Described in *The Octopus*"

This map, included with early editions of Norris' *The Octopus: A Story of California* (1901), shows why a Mussel Slough resident of 1880 might have had a tough time recognizing the district as depicted in Norris' novel. Norris has not only changed the names of southern San Joaquin towns, he's erected a completely fictional Spanish mission and does not do justice to the network of irrigation canals built by local mutual irrigation companies. That work is here represented only by the single ditch that links the Rancho de Los Muertos and the Quien Sabe Rancho. Runing directly beneath the tracks of the Pacific and Southwestern Railroad, it symbolically links the prosperity of the great ranchos to two emerging technologies, irrigation and transportation.

"Combined Harvester, Tulare, Cal."
Combine harvesters like the one shown here were commonly used throughout
the southern San Joaquin to cut and thresh wheat. (Courtesy California Historical
Society; FN-35877)

"Ditch Digging"
This photograph from around 1883 shows settlers digging an irrigation ditch
using hand tools and horse-drawn earth scrapers. (Courtesy William Hammond
Hall Collection, California Historical Society; FN-22654)

"Building of Dam, Kings River"
This dam under construction in 1873 was designed to divert water from the Kings River into People's Ditch.[1] (Courtesy Kings County Museum, Box: Oversize Photos, Daggs Market, Item 87.769)

[1] Kings County Centennial Committee, *Kings County: A Pictorial History* (Hanford, CA: County Government Center, 1992), 28.

"Irrigated Field"
This field is irrigated by a system of shallow cuts that carry water from one of the larger irrigation ditches. (Courtesy Kings County Museum, File: Ag-Irrigation, Water, Item 87.2142)

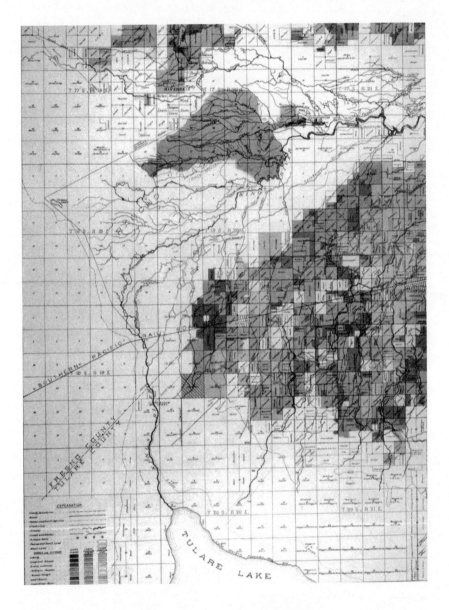

"Irrigation Map Detail, Lemoore and Hanford Sheet"

This 1885 map details the irrigation system in the Mussel Slough region. (Courtesy California Historical Society, Collection of William Hammond Hall, C. E.)

George Frederick Keller, "Devilfish"

George Frederick Keller published a number of political cartoons in the satirical
San Francisco magazine *The Wasp,* many of which took their themes from the
Mussel Slough incident. In this 1882 drawing, the devilfish—or octopus—represents
the railroad monopoly whose tentacles put the squeeze on other California
industries. In his cartoon, Keller gives special attention to the farmers of Mussel
Slough, who, despite their community solidarity, are strangled near to death by
the mighty tentacles of the Octopus.

THE MUSSEL SLOUGH EVICTION.

R. R. King.— Come now Slaves, vacate, my wife is traveling in Europe, and your little home, improved as it is, will bring a nice
little pile of Pin Money for her.
Settler's Daughter.—Oh, Mr. Stanford, good Mr. Stanford, please do not drive poor old Father and Mother from our Home.
R. R. King.— Marshal, do your duty!

Carl Browne, "The Mussel Slough Eviction"

Carl Browne drew political cartoons for the *Daily Graphic* and *Weekly Graphic* in San Francisco. He was also a member of the committee designing a monument to the slain Mussel Slough farmers. In this 1880 drawing from the *Graphic*, Leland Stanford is personally evicting a family from its Mussel Slough home—just for the pin money.

Brewer's Homestead

Henry Brewer's homestead was the site of the gunfight. (Courtesy Carnegie
Museum, Hanford)

Tragedy Oak

The casualties from the Mussel Slough gunfight were placed beneath this oak
tree in Henry Brewer's front yard. The tree was marked with a state historical
plaque in 1948,[2] but has since died and been cut down. (Courtesy Carnegie
Museum, Hanford)

[2] Richard B. Rice, William A. Bullough, Richard J. Orsi, *The Elusive Eden:
A New History of California*, 3rd ed. (Boston: McGraw-Hill, 2002), 251.

Carl Browne, "Affair of May Last"

This drawing by Carl Browne depicts the whole cast of characters appearing in the court trial after the Mussel Slough gunfight. An inset illustrates the gunfight itself, with Marshal Poole's "tools"—Hartt and Crow—firing on the settlers.

Convicted Mussel Slough Settlers

Left to right, John D. Purcell, John J. Doyle, James N. Patterson, Wayman
L. Pryor, and William Braden served eight months in the Santa Clara County
Jail, convicted of obstruction of a federal officer. They became local heroes and
received while in jail telegrams of sympathy from across the nation and two
cablegrams from England. One of the five, William Braden, married the jailer's
daughter upon his release.[3] (Courtesy Carnegie Museum, Hanford)

[3] Wallace Smith, *Garden of the Sun: A History of the San Joaquin Valley*
  (Los Angeles: Lymanhouse, 1939), 286–287.

THE WEEKLY GRAPHIC,
AND ANTI-MONOPOLIST.

VOL. 2.   SAN FRANCISCO, THURSDAY, JULY 28, 1881.   NO. 87.

Carl Browne, "Mussel Slough Memorial"

This 1881 drawing from San Francisco's *Weekly Graphic and Anti-Monopolist*
shows one of several versions of a planned memorial to the slain farmers of
Mussel Slough. Inset into the base is a depiction of a pioneer at work digging
an irrigation ditch.

RAILROAD LANDS.

CENTRAL PACIFIC RAILROAD,
SOUTHERN PACIFIC RAILROAD,
LAND DEPARTMENTS,
Corner of Fourth and Townsend Streets,

SAN FRANCISCO, CALIFORNIA, July 1st, 1876.

The following statement is made for the information of those who desire to purchase Lands from said Companies:

1st. Congress, to aid in the construction of the above mentioned Railroads, granted all the odd numbered Sections of non-mineral public land, within certain limits, excepting such as were reserved by the United States, and those to which a valid homestead or preemption right had attached prior to such grant, as follows: To the Central Pacific Railroad (main line), all within twenty miles on each side of its road; to the California and Oregon branch of the C. P. R. R., all within twenty miles on each side of its line, and, where the odd numbered sections within said twenty miles have been taken by preemption, or otherwise, the Company has the right to select other vacant odd numbered sections as indemnity within the twentieth and thirtieth mile on each side of its line; and to the Southern Pacific Railroad, all within twenty miles on each side of its line, with an indemnity grant similar to that of the California and Oregon Railroad.

2d. The Companies have no interest in even numbered sections.

3d. To constitute a valid homestead or preemption claim, within the above exception, the party must have resided on the land prior to the grant to the Railroad, and continuously from that time. He must also, at that time, have been an American citizen (or declared his intentions), over twenty-one years of age, or the head of a family, and have filed his claim in the United States Land Office within the time required by law. If he has not these requisites, or has neglected to file, he will have to buy from the Railroad Company.

4th. All persons who desire to purchase lands from the Railroad Companies should make application to the Land Agents, at the Land Offices of the Companies, in San Francisco, California, either personally or by letter, describing the land by Section, Township and Range, according to legal subdivisions. This application will be filed, and the party allowed three months to complete the purchase, and during this time the land will not be sold to another without giving the applicant thirty days previous notice. If the purchase is not completed within three months after sale of land shall commence in the locality where the tract is situated, it can be bought by other persons.

5th. An application for land confers no right or privilege on the applicant. It is merely a notice that he wishes to buy. *The first application is not given precedence over those which may be filed later.* Settlers and actual occupants, who in good faith cultivate and improve lands belonging to either of the Companies, will generally be given preference of purchase at the regular price, and they are invited to settle upon and improve the *vacant lands* whether they are applied for or not by other persons. Where there are conflicting claimants who apply to purchase, an adjudication of their respective claims will be made by the Land Agent, upon due notice given to the parties. Applications to purchase lands can be filed in the Land Offices of the Companies at any time after survey by the Government, but no application will be acted upon until three months after the Township plats shall have been filed in the United States Land Office. Blank applications will be furnished to all who desire to purchase. No sales will be made except by legal subdivisions, according to Government surveys. Purchasers must not be limited as to the amount of vacant lands they can buy. It must be borne in mind, however, that 640 acres is the largest tract that can be sold in any one place, the Railroad sections not being contiguous to each other, or *adjoining.*

In filling in the blanks, it is requested that a separate application be made for the lands in each township; or, in other words, that lands in two or more Townships shall not be applied for in the same blank.

6th. The Companies sell ordinary agricultural, vineyard and grazing lands, at from $2 50 upwards per acre, according to quality. They will be sold for cash; or in tracts of not less than eighty acres, upon a credit of five years, if desired; that is,—twenty per cent. in cash and the remainder payable at any time within five years, with interest at ten per cent. per annum. The interest must be paid yearly in advance, thus:

For example, take 160 acres of land and suppose the price to be $5 00 per acre,
If paid for in full, at time of purchase, the amount would be:

160 acres at $5 per acre.. $800 00 U. S. Coin.

If bought on the credit system, the amount required for the first payment would be:

20 per cent. of $800 00... $160 00
1st year's interest on remainder, $640 00, at 10 per cent...................... 64 00

Total amount of 1st payment... $224 00 U. S. Coin.

The other payments would be $64 00 each year—the annual interest, in advance—and at the end of five years, $640 00—the remainder of the principal. The $640 00 can be paid, and the interest stopped at any time within five years, but no installment of it will be received. No part of any interest paid will be refunded. Timber and wood land is from $5 00 to $10 00 per acre, according to quality, and payment in full must be made at time of purchase.

7th. Purchasers of Railroad lands have many advantages over those purchasing from the Government. There are no lawyers or witness fees to pay, as is the case in "proving up" at the United States Land Office. Title can be perfected in less time. The land can be bought on credit, and in the interim between buying and final payment, the buyer can reside wherever he pleases; and he can, if he desires, mortgage or sell it.

8th. As the lands are listed by the United States Land Office to the Companies, competent and reliable men are sent to grade them and report the value of each particular piece. The report is examined, and if found correct, a price is established. It is that of unimproved land of the same quality in the immediate vicinity, at the time of the grading. In fixing the value, improvements made on the land are not taken into consideration, and the price is not increased in consequence.. There is but one price—that fixed by the Company—and land will be sold at that rate to those entitled in equity to buy, even if a larger sum should be offered by others. The actual settler, therefore, in addition to being accorded the first privilege of purchase, is secured in his improvements.

9th. No deeds are made by the Companies until after the receipt of United States Patent.

B. B. REDDING, Land Agent, C. P. R. R. Co.
JEROME MADDEN, Land Agent, S. P. R. R. Co.

"Railroad Lands"

Railroad flyers like this one were widely distributed by the Central Pacific and Southern Pacific Railroads in order to advertise lands that the railroads wanted to offer for sale. Unfortunately, many settlers failed to read the fine print that reserved railroads the privilege of fixing the final sale price. The full text of this flyer is reproduced on pages 96–99. (Courtesy Kings County Museum, "Mussel Slough Scrapbook 93.4," no item number)

Section III:

I Only Know My Duty

On May 11, 1880, Mussel Slough settlers planned a local picnic at which former State Supreme Court Justice David Terry—a notorious hothead and firebrand speaker—was to give a speech concerning the farmers' legal battle with the Southern Pacific. Judge Terry was unable to come, but in the meantime another notable public servant had arrived in the region, U.S. Marshal Alonzo W. Poole, who carried instructions to evict some settlers from railroad land and install in their place Walter Crow and Mills Hartt, who were purchasing the land directly from the Southern Pacific. Along with railroad land grader William Clark, Poole, Crow, and Hartt made their way to the home of William B. Braden in order to evict the Mussel Slough resident from the property. Finding no one at home, the party removed Braden's belongings and set them on the side of the road, leaving behind a row of shotgun shells on the doorstep of Braden's house, a warning to anyone aiming to stop the eviction. Hartt was officially placed in possession of the property. When this news reached settlers gathering for the picnic, members of the Settlers' League set out to stop the marshal and his companions. No one planned on bloodshed.

Each of the Mussel Slough novelists depicted the gunfight according to the narrative logic of their own stories. Most often, they preserved the bare facts: that the marshal clearly did not relish performing such an unpopular duty; that a stumbling horse accidentally knocked the marshal down and caused enough confusion at the tense gathering to set off the shooting; and that everyone shared intense feelings of remorse after the tragic gunfight. Each novelist, however, emphasized a different motif and strayed from the accepted facts whenever it seemed right to the story. Frank Norris, for example, arrayed the farmers defensively in an irrigation ditch and had one of their own number shoot first, thus emphasizing the idea that the settlers shared blame with the railroad for the tragedy. C. C. Post used Walter Crow's true name for the gunfighter character he saw as a tool of the railroad, and furthered the theory that the railroad had initiated the disastrous events. William Morrow focused on the tragic loss of life, revealing the common humanity shared by all the belligerents, despite their enmity. Josiah Royce exaggerated the number of deaths, expanding the scale of the tragedy. Finally May Merrill Miller gave readers the fullest, most closely observed version of the grievous loss suffered by the family and friends of the slain.

In this section, bravery and virtue square off against human greed, the irresistible forces of laissez-faire capitalism, and pure, dumb chance.

Frank Norris
"Iron-Hearted Monster of Steel"

Magnus and Harran Derrick are guests of the capitalist Cedarquist at his San Francisco club. Cedarquist has given Magnus the idea of selling his wheat in Asia, where the need is acute and the market wide open. As Magnus ponders the magnificence of the grand plan—a sort of Anglo-Saxon mercantile assault on the gates of the Orient—he and Harran overhear the details of the most recent court decision regarding the settlers.

"Harran," said the Governor, with decision, "there is a deal, there, in what Cedarquist says. Our wheat to China, hey, boy?"

"It is certainly worth thinking of, sir."

"It appeals to me, boy; it appeals to me. It's big and there's a fortune in it. Big chances mean big returns; and I know—your old father isn't a back number yet, Harran—I may not have so wide an outlook as our friend Cedarquist, but I am quick to see my chance. Boy, the whole East is opening, disintegrating before the Anglo-Saxon. It is time that bread stuffs, as well, should make markets for themselves in the Orient. Just at this moment, too, when Lyman will scale down freight rates so we can haul to tidewater at little cost."

Magnus paused again, his frown beetling, and in the silence the excited murmur from the main room of the club, the soprano chatter of a multitude of women, found its way to the deserted library.

"I believe it's worth looking into, Governor," asserted Harran.

Magnus rose, and his hands behind him, paced the floor of the library a couple of times, his imagination all stimulated and vivid. The great gambler perceived his Chance, the kaleidoscopic shifting of circumstances that made a Situation. It had come silently, unexpectedly. He had not seen its approach. Abruptly he woke one morning to see the combination realised. But also he saw a vision. A sudden and abrupt revolution in the Wheat. A new world of markets discovered, the matter as important as the discovery of America. The torrent of wheat was to be diverted, flowing back upon itself in a sudden, colossal eddy, stranding the middleman, the *entre-preneur*, the elevator—and mixing-house men dry and despairing, their occupation gone. He saw the farmer suddenly emancipated, the world's food no longer at the mercy of the speculator, thousands upon thousands of men set free of the grip of Trust and ring and monopoly acting for themselves, selling their own wheat, organising into one gigantic trust, themselves, sending their agents to all the entry ports of China. Himself, Annixter, Broderson and Osterman would pool their issues. He would convince them of the magnificence of the new movement. They would be its pioneers. Harran would be sent to Hong Kong to represent the four. They would charter—probably buy—a ship, perhaps one of Cedarquist's, American built, the nation's flag at the peak, and the sailing of that ship, gorged with the crops from Broderson's and Osterman's ranches, from Quien Sabe and Los Muertos, would be like the sailing of the caravels from Palos. It would mark a new era; it would make an epoch.

With this vision still expanding before the eye of his mind, Magnus, with Harran at his elbow, prepared to depart.

They descended to the lower floor and involved themselves for a moment in the throng of fashionables that blocked the hallway and the entrance to the main room, where the numbers of the raffle were being drawn. Near the head of the stairs they encountered Presley and Cedarquist, who had just come out of the wine room.

Magnus, still on fire with the new idea, pressed a few questions upon the manufacturer before bidding him good-bye. He wished to talk further upon the great subject, interested as to details, but Cedarquist was vague in his replies. He was no farmer, he hardly knew wheat when he saw it, only he knew the trend of the world's affairs; he felt them to be setting inevitably eastward.

However, his very vagueness was a further inspiration to the Governor. He swept details aside. He saw only the grand *coup,* the huge results, the East conquered, the march of empire rolling westward, finally arriving at its starting point, the vague, mysterious Orient. He saw his wheat, like the crest of an advancing billow, crossing the Pacific, bursting upon Asia, flooding the Orient in a golden torrent. It was the new era. He had lived to see the death of the old and the birth of the new; first the mine, now the ranch; first gold, now wheat. Once again he became the pioneer, hardy, brilliant, taking colossal chances, blazing the way, grasping a fortune—a million in a single day. All the bigness of his nature leaped up again within him. At the magnitude of the inspiration he felt young again, indomitable, the leader at last, king of his fellows, wresting from fortune at this eleventh hour, before his old age, the place of high command which so long had been denied him. At last he could achieve.

Abruptly Magnus was aware that some one had spoken his name. He looked about and saw behind him, at a little distance, two gentlemen, strangers to him. They had withdrawn from the crowd into a little recess. Evidently having no women to look after, they had lost interest in the afternoon's affair. Magnus realised that they had not seen him. One of them was reading aloud to his companion from an evening edition of that day's newspaper. It was in the course of this reading that Magnus caught the sound of his name. He paused, listening, and Presley, Harran and Cedarquist followed his example. Soon they all understood. They were listening to the report of the judge's decision, for which Magnus was waiting—the decision in the case of the League vs. the Railroad. For the moment, the polite clamour of the raffle hushed itself—the winning number was being drawn. The guests held their breath, and in the ensuing silence Magnus and the others heard these words distinctly:

"…It follows that the title to the lands in question is in the plaintiff—the Pacific and Southwestern Railroad, and the defendants have no title, and their possession is wrongful. There must be findings and judgment for the plaintiff, and it is so ordered."

In spite of himself, Magnus paled. Harran shut his teeth with an oath. Their exaltation of the previous moment collapsed like a pyramid of cards. The vision of the new movement of the wheat, the conquest of the East, the invasion of the Orient, seemed only the flimsiest mockery. With a brusque wrench, they were snatched back to reality.

Between them and the vision, between the fecund San Joaquin, reeking with fruitfulness, and the millions of Asia crowding toward the verge of starvation, lay the iron-hearted monster of steel and steam, implacable, insatiable, huge—its entrails gorged with the life blood that it sucked from an entire commonwealth, its ever hungry maw glutted with the harvests that should have fed the famished bellies of the whole world of the Orient.

Josiah Royce
"Steady Here"

The main characters of The Feud of Oakfield Creek—*Alonzo Eldon and Alf Escott—share a complicated personal history. As young men they fought Indians together and at one point they looked forward to uniting their families through the marriage of Escott's daughter Ellen to Eldon's son Tom. But when Tom rejects Ellen in favor of someone else, she descends into despair and madness. Soon, she dies, a death for which the Escotts hold Tom at least figuratively responsible. What follows is the showdown between the wealthy Alonzo Eldon, president of the fictional Land and Improvement Company, and Alf Escott, an intellectual and a champion of social reform.*

In this scene, Alonzo and Tom finally face the eloquent Alf, who heads a contingent of settlers who won't be moved by the marshal sent to evict them from the Land and Improvement Company's holdings in favor of new purchasers, Buzzard and Foster. In Royce's version of the gunfight, perspective focuses briefly on Alf's other son, Sam Escott, struck not by a bullet but by "a numb sense of wonder." Royce sticks to the bare outline of the Mussel Slough shootout, but in his fictional version there are more wounded, making it significant that, in the end, capitalist land mogul Alonzo Eldon survives unscathed.

A few moments later, Sam, who had ridden beside his father and Harold as long as he was allowed to, was watching the scene from the front rank of the irregular line of settlers, while Peterson, Escott, and Harold, a little in advance of the main body, were confronting the marshal's armed men. These were drawn up in a field near the roadside; they were clustered under an oak-tree, and about the wagon in which they had been carrying their arms and equipments. The marshal was calling out in a loud voice to the new-comers:

"I want to hear no word from you men. I am doing my duty. I cannot parley with armed bands. I have no quarrel with any of you. I have come to put these here parties in possession of certain tracts. You must not bar my way. Disperse, I tell you, disperse." The marshal was a great heavy man, like Alonzo, but his face was red, smooth, dull, and fat, and his little black eyes looked mean and wicked. Yet he was plainly a brave fellow, who meant to do his official duty. Beside him, just in front of the wagon, were Alonzo and Tom, both on horseback. Buzzard and Foster, armed with repeating rifles, stood up in the wagon, behind the other men. Sam, who himself had a rifle slung over his shoulder, found himself uneasily fingering it, as he looked at Tom. "That is my sister's murderer," he said to himself. But now Escott was speaking.

"Alonzo Eldon," he said, "it's with you that I want a word here, before all these people; and not on my behalf, but on theirs. You don't want the shedding of innocent blood, man, and so"—

"That's a brave word there, Escott!" shouted out with a harsh and unnatural exertion the usually so soft voice of Tom Eldon. Tom was terribly excited. His black eyes flashed, his body quivered with rage; the horse on which he rode took impatiently a step or two forwards, as Tom spoke. "It's a brave word that, about innocent blood, when you lead here these innocent men armed for a fight in your own cause. Disperse them first, and then there'll be no blood shed here, at least no innocent blood."

"Tom Eldon," said Escott sternly, "with you I've no reckoning now, nor do I come here to talk to any but men who can hear a fair speech to its end. To you, Alonzo Eldon, I have something to say that may end this land trouble at once. Will you hear me, I ask you again? Will you hear me on behalf of these innocent men, whose property you seem to be threatening?"

"Your own bogus property, Escott," answered Alonzo sternly, "is what's now in danger. For to-day I have come here to dispossess traitors. Innocent men and quiet citizens have nothing to do but stay at home."

"I'm glad to hear you say that, Alonzo. I don't come here on my own account. Take my property if you will. Call me traitor if you must. What I ask of you is a word on behalf of these men."

"Not a word, sir, until you and they lay down your arms."

"I myself have not asked them to arm and come here, Eldon. Finding them armed, I have joined them, unarmed myself, to inter-cede with you, and plead for a prevention of bloodshed."

"Fine interceders you and Harold make, sir!" Tom again broke in.

"If, Mr. Eldon," said Harold now, and in his clearest tone, "*if*, as I well know, you and your son have come here to-day more on my account than on that of any other man living, I may join my voice to ask that you should behave like honest men, and that you should fight out your quarrels elsewhere with me whom you call your enemy. But don't come here to vex the peace of this place merely because you hate me. You know what you are here for. You are here because you believe that *I* have wronged you. If so, meet me as you will and where you will; I am ready for you. But, now that you are here, say plainly to this company that your fight isn't with them, but with Escott on my sole account, and with me for myself. Then, when you have pledged your word not to molest them, take Escott's land as you will, and leave the settlers in peace. He and I can be ready for you else-where."

"Our fight," came back Tom's voice, "is with traitors, old and young, and with all who follow them, and bear arms here to help them against the law and the courts of the land."

"I'll not hear my father called traitor!" cried Sam Escott. As he spoke, his horse was becoming very restive. Peterson roughly ordered silence, and Alf Escott's stern voice joined itself to Peterson's. But a certain confused murmur from behind encouraged Sam. The marshal had been, meanwhile, very quietly removing his hat and wiping his forehead, for the sun was hot and the marshal's courage was cool; but at Sam's words the marshal was once more on the alert. His hand seized the bridle, which had fallen on his horse's neck. He laid his other hand by his belt.

"Steady here, all of you!" he shouted to his own men, perceiving that they were excited. The two main bodies were not more than fifteen or twenty paces apart, and the situation was growing momentarily worse. Nearly every one heard all that was said at the front, for the speaking was loud and clear, and an almost perfect silence had prevailed in the main bodies. Sam, however, went on: "You, Tom Eldon, are no man to call Alf Escott traitor,—you, whose whole soul is nothing but an accursed lie." Sam had once heard his father use this expression, and it pleased him now in his rage. Alf and Peterson vainly tried to quiet the young man or to drown his voice. As for Tom Eldon, his Spanish eyes glowed none the less for this word. He drew his pistol—

The next instant firing began. Nobody could ever afterwards be sure whence came the first shot. Most witnesses declared that Buzzard fired first from the wagon, over Tom Eldon's head. There was, however, much conflict of testimony; and Sam, who was indicted later for murder, was never tried on that charge, just because of this conflict of testimony. At all events, he himself was sure that he heard several bullets whiz by him, and at least a dozen shots fired, before he did more than to try to control his terrified horse. But thereafter, as soon as he realized what it all meant, he sprang from the saddle, let the horse go, raised his own rifle deliberately, and shot full at Tom Eldon. By that time more than half of the marshal's party were in flight, the settlers were discharging their guns from all sides, and a number of settlers also had either fallen or fled. Buzzard, a tall, fierce, dark, heavily-bearded man, fired steadily and coolly with his repeating rifle from his standing-place in the wagon. Alonzo Eldon, like Escott, had carried no arms to the battle-field, and at first sat, grim and stiff, on his great black horse, which seemed as cool as himself.

All these things Sam saw, but like a man in a dream. He seemed, after his one shot, to stand for a moment paralyzed,—not with fear, for he was positively amused at the sights before him, but with a numb sense of wonder, and a feeling that something unheard of had happened. What! had he actually shot his man? And Tom Eldon? The ancient wrong avenged! For Tom had fallen. The next moment, however, Sam saw his own father close by his side, felt that he himself was staggering, saw strange colors before his eyes, and then knew no more for a long time—

Harold, five minutes later, found himself at the centre of the excited group. The firing had ceased. Buzzard lay dead where the wagon had left him, when the horses at last grew unmanageable and ran away. Tom Eldon was close beside him, whether dead or alive could not be told as yet. Escott and his son were just being carried off by some settlers. Alf Escott was not senseless, but had received two or three ugly-looking hurts. Alonzo Eldon, uninjured, was kneeling beside Tom. The marshal, also unhurt, was now disarmed, and a prisoner in the hands of the score of Rangers who, with shot-gun, pistol, and rifle, had borne the brunt of the battle. These men also surrounded Alonzo. The firing had been remarkably effective, owing to the very short range. Somewhere between two and three hundred shots had been fired, and, on both sides, as many as sixteen men had been struck. Of these, five were already certainly dead, among them Collins. Peterson was helpless with a bad wound. The most effective work, during the skirmish, had been undoubtedly done by Buzzard's repeating rifle. Six or eight men must have been struck by him. How Alonzo Eldon had escaped unhurt was thenceforth a mystery.

William C. Morrow
"Baptism of Blood"

Because of a "great meeting" in Hanford, many of the homes in Mussel Slough territory are left unattended, even though word has circulated that a marshal is in the area looking to evict settlers from their homes. Soon word arrives that "on Storer's ranch they are butchering the settlers like hogs!" John Graham and his neighbor Newton go in search of the marshal and witness the grisly spectacle of "man set against man, and neighbor against neighbor."

Leaving Hanford, Graham and Newton rode away in the direction the Marshal and the three men with him had taken. As they went, they met many persons going to Hanford.

"Have you seen the Marshal and his party?" Newton asked some of them.

"The Marshal? Is he here?"

This was depressing news, but it had been expected for some time, and his mission was known at once.

"He is on the road," replied Newton, "and we are going to see what he will do. Of course he will eject some settlers."

Some of the men they thus met joined them and turned about.

"I heard something just as I was leaving town," said Graham, "that does not sound encouraging."

"What is that?" eagerly asked Newton.

"That the two men who drove to Hanford this morning, and went out with the Marshal and the land grader for the railroad company, had two shotguns and a rifle in their buggy, and that each had a pair of revolvers."

"What is that for?" asked one of the party.

"I don't know."

Newton looked downcast.

"Surely," he said, "they don't expect a fight. Why, we are unarmed, and we never thought of a fight."

"No," said one; "there mustn't be anything of the kind."

Thus they rode along, increasing their pace; for an indefinable dread took possession of them. One man, who was incredulous, said:

"Why, the railroad company promised us only the other day that it would not prosecute any ejectment suits until our cases should be decided. How can it do such a thing?"

Newton smiled with some bitterness.

"I am not surprised at what has happened," he said.

They had gone four or five miles when they were joined by a man who was considerably excited.

"What has happened?" asked Newton.

"They have thrown Braden's goods into the road," replied the man. "And that isn't all: they left four loaded cartridges on the door-sill."

This was indeed discouraging news.

"Did Braden make any objection?" asked Graham.

"He expostulated with them; but the Marshal told him that, although it was an unpleasant duty, it had to be done."

"What do those cartridges mean?" asked Graham of the man.

"I don't know. Perhaps they were put there as a warning to the settlers of what they may expect if they offer any resistance."

"But we don't want to fight!" exclaimed Newton, with some impatience. "We want merely to see if this thing can't be delayed. Why, it would be a terrible thing to turn us out now, after we have done all the work and spent all the money that is required until harvest. What in the world will become us? We must reason with the Marshal. They say he is a good man; and I think we can get him to defer the service of these writs of ejectment until after harvest, or until our cases have been decided."

The eviction was the sole topic of conversation. The men discussed it from every point of view, and felt dispirited and crushed.

By this time the number of settlers had increased to fifteen, and it was learned that the Marshal and his party had gone northward after dispossessing Braden. The fifteen men were not far behind the Marshal, as they learned from persons they met on the road. A feeling of gloom depressed them, and they rode in silence. Soon they arrived at a turn in the road, and looking before them, across the field that intervened, they saw the Marshal and the three men who were with him. These had just emerged into the field from the yard surrounding the farm-house belonging to Storer and Brewer.

"There they are," said Graham.

Instead of following the turn in the road to the eastward, the settlers removed a panel of the fence, and rode straight across the field toward the Marshal. That officer sat in one buggy with the rail-road land grader, and the other was occupied by the two men who were to be placed in possession of the land from which the Marshal was evicting the settlers, and who had bought the land from the rail-road company.

Seeing them coming, the Marshal advanced on foot toward them, and met them about sixty yards from where the buggies were. A short parley ensued, in which the settlers endeavored to make some arrangement with the Marshal, whereby the service of the writs of ejectment might be delayed. The meeting was a friendly one, and the Marshal deplored the unfortunate position in which he was placed.

"It is an unpleasant duty," he said, "but I have to do it."

Some of the men were becoming excited; and as an outbreak seemed possible, on account of the exasperation to which the settlers were driven at seeing themselves betrayed, a guard was placed over the Marshal.

While this was transpiring, two or three settlers rode toward the three men who still sat in the buggies, and they were somewhat more than half-way, when a terrible thing occurred. The sight made Graham's heart stand still.

One of the men in the buggy, seeing the settlers approach near, reached for a gun that leaned against the seat, when the other said:

"Don't shoot yet: it isn't time."

A moment afterward a shot was fired, and one of the advancing settlers fell from his horse, with twelve buckshot in his breast.

The battle had opened. Shot followed shot in rapid succession between the settlers and the two men who occupied the buggy in which were the guns.

Graham and Newton stood apart from the others, and saw this sickening spectacle: saw man set against man, and neighbor against neighbor, and dragged into the jaws of death by that far-reaching thing that saw fit on this occasion to masquerade in the sacred vestments of the law: saw brave men slaughter one another as though heaven instead of hell had brought them to such bloody work.

It was a terrible sight! One of the men in the wagon received a pistol-ball in the abdomen. The other sprung to the ground; and with a shotgun in one hand and a revolver in the other, boldly advanced upon one of the two men who were guarding the Marshal. Between this guard and the advancing man an old feud existed. The guard, see-ing the fate that awaited him, endeavored to get behind his horse, which he was holding. The pursuing man went around, and sent a bullet full into the breast of the guard. The wounded man dropped to his knees, clasped his breast, and exclaimed:

"My God! I'm shot!"

Then he staggered to his feet, and received another bullet in the breast. He reeled away, mortally wounded, in the direction of a pool of water. This man was unarmed; and it may here be said that of the fifteen men only seven had pistols, and they were nearly all inefficient weapons.

As this man staggered to his feet and started for the pool, the other guard, who carried a small revolver which was so inferior that the thumb was required to revolve the chamber, advanced and opened fire on the assailant. He emptied his pistol, but none of the shots took effect. The other man fired twice, missing both times. The third shot made a hole in the guard's breast. He staggered backward three or four steps, stopped, straightened himself, and then fell backward.

The scene was becoming more exciting. Riderless horses dashed about.

"For God's sake, bring me my rifle!" cried the man who had finished the two guards, addressing his companion. This man, suffer-ing from a terrible wound, had descended from the buggy, and was lying on the ground. Besides, the horses, becoming frightened, had run away with the buggy containing the rifle.

The frightful details of that affair are apart from the requirements of this tale. Let it be hoped that at some time they will be written by an abler pen than the one which indites this simple tale. Suffice it to say, that as Graham sat there on his horse, he saw a rapid hurrying of men hither. and thither; shouts of the excited, and groans of the wounded and dying; a rapid and deadly discharge of firearms; and then all was still.

The fight had lasted but a moment—perhaps less than three minutes—but it seemed an age. One of the men who had come to be placed in possession of the settler's land by the marshal lay writhing in agony, with a bullet in his vitals. The other, a bold, fearless man, was walking away. He walked down the road, turned out into a field, and two hours later he was found lying on his face, a blackened corpse.

It was immediately after the fight that the messenger started for Hanford with the news that changed the holiday into a day of mourning.

Men and women drove rapidly to the spot; and when they arrived, an awful scene greeted them. Three settlers lay dead upon the porch of the farm-house; and one of the two men who had been in the wagon lay alongside them, in the throes of death. Two wounded settlers lay inside the house. They afterward died. So strange was the fatality of that day, that another settler, who had received merely a scalp wound, and who walked about all day, afterward died from the injury.

No man who was wounded came out of it alive; and eight brave men were slaughtered that day. All of these were married but two; and when their wives and children arrived, the cries of anguish that went up to heaven might have melted to pity even the hearts of stone that had permitted such a scene to be possible. Women fell upon the prostrate forms of their husbands, and begged them to speak but a single word. Little children, brightly arrayed in holiday attire, fondled the cold hands, and wondered at it all.

One by one the bodies were taken away; and toward evening a storm of wind arose, and howled and groaned, tearing over the plains as though the very elements were outraged and driven to furious anger; and then, adding to its groans the cries of the widow and the orphan, it passed furiously on, howling with rage and screaming in agony—on it madly flew, passing over the lake, and lashing its broad bosom, and then on and on, over the plains, over the fields, over the mountains and far away, until it was lost in the night.

The eleventh of May has passed into the history of California. The widows and the orphans that then were made are the fittest monument to commemorate that day. As the years roll by, crowding one upon another, until they seem small in the perspective, the eleventh of May will yet stand out alone and ever conspicuous, broad and bloody, raising its red hand in suppliance to the throne in heaven.

Frank Norris
"I Only Know My Duty"

While the settlers enjoy a community picnic, they receive word that a U.S. marshal is in the area evicting some of them from their homes. Magnus Derrick and Buck Annixter both insist that bloodshed still isn't necessary, but they nevertheless direct the Leaguers to take up defensive positions in the irrigation ditch that cuts between their two properties. When the marshal arrives—accompanied by representatives of the railroad and purchasers Delaney and Christian—angry words are exchanged. As in the actual gunfight, an accidental stumble is misinterpreted by a trigger-nervous shooter, in this case the farmer Hooven.

By now everyone was eating. It was the feeding of the People, elemental, gross, a great appeasing of appetite, an enormous quenching of thirst. Quarters of beef, roasts, ribs, shoulders, haunches were consumed, loaves of bread by the thousands disappeared, whole barrels of wine went down the dry and dusty throats of the multitude. Conversation lagged while the People ate, while hunger was appeased. Everybody had their fill. One ate for the sake of eating, resolved that there should be nothing left, considering it a matter of pride to exhibit a clean plate.

After dinner, preparations were made for games. On a flat plateau at the top of one of the hills the contestants were to strive. There was to be a footrace of young girls under seventeen, a fat men's race, the younger fellows were to put the shot, to compete in the running broad jump, and the standing high jump, in the hop, skip, and step and in wrestling.

Presley was delighted with it all. It was Homeric, this feasting, this vast consuming of meat and bread and wine, followed now by games of strength. An epic simplicity and directness, an honest Anglo-Saxon mirth and innocence, commended it. Crude it was; coarse it was, but no taint of viciousness was here. These people were good people, kindly, benignant even, always readier to give than to receive, always more willing to help than to be helped. They were good stock. Of such was the backbone of the nation—sturdy Americans everyone of them. Where else in the world round were such strong, honest men, such strong, beautiful women?

Annixter, Harran, and Presley climbed to the level plateau where the games were to be held, to lay out the courses, and mark the distances. It was the very place where once Presley had loved to lounge entire afternoons, reading his books of poems, smoking and dozing. From this high point one dominated the entire valley to the south and west. The view was superb. The three men paused for a moment on the crest of the hill to consider it.

Young Vacca came running and panting up the hill after them, calling for Annixter.

"Well, well, what is it?"

"Mr. Osterman's looking for you, sir, you and Mr. Harran. Vanamee, that cow-boy over at Derrick's, has just come from the Governor with a message. I guess it's important."

"Hello, what's up now?" muttered Annixter, turned back.

They found Osterman saddling his horse in furious haste. Near-by him was Vanamee holding by the bridle an animal that was one lather of sweat. A few of the picnickers were turning their heads curiously in that direction. Evidently something of moment was in the wind.

"What's all up?" demanded Annixter, as he and Harran, followed by Presley, drew near.

"There's hell to pay," exclaimed Osterman under his breath. "Read that. Vanamee just brought it."

He handed Annixter a sheet of note paper, and turned again to the cinching of his saddle.

"We've got to be quick," he cried. "They've stolen a march on us."

Annixter read the note, Harran and Presley looking over his shoulder.

"Ah, it's them, is it," exclaimed Annixter.

Harran set his teeth. "Now for it," he exclaimed.

"They've been to your place already, Mr. Annixter," said Vanamee. "I passed by it on my way up. They have put Delaney in possession, and have set all your furniture out in the road."

Annixter turned about, his lips white. Already Presley and Harran had run to their horses.

"Vacca," cried Annixter, "where's Vacca? Put the saddle on the buckskin, *quick*. Osterman, get as many of the League as are here together at *this* spot, understand. I'll be back in a minute. I must tell Hilma this."

Hooven ran up as Annixter disappeared. His little eyes were blazing, he was dragging his horse with him.

"Say, dose fellers come, hey? Me, I'm alretty, see I hev der guhn."

"They've jumped the ranch, little girl," said Annixter, putting one arm around Hilma. "They're in our house now. I'm off. Go to Derrick's and wait for me there."

She put her arms around his neck.

"You're going?" she demanded.

"I must. Don't be frightened. It will be all right. Go to Derrick's and—good-bye."

She said never a word. She looked once long into his eyes, then kissed him on the mouth.

Meanwhile, the news had spread. The multitude rose to its feet. Women and men, with pale faces, looked at each other speechless, or broke forth into inarticulate exclamations. A strange, unfamiliar murmur took the place of the tumultuous gaiety of the previous moments. A sense of dread, of confusion, of impending terror weighed heavily in the air. What was now to happen?

When Annixter got back to Osterman, he found a number of the Leaguers already assembled. They were all mounted. Hooven was there and Harran, and besides these, Garnett of the Ruby ranch and Gethings of the San Pablo, Phelps the foreman of Los Muertos, and, last of all, Dabney, silent as ever, speaking to no one. Presley came riding up.

"Best keep out of this, Pres," cried Annixter.

"Are we ready?" exclaimed Gethings.

"Ready, ready, we're all here."

"*All*. Is this all of us?" cried Annixter. "Where are the six hundred men who were going to rise when this happened?"

They had wavered, these other Leaguers. Now, when the actual crisis impended, they were smitten with confusion. Ah, no, they were not going to stand up and be shot at just to save Derrick's land. They were not armed. What did Annixter and Osterman take them for? No, sir; the Railroad had stolen a march on them. After all his big talk Derrick had allowed them to be taken by surprise. The only thing to do was to call a meeting of the Executive Committee. That was the only thing. As for going down there with no weapons in their hands, *no*, sir. That was asking a little *too* much.

"Come on, then, boys," shouted Osterman, turning his back on the others. "The Governor says to meet him at Hooven's. We'll make for the Long Trestle and strike the trail to Hooven's there."

They set off. It was a terrible ride. Twice during the scrambling descent from the hills, Presley's pony fell beneath him. Annixter, on his buckskin, and Osterman, on his thoroughbred, good horsemen both, led the others, setting a terrific pace. The hills were left behind. Broderson Creek was crossed and on the levels of Quien Sabe, straight through the standing wheat, the nine horses, flogged and spurred, stretched out to their utmost. Their passage through the wheat sounded like the rip and tear of a gigantic web of cloth. The landscape on either hand resolved itself into a long blur. Tears came to the eyes, flying pebbles, clods of earth, grains of wheat flung up in the flight, stung the face like shot. Osterman's thoroughbred took the second crossing of Broderson's Creek in a single leap. Down under the Long Trestle tore the cavalcade in a shower of mud and gravel; up again on the further bank, the horses blowing like steam engines; on into the trail to Hooven's, single file now, Presley's pony lagging, Hooven's horse bleeding at the eyes, the buckskin, game as a fighting cock, catching her second wind, far in the lead now, distancing even the English thoroughbred that Osterman rode.

At last Hooven's unpainted house, beneath the enormous live oak tree, came in sight. Across the Lower Road, breaking through fences and into the yard around the house, thundered the Leaguers. Magnus was waiting for them.

The riders dismounted, hardly less exhausted than their horses.

"Why, where's all the men?" Annixter demanded of Magnus.

"Broderson is here and Cutter," replied the Governor, "no one else. I thought *you* would bring more men with you."

"There are only nine of us."

"And the six hundred Leaguers who were going to rise when this happened!" exclaimed Garnett, bitterly.

"Rot the League," cried Annixter. "It's gone to pot—went to pieces at the first touch."

"We have been taken by surprise, gentlemen, after all," said Magnus. "Totally off our guard. But there are eleven of us. It is enough."

"Well, what's the game? Has the marshal come? How many men are with him?"

"The United States marshal from San Francisco," explained Magnus, "came down early this morning and stopped at Guadalajara. We learned it all through our friends in Bonneville about an hour ago. They telephoned me and Mr. Broderson. S. Behrman met him and provided about a dozen deputies. Delaney, Ruggles, and Christian joined them at Guadalajara. They left Guadalajara, going towards Mr. Annixter's ranch house on Quien Sabe. They are serving the writs in ejectment and putting the dummy buyers in possession. They are armed. S. Behrman is with them."

"Where are they now?"

"Cutter is watching them from the Long Trestle. They returned to Guadalajara. They are there now."

"Well," observed Gethings, "from Guadalajara they can only go to two places. Either they will take the Upper Road and go on to Osterman's next, or they will take the Lower Road to Mr. Derrick's."

"That is as I supposed," said Magnus. "That is why I wanted you to come here. From Hooven's, here, we can watch both roads simultaneously."

"Is anybody on the lookout on the Upper Road?"

"Cutter. He is on the Long Trestle."

"Say," observed Hooven, the instincts of the old-time soldier stirring him, "say, dose feller pretty demn schmart, I tink. We got to put some picket way oudt bei der Lower Roadt alzoh, und he tek dose glassus Mist'r Ennixt'r got bei um. Say, look at dose irregation ditsch. Dot ditsch he run righd across *both* dose road, hey? Dat's some fine entrenchment, you bedt. We fighd um from dose ditsch."

In fact, the dry irrigating ditch was a natural trench, admirably suited to the purpose, crossing both roads as Hooven pointed out and barring approach from Guadalajara to all the ranches save Annixter's—which had already been seized.

Gethings departed to join Cutter on the Long Trestle, while Phelps and Harran, taking Annixter's field glasses with them, and mounting their horses, went out towards Guadalajara on the Lower Road to watch for the marshal's approach from that direction.

After the outposts had left them, the party in Hooven's cottage looked to their weapons. Long since, every member of the League had been in the habit of carrying his revolver with him. They were all armed and, in addition, Hooven had his rifle. Presley alone carried no weapon.

The main room of Hooven's house, in which the Leaguers were now assembled, was barren, poverty-stricken, but tolerably clean. An old clock ticked vociferously on a shelf. In one corner was a bed, with a patched, faded quilt. In the centre of the room, straddling over the bare floor, stood a pine table. Around this the men gathered, two or three occupying chairs, Annixter sitting sideways on the table, the rest standing.

"I believe, gentlemen," said Magnus, "that we can go through this day without bloodshed. I believe not one shot need be fired. The Railroad will not force the issue, will not bring about actual fighting. When the marshal realises that we are thoroughly in earnest, thoroughly determined, I am convinced that he will withdraw."

There were murmurs of assent.

"Look here," said Annixter, "if this thing can by any means be settled peaceably, I say let's do it, so long as we don't give in."

The others stared. Was this Annixter who spoke—the Hotspur of the League, the quarrelsome, irascible fellow who loved and sought a quarrel? Was it Annixter, who now had been the first and only one of them all to suffer, whose ranch had been seized, whose household possessions had been flung out into the road?

"When you come right down to it," he continued, "killing a man, no matter what he's done to you, is a serious business. I propose we make one more attempt to stave this thing off. Let's see if we can't get to talk with the marshal himself: at any rate, warn him of the danger of going any further. Boys, let's not fire the first shot. What do you say?"

The others agreed unanimously and promptly; and old Broderson, tugging uneasily at his long beard, added:

"No—no—no violence, no *unnecessary* violence, that is. I should hate to have innocent blood on my hands—that is, if it *is* innocent. I don't know, that S. Behrman—ah, he is a—a—surely he had innocent blood on *his* head. That Dyke affair, terrible, terrible; but then Dyke *was* in the wrong driven to it, though; the Railroad did drive him to it. I want to be fair and just to everybody—"

"There's a team coming up the road from Los Muertos," announced Presley from the door.

"Fair and just to everybody," murmured old Broderson, wagging his head, frowning perplexedly. "I don't want to—to—to harm anybody unless they harm me."

"Is the team going towards Guadalajara?" enquired Garnett, getting up and coming to the door.

"Yes, it's a Portuguese, one of the garden truck men."

"We must turn him back," declared Osterman. "He can't go through here. We don't want him to take any news on to the marshal and S. Behrman."

"I'll turn him back," said Presley.

He rode out towards the market cart, and the others, watching from the road in front of Hooven's, saw him halt it. An excited interview followed. They could hear the Portuguese expostulating volubly, but in the end he turned back.

"Martial law on Los Muertos, isn't it?" observed Osterman. "Steady all," he exclaimed as he turned about, "here comes Harran."

Harran rode up at a gallop. The others surrounded him.

"I saw them," he cried. "They are coming this way. S. Behrman and Ruggles are in a two-horse buggy. All the others are on horseback. There are eleven of them. Christian and Delaney are with them. Those two have rifles. I left Hooven watching them."

"Better call in Gethings and Cutter right away," said Annixter. "We'll need all our men."

"I'll call them in," Presley volunteered at once. "Can I have the buckskin? My pony is about done up."

He departed at a brisk gallop, but on the way met Gethings and Cutter returning. They, too, from their elevated position, had observed the marshal's party leaving Guadalajara by the Lower Road. Presley told them of the decision of the Leaguers not to fire until fired upon.

"All right," said Gethings. "But if it comes to a gun-fight, that means it's all up with at least one of us. Delaney never misses his man."

When they reached Hooven's again, they found that the Leaguers had already taken their position in the ditch. The plank bridge across it had been torn up. Magnus, two long revolvers lying on the embankment in front of him, was in the middle, Harran at his side. On either side, some five feet intervening between each man, stood the other Leaguers, their revolvers ready. Dabney, the silent old man, had taken off his coat.

"Take your places between Mr. Osterman and Mr. Broderson," said Magnus, as the three men rode up. "Presley," he added, "I forbid you to take any part in this affair."

"Yes, keep him out of it," cried Annixter from his position at the extreme end of the line. "Go back to Hooven's house, Pres, and look after the horses," he added. "This is no business of yours. And keep the road behind us clear. Don't let *any one* come near, not *any one*, understand?"

Presley withdrew, leading the buckskin and the horses that Gethings and Cutter had ridden. He fastened them under the great live oak and then came out and stood in the road in front of the house to watch what was going on.

In the ditch, shoulder deep, the Leaguers, ready, watchful, waited in silence, their eyes fixed on the white shimmer of the road leading to Guadalajara.

"Where's Hooven?" enquired Cutter.

"I don't know," Osterman replied. "He was out watching the Lower Road with Harran Derrick. Oh, Harran," he called, "isn't Hooven coming in?"

"I don't know what he is waiting for," answered Harran. "He was to have come in just after me. He thought maybe the marshal's party might make a feint in this direction, then go around by the Upper Road, after all. He wanted to watch them a little longer. But he ought to be here now."

"Think he'll take a shot at them on his own account?"

"Oh, no, he wouldn't do that."

"Maybe they took him prisoner."

"Well, that's to be thought of, too."

Suddenly there was a cry. Around the bend of the road in front of them came a cloud of dust. From it emerged a horse's head.

"Hello, hello, there's something."

"Remember, we are not to fire first."

"Perhaps that's Hooven; I can't see. Is it? There only seems to be one horse."

"Too much dust for one horse."

Annixter, who had taken his field glasses from Harran, adjusted them to his eyes.

"That's not them," he announced presently, "nor Hooven either. That's a cart." Then after another moment, he added, "The butcher's cart from Guadalajara."

The tension was relaxed. The men drew long breaths, settling back in their places.

"Do we let him go on, Governor?"

"The bridge is down. He can't go by and we must not let him go back. We shall have to detain him and question him. I wonder the marshal let him pass."

The cart approached at a lively trot.

"Anybody else in that cart, Mr. Annixter?" asked Magnus. "Look carefully. It may be a ruse. It is strange the marshal should have let him pass."

The Leaguers roused themselves again. Osterman laid his hand on his revolver.

"No," called Annixter, in another instant, "no, there's only one man in it."

The cart came up, and Cutter and Phelps, clambering from the ditch, stopped it as it arrived in front of the party.

"Hey—what—what?" exclaimed the young butcher, pulling up. "Is that bridge broke?"

But at the idea of being held, the boy protested at top voice, badly frightened, bewildered, not knowing what was to happen next.

"No, no, I got my meat to deliver. Say, you let me go. Say, I ain't got nothing to do with you."

He tugged at the reins, trying to turn the cart about. Cutter, with his jack-knife, parted the reins just back of the bit.

"You'll stay where you are, m' son, for a while. We're not going to hurt you. But you are not going back to town till we say so. Did you pass anybody on the road out of town?"

In reply to the Leaguers' questions, the young butcher at last told them he had passed a two-horse buggy and a lot of men on horseback just beyond the railroad tracks. They were headed for Los Muertos.

"That's them, all right," muttered Annixter. "They're coming by this road, sure."

The butcher's horse and cart were led to one side of the road, and the horse tied to the fence with one of the severed lines. The butcher, himself, was passed over to Presley, who locked him in Hooven's barn.

"Well, what the devil," demanded Osterman, "has become of Bismarck?"

In fact, the butcher had seen nothing of Hooven. The minutes were passing, and still he failed to appear.

"What's he up to, anywise?"

"Bet you what you like, they caught him. Just like that crazy Dutchman to get excited and go too near. You can always depend on Hooven to lose his head."

Five minutes passed, then ten. The road towards Guadalajara lay empty, baking and white under the sun.

"Well, the marshal and S. Behrman don't seem to be in any hurry, either."

"Shall I go forward and reconnoitre, Governor?" asked Harran.

But Dabney, who stood next to Annixter, touched him on the shoulder and, without speaking, pointed down the road. Annixter looked, then suddenly cried out:

"Here comes Hooven."

The German galloped into sight, around the turn of the road, his rifle laid across his saddle. He came on rapidly, pulled up, and dismounted at the ditch.

"Dey're commen," he cried, trembling with excitement. "I watch um long dime bei der side oaf der roadt in der busches. Dey shtop bei der gate oder side der relroadt trecks and talk long dime mit one n'udder. Den dey gome on. Dey're gowun sure do zum monkey-doodle pizeness. Me, I see Gritschun put der kertridges in his guhn. I tink dey gowun to gome *my* blace first. Dey gowun to try put me off, tek my home, bei Gott."

"All right, get down in here and keep quiet, Hooven. Don't fire unless—"

"Here they are."

A half-dozen voices uttered the cry at once.

There could be no mistake this time. A buggy, drawn by two horses, came into view around the curve of the road. Three riders accompanied it, and behind these, seen at intervals in a cloud of dust were two—three—five—six others.

This, then, was S. Behrman with the United States marshal and his posse. The event that had been so long in preparation, the event which it had been said would never come to pass, the last trial of strength, the last fight between the Trust and the People, the direct, brutal grapple of armed men, the law defied, the Government ignored, behold, here it was close at hand.

Osterman cocked his revolver, and in the profound silence that had fallen upon the scene, the click was plainly audible from end to end of the line.

"Remember our agreement, gentlemen," cried Magnus, in a warning voice. "Mr. Osterman, I must ask you to let down the hammer of your weapon."

No one answered. In absolute quiet, standing motionless in their places, the Leaguers watched the approach of the marshal.

Five minutes passed. The riders came on steadily. They drew nearer. The grind of the buggy wheels in the grit and dust of the road, and the prolonged clatter of the horses' feet began to make itself heard. The Leaguers could distinguish the faces of their enemies.

In the buggy were S. Behrman and Cyrus Ruggles, the latter driving. A tall man in a frock coat and slouched hat—the marshal, beyond question—rode at the left of the buggy; Delaney, carrying a Winchester, at the right. Christian, the real estate broker, S. Behrman's cousin, also with a rifle, could be made out just behind the marshal. Back of these, riding well up, was a group of horsemen, indistinguishable in the dust raised by the buggy's wheels.

Steadily the distance between the Leaguers and the posse diminished.

"Don't let them get too close, Governor," whispered Harran.

When S. Behrman's buggy was about one hundred yards distant from the irrigating ditch, Magnus sprang out upon the road, leaving his revolvers behind him. He beckoned Garnett and Gethings to follow, and the three ranchers, who, with the exception of Broderson, were the oldest men present, advanced, without arms, to meet the marshal.

Magnus cried aloud:

"Halt where you are."

From their places in the ditch, Annixter, Osterman, Dabney, Harran, Hooven, Broderson, Cutter, and Phelps, their hands laid upon their revolvers, watched silently, alert, keen, ready for anything.

At the Governor's words, they saw Ruggles pull sharply on the reins. The buggy came to a standstill, the riders doing likewise. Magnus approached the marshal, still followed by Garnett and Gethings, and began to speak. His voice was audible to the men in the ditch, but his words could not be made out. They heard the marshal reply quietly enough and the two shook hands. Delaney came around from the side of the buggy, his horse standing before the team across the road. He leaned from the saddle, listening to what was being said, but made no remark. From time to time, S. Behrman and Ruggles, from their seats in the buggy, interposed a sentence or two into the conversation, but at first, so far as the Leaguers could discern, neither Magnus nor the marshal paid them any attention. They saw, however, that the latter repeatedly shook his head and once they heard him exclaim in a loud voice:

"I only know my duty, Mr. Derrick."

Then Gethings turned about, and seeing Delaney close at hand, addressed an unheard remark to him. The cow-puncher replied curtly and the words seemed to anger Gethings. He made a gesture, pointing back to the ditch, showing the intrenched Leaguers to the posse. Delaney appeared to communicate the news that the Leaguers were on hand and prepared to resist, to the other members of the party. They all looked toward the ditch and plainly saw the ranchers there, standing to their arms.

But meanwhile Ruggles had addressed himself more directly to Magnus, and between the two an angry discussion was going forward. Once even Harran heard his father exclaim:

"The statement is a lie and no one knows it better than yourself."

"Here," growled Annixter to Dabney, who stood next him in the ditch, "those fellows are getting too close. Look at them edging up. Don't Magnus see that?"

The other members of the marshal's force had come forward from their places behind the buggy and were spread out across the road. Some of them were gathered about Magnus, Garnett, and Gethings; and some were talking together, looking and pointing towards the ditch. Whether acting upon signal or not, the Leaguers in the ditch could not tell, but it was certain that one or two of the posse had moved considerably forward. Besides this, Delaney had now placed his horse between Magnus and the ditch, and two others riding up from the rear had followed his example. The posse surrounded the three ranchers, and by now, everybody was talking at once.

"Look here," Harran called to Annixter, "this won't do. I don't like the looks of this thing. They all seem to be edging up, and before we know it they may take the Governor and the other men prisoners."

"They ought to come back," declared Annixter.

"Somebody ought to tell them that those fellows are creeping up."

By now, the angry argument between the Governor and Ruggles had become more heated than ever. Their voices were raised; now and then they made furious gestures.

"They ought to come back," cried Osterman. "We couldn't shoot now if anything should happen, for fear of hitting them."

"Well, it sounds as though something were going to happen pretty soon."

They could hear Gethings and Delaney wrangling furiously; another deputy joined in.

"I'm going to call the Governor back," exclaimed Annixter, suddenly clambering out of the ditch.

"No, no," cried Osterman, "keep in the ditch. They can't drive us out if we keep here."

Hooven and Harran, who had instinctively followed Annixter, hesitated at Osterman's words and the three halted irresolutely on the road before the ditch, their weapons in their hands.

"Governor," shouted Harran, "come on back. You can't do anything."

Still the wrangle continued, and one of the deputies, advancing a little from out the group, cried out:

"Keep back there! Keep back there, you!"

"Go to hell, will you?" shouted Harran on the instant. "You're on my land."

"Oh, come back here, Harran," called Osterman. "That ain't going to do any good."

"There—listen," suddenly exclaimed Harran. "The Governor is calling us. Come on; I'm going."

Osterman got out of the ditch and came forward, catching Harran by the arm and pulling him back.

"He didn't call. Don't get excited. You'll ruin everything. Get back into the ditch again."

But Cutter, Phelps, and the old man Dabney, misunderstanding what was happening, and seeing Osterman leave the ditch, had followed his example. All the Leaguers were now out of the ditch, and a little way down the road, Hooven, Osterman, Annixter, and Harran in front, Dabney, Phelps, and Cutter coming up from behind.

"Keep back, you," cried the deputy again.

In the group around S. Behrman's buggy, Gethings and Delaney were yet quarrelling, and the angry debate between Magnus, Garnett, and the marshal still continued.

Till this moment, the real estate broker, Christian, had taken no part in the argument, but had kept himself in the rear of the buggy. Now, however, he pushed forward. There was but little room for him to pass, and, as he rode by the buggy, his horse scraped his flank against the hub of the wheel. The animal recoiled sharply, and, striking against

Garnett, threw him to the ground. Delaney's horse stood between the buggy and the Leaguers gathered on the road in front of the ditch; the incident, indistinctly seen by them, was misinterpreted.

Garnett had not yet risen when Hooven raised a great shout:

"Hoch, der Kaiser! Hoch, der Vaterland!"

With the words, he dropped to one knee, and sighting his rifle carefully, fired into the group of men around the buggy.

Instantly the revolvers and rifles seemed to go off of themselves. Both sides, deputies and Leaguers, opened fire simultaneously. At first, it was nothing but a confused roar of explosions; then the roar lapsed to an irregular, quick succession of reports, shot leaping after shot; then a moment's silence, and, last of all, regular as clock-ticks, three shots at exact intervals. Then stillness.

Delaney, shot through the stomach, slid down from his horse, and, on his hands and knees, crawled from the road into the standing wheat. Christian fell backward from the saddle toward the buggy, and hung suspended in that position, his head and shoulders on the wheel, one stiff leg still across his saddle. Hooven, in attempting to rise from his kneeling position, received a rifle ball squarely in the throat, and rolled forward upon his face. Old Broderson, crying out, "Oh, they've shot me, boys," staggered sideways, his head bent, his hands rigid at his sides, and fell into the ditch. Osterman, blood running from his mouth and nose, turned about and walked back. Presley helped him across the irrigating ditch and Osterman laid himself down, his head on his folded arms. Harran Derrick dropped where he stood, turning over on his face, and lay motionless, groaning terribly, a pool of blood forming under his stomach. The old man Dabney, silent as ever, received his death, speechless. He fell to his knees, got up again, fell once more, and died without a word. Annixter, instantly killed, fell his length to the ground, and lay without movement, just as he had fallen, one arm across his face.

May Merrill Miller
"My Sympathy Is with You"

Amelie Blansford watches her neighbors with pleasure as they enjoy a community celebration. But soon she notes that the mood is soured, as some terrible message is passed from farmer to farmer. When she leaves the picnic to meet Edwin at the railroad depot, it is with a sense of dread.

When Mary rose to look after Sean, Letitia whispered to Amelie: "Horace just told me he heard the United States Marshal is in town with a writ to put Cole in possession of Tim's place, and Tim has said he'll not be for waiting for any law or League or even night to be put back. Here comes Mary now. Don't tell her. Try to keep her talking."

When Mary returned she was smiling. "The littles are having such a good time, it does me good to see them."

Amelie was glad Mary started after the small wanderers again when she looked over at the knot of men standing under the farther locusts past the outer benches. Someone from behind whispering to Tim, and Tim, startled, turning to the head at his shoulder, Tim's face glowing as he listened, with anger—and something else—beneath the freckles.

Quietly, without a sign or a signal, Tim and Jed leaving, Arne with them, and Ralph Walker and Harry Gordon and Orrin Moore. Horace too; Amelie hoped Letitia had not seen him, but she had. Letitia's face was white. Stone again—like the framed pasteboards of Letitia's father and mother, who kept the cold winter of Deerfield in their eyes. Yankee strength—perhaps it hurt worse inside when you were stone outside.

But Tim Connery's reddening face had not been stone, or Jed's, or even Horace's, only something held back before, released and ready.

Amelie was sick when she rose to go to the station to meet Edwin. As she walked to the hitching-rack to her buggy and untied her horse she saw Tim and Jed and the others riding away on horseback. They would miss what the Judge had to say about the law. And although it was the day of the planned picnic, not a one was wearing his Sunday suit, but old clothes as if they were going hunting...hunting....Stand here rooted to the ground....They will go hunting and leave you whenever they are ready. They always have.

When Amelie met Edwin at the station she rubbed her eyes. Here was a man in a Sunday suit. He told her he was glad to be home. He was anxious to go to the speaking and the picnic to see the men, to tell them what the Governor had said. The Governor thought there was a good chance the railroad might arbitrate. He had promised to talk to the president of the El Dorado Pacific himself and appoint a committee. And the California state legislature had passed a resolution asking Congress to act, and for consultation with the Attorney General. In a few weeks…

"Why, you look tired, Amelie," he said after a minute. "Is anything wrong?"

"No, I guess it's just the heat." Time enough for him to find out when he got there. Probably just a rumor. But when she thought of the men leaving so quietly, her heart was cold.

Edwin left her at a bench near the platform to talk to some of the men. She knew he would. He came back in a minute and said he must go along for a while. She knew he would.

"Do you have to go?" she said. It was hard to force her tongue to form the words.

"Yes."

He would not like it if she kissed him, he wanted to leave these benches and go to his friends quickly. She must help him. "Please try to be careful," she allowed herself to whisper.

"Mamma, where is Papa going?" Roger demanded. "Can't I go too?"

"No, you stay right here with me"—she would have to tell him some other time it was not anger making her voice break like this— "we must stay here and wait—to hear the Judge make a speech about the law."

When Edwin left Amelie he hurried back to Colonel Becker, who had signaled to him from the edge of the picnic crowd.

"I got a saddle-horse for you from Hennesy's," the colonel said at the hitching-rack. "I thought you would need it."

"But if you knew this was going to happen, why didn't you send me some word, why didn't you telegraph?" Edwin implored as he urged on his horse, not so fleet a one as the colonel's own.

"I tell you, Blansford, we didn't know anything until late last night, and then we were not sure. We just heard the Marshal had come to town, that was all. He didn't stay at the hotel. Somebody said they had seen him, and Cole boasted his writ for Tim's place had come and it got around."

"Then there hasn't been any meeting of the League since I left?"

"No, we were waiting for you to come back from seeing the Governor."

Edwin sighed in relief and mopped his brow. It was hot riding in these good clothes. His relief was cut short by the next words of the colonel.

"No, we didn't have any meeting, but I did have a paper drawn up. I am going to present it to the Marshal. What do you think of this, Blansford?"

He pulled a paper from his pocket.

"Colonel, there isn't time now for any paper," Edwin cried, but the colonel pulled his horse down to a slow trot.

"It will take just a minute."

"A minute," Edwin thought, "it just takes a minute to fire a gun." But the colonel was reading:

"To the United States Marshal.

"Sir: We understand that you hold writs of ejectment issued against the settlers of Tulare and Fresno counties for the purpose of putting the El Dorado Pacific Railroad in possession of our lands. We hereby notify you that we have had no chance to present our equities, etc., and that we have, therefore, determined that we will not leave our homes unless forced to do so by superior force; in other words, it will require an army of at least a thousand good soldiers against the local forces that we can rally for self-defense; and we further expect the moral support of the good law-abiding citizens of the United States sufficient to resist all force that can be brought to bear to perpetuate such an outrage."

"Why, you can't do that without a League vote. That's resistance. That's too strong, colonel," Edwin objected, but glad the colonel had started his horse to galloping once more.

"No, it isn't." The colonel's words were partly cut off by the sound of the horses' hoofs. "In Tennessee it would be literature....I wrote at the bottom the reasons—these lands were never granted to the railroad...in the first place...change of route...road never completed... certain equities that must be respected and shall be respected...in the second...we as American citizens cannot respect rights claimed by El Dorado Pacific...."

They were at the crossroads; Edwin would talk to the colonel later about his paper. They turned at the corner toward Tim Connery's place.

"Oh, my God..." Edwin whispered. It was a prayer to hurry, that he might be there with the others a quarter of a mile away. If he could only tell them what the Governor had said...a few weeks. Edwin looked back; the colonel had slowed his horse and was carefully replacing his paper in his pocket. Edwin dug his heels into his horse's flanks and longed for spurs.

To the right the shanty of Cole and Ellis, to the left Tim's cabin; on the road just beyond, a knot of men on horseback. Just past Cole's cabin Ralph Walker's hired man was plowing Ralph's corn patch under for summer fallow; across the road, beside the horsemen and beyond, all the way from Tim's house Tim's field of wheat blazing in the sun. Edwin saw with a sinking wrench of despair the wheat was headed, ready to be cut. He had watched Tim sow it, he had heard Tim proclaim it the heaviest stand in the valley—and all the while Cole living across the road in his cabin furnished only with guns and cartridges, boasting he would not bother to take possession of Tim's place yet, he would wait until Tim's wheat was ready to harvest. Well, it was ripe now.

Ahead of him in the road Edwin could see the dark knot of horseback riders more closely; he spotted Tim and Arne and Jed in front—they would be. Horace Whitney, quiet, but you could always count on him, August Schumacher, Dan Fleming, Pierre, Wade Norris, Orrin, solemn scarecrow on a plow-horse, Ralph Walker—not more than a dozen, the horses too close together to count.

About seventy-five yards beyond the men stood a buggy with Matthews, the El Dorado Pacific's grader in it, and beside it an empty grain wagon, with Cole and Ellis on the high seat, blocking the road.

With his back to the wagon and buggy, about fifteen paces away from and facing the horsemen, a man with a silver star on his vest stood on the road alone.

They were all so still. The hoof-beats of Edwin's horse echoed; one by one the men jerked their heads back and to the front again as if pulled by unseen strings. Edwin slowed his horse; when he got a little nearer he would tell them about the Governor....

Edwin drew abreast of Ralph Walker.

"What's happening?" Edwin whispered.

"It's the Marshal."

Young Harry Gordon in a white shirt without a coat, his hair rumpled, red cheeks redder than ever in this hot sun, looking like a boy, was leaving his neighbors to stand holding the bridle of the Marshal's horse. One glance at the Marshal's sharply cramped buggy showed Matthews left on the seat, his face white in the buggy-top's shadow, the lines limp and loose in his hands.

Now, everything must be all right or Harry wouldn't be there holding the horse, helping the Marshal....No, Harry was holding the horse because it would shy when a gun was shot...Edwin was sick with pity...Harry's too young, he shouldn't be here. If he only had sense enough to wear a coat over that white shirt...

How far above them all sat Cole and Ellis, how high the seat of that wagon beside the buggy, blocking the road, how tall Cole was in black suit and black Stetson, looking down on those he faced, his quick eyes never leaving them! Ellis, heavier, slower, beside him, looked harmless enough. But the colonel had said this morning Ellis had got his writ for Arne's place.

Beneath them the Marshal still stood midway on the strip of road, facing the horsemen. He had grit to stand alone like that...dark suit on a white dusty road...just talking....

"My name is Nash and I am a United States Marshal and I've come to do my duty, gentlemen." How still that voice was! He was a nice-looking man, how different from white-faced Matthews, crouched back in the buggy-top's shadow! The Marshal was holding a pistol in his hand, but loosely, not even cocked. "And it isn't a pleasant duty....I did not know till I came here this morning that I would find my old friend Moore here, I used to know in Calaveras County, among you. I'm doubly sorry one of these writs is for him....I have six writs here and I must serve them all."

Jed Fassett, up in front, rode closer to the Marshal, scowling. "We've had enough of your writs. Give me your pistol. I'm going to take you prisoner. Give me that gun...."

"Jed!"

Edwin could not get closer, but he rose in his stirrups and shouted: "Don't touch him! Don't touch his arms! He's a United States Marshal and he's got a right to carry them!"

"He's right," Ralph Walker called. "We didn't bargain for this."

In the wagon Ellis was leaning down to get something at his feet. When he straightened up he handed Cole a Henry rifle, keeping a number-ten shotgun for himself. Cole took the gun without looking at it, shouting at Ellis: "It isn't time to shoot yet."

"There's no need to shoot at all," Edwin cried. "Wait a minute, boys....Mr. Nash, these men don't want any trouble. We've all got equities in these lands and we're just waiting till the cases are decided in the United States Supreme Court...I've just got back from seeing the Governor—he says he hopes in a few weeks..."

But the Marshal interrupted. "I'm sorry—my sympathy is with you, but I am here by the authority of the President of the United States...I must do my duty...."

The Marshal drew a long folded paper from his pocket.

"Jed! For God's sake—"

But Jed's horse, close upon the Marshal, was wheeling and struck the Marshal, knocking him down on the road, kicking him as he fell.

Cole, in the seat beside Ellis, was drawing his Henry rifle. How slowly he was lifting it, his eyes steady under his black hat!

Guns cocking now, cocking, popping, clicking, Edwin with none. Cole's gun higher now.

A shot from Cole...echoing, forever, forever....It's started. Smoke now, blue and the stench of it strong, the wind blowing it from Cole's wagon toward Edwin and his neighbors. Edwin saw he could not get to the Marshal to help him. A tiny spurt of dust was rising from the road where the Marshal was lying, hitting him in the face.

Cole, in the wagon seat, shouting to Ellis: "Get me that other rifle."

Another shot now. From Jed? Tim? Arne? Edwin could not see.

Cole, loading the rifle in his hand, howling at slow Ellis beside him: "God damn it, you gave me the wrong rifle. Get me the other one!"

Ellis slumping down suddenly from the seat, stumbling over the wheel, dragging the horses' lines with him, letting them fall in the road, clutching his hands to his left groin.

Cole, paying no attention to Ellis, kept on loading his gun.

Through the horses in between, Edwin saw the Marshal trying to get up from the road, horses almost upon him.

No time to protest. No one would listen.

Jed Fassett with six-shooter smoking. It would be Jed. Beside Jed, Arne, his fair head lifted, Cole's gun at his shoulder again, no one paying any attention to Ellis, staggering around on the road near the buggy in circles, clutching his groin, his face grimacing.

And behind them all the white ghost face of Matthews in the Marshal's buggy, not even getting out to help Ellis...and white-shirted Harry, holding the Marshal's horse.

Edwin felt a strange lightness....It could not be happening...too fast...shots echoing....Edwin could see only Tim's back up in front and his sweaty old hat and his red hair and his drawn gun smoking... Jed, slipping off his horse, falling onto the road, Pierre following... Arne drawing his shotgun with his blue eyes fixed on Cole—Arne's horse turning, another shot, Cole firing this time, Arne getting it in the back, his coat blown open, the blood running in a great stain across Arne's back as he turned and fell, his foot still in the stirrup.

Edwin was sick, sick with the helplessness of a watcher. He did not have a gun. He checked his horse tighter as the lean black figure of Cole jumped down from the wagon without a word to Ellis, past him now, Ellis still staggering behind him like a crazy man, his hands at his groin, what a pair!...Good God, they were stumbling over Arne, fallen now in the road, but still living, Edwin could tell that.... August...Pierre too, huddled over in strange positions like children thrusting out an arm or leg in their sleep.

Suddenly a great clatter, even Cole turning. No driver now in the empty grain wagon, with the lines dragging, Cole's team began running, swerving, just missing the fallen men, plunging straight at Edwin and the knot of men on horseback.

Edwin reined his horse to the side, helpless, between the others.

The heavy empty wagon parted the knot of horsemen, rolled thundering past Edwin on the hard road, horses snorting, frightened eyes white. Edwin could hardly hold his own horse, he felt it trying to turn and run, but the horses of his neighbors closed in upon him, stirrups locked. As they shifted, Edwin glimpsed Ralph Walker's hired man at the fence by the side of the road, white-faced, staring, his plow stilled.

When Edwin looked back at the road, Cole had turned and was making straight for Harry Gordon, who was still holding the Marshal's frightened horse.

"Cole can't go after Harry like that," Ralph gasped beside Edwin, "Harry's just trying to help the Marshal. Pull over, Edwin...I must go to him."

"Harry hasn't a gun," Tim Connery yelled from the front row of men, leaving them, riding straight at Cole, his own gun drawn. "Sure, and you can't do that!"

Harry, holding on the horse's mane, swinging under its neck, had no refuge from Cole, running around the horse after him. How young, how surprised, how gentle he looked standing there, one hand on the horse's mane, the other still clutching the bridle!...Only two feet away, Cole was aiming straight at Harry's breast. Two shots, so quick, almost together. "I never knew bullets would go right through a man, but they do." Edwin saw Harry whirl and turn, two red spots appearing on the back of his white shirt as if they had been thrown there.

Tim, riding toward Cole, was above him now; Cole, standing still, his black Stetson rakish to one side, his lips almost smiling, was looking up into Tim's freckled twisted face, standing at Tim's stirrup, their guns almost touching. Four shots. Two from each gun. Tim was slumping in his saddle, his old sweaty hat falling off his red hair....

More gun smoke, stench...more shots...why, it was Cole running...he must have left his cartridges in the wagon...leaving the road now...running into Tim's field of wheat...keeping time to the shots...leaping like a jack-rabbit seeking shelter...deeper...deeper... into the field he had sworn to harvest...into the field he had not sown.

Breaking down the heads of the wheat.

How ripe it is!

He should not run through it like that.

Falling, his arms out, his gun flung away at the side, falling into Tim's field...Tim's wheat covering him....

A swirl, a bending, an eddy in the stalks.

The black Stetson lay alone, a solitary crow upon a field of golden-headed wheat.

The sun shone down warmly upon the seed it had ripened.

Edwin was still for a moment, staring. Voices about him broke the quiet that had fallen.

Edwin ran to Tim then, to Tim just falling from his horse. Edwin caught the limp weight on his shoulder as it curved over him. He had not known it would be so heavy. His knees giving way; Ralph Walker beside him—and a sudden shifting as Ralph helped with the weight between them. The shock of Tim's red hair brushed against Edwin's coat as he lowered Tim to take him by the shoulders. When he looked into Tim's face, Edwin almost let go of him. For Tim's blank eyes were staring past all of them at a field of fully ripened wheat.

As the others helped Edwin and Ralph with their slumping burden, Edwin looked back to see the colonel handing the Marshal a folded white paper.

Edwin set his teeth.

"Let us take Tim to his own house," he said, "and Arne and Harry and the others with him."

In a little while after Edwin had left Amelie, the platform built for today's oratory was filled. There was a hush. It was a warm day. No need for her heart to beat like this....They have just gone to talk to the Marshal, that is all. The League had decided to take no action yet; there is no need to worry. The Governor said in a few weeks....This is a picnic. Everybody in his best clothes, the children restless, watching the lemonade-stand beyond the benches, Stella Moore and Rhoda Walker waiting with tin dippers to ladle it out of the deep black casks.

This is a picnic. Only it is a strange warm sweet hush with the first white blossom clusters of the young locust trees hanging heavy with scent. Only it is a dream—nothing is real but those men riding away in their old clothes, Edwin following. But there is Reverend Gilmer standing so still in his square-tailed coat, giving the invocation. "Our heavenly Father, we come not to beseech Thee, but to endeavor to know Thy will. Look down upon us, help us to find a way."

Anna Halvorson, standing near the parlor organ on the platform in her new white lawn dress. How beautiful, like her mother Sigrid, strong underneath, younger! Sigrid would say nothing about it, but Amelie knew she and Arne were proud Anna was receiving the most votes at Bailey's Dry Goods Store for Goddess of Liberty. She would surely be the Goddess in this year's parade on the Fourth of July. She stood so quietly, her golden hair braided in a coronet like Sigrid's as she waited for Eileen Connery to pick up the music which had fallen to the floor.

Amelie's eyes were wet...something...it's that dress, white ruffles...how long it took Hester to iron them, around and around... another May morning in Missouri...and the rows of white handkerchief tents bleaching on the grass of Camp Jackson and Jason looking down at the white ruffles, his hand on one of them, his eyes on your cheeks..."You don't need any red to wear with the white." And yourself within, all that steel ringing you round...wanting to be with him... nearer...and you thought you would and you never did...youth, believing, unhurt as yet....

Amelie hoped Anna did not know that her father had left and would not be there to hear his daughter sing.

When the organ and the young voice began *The Star Spangled Banner*, rebellious words trembled upon Amelie's lips. She was surprised, she had not thought of them for so long, why should she think of them on this May morning? Perhaps May is the month for rebellion. She kept the words silent, but she framed her lips over them in time to the lift and fall of the tune:

> "All they ask is the right, the old Banner's great stand,
> The right to be ruled by the voice of the land.
> The right is denied, can the Banner now wave
> O'er the land of the free and the home of the brave?"

But suddenly Amelie stopped these words short and sang the others—the ones she had learned first before she ever quelled bitter stanzas in the black book. These first words are the right ones. They always have been. She had to make herself hate to learn those others. Even if her father then and Edwin now decided action for her, she could decide within. She knew she was right. Women have to know how to wait to receive what happens...if men would...but perhaps they can't....

Roger had been looking up at his mother in surprise; he turned toward the platform again and joined Amelie in the proper song.

When Anna sat down, the young white-blossom-burdened trees moved in the slight stir of the breeze before people remembered to applaud. Amelie looked at her gold watch. Three quarters of an hour since the men had gone.

The Judge stood up. He was a fine-looking man from Virginia. Amelie usually listened with joy, for his tongue spoke the speech of her youth. Not today. Her hands were cramped upon the new board bench. She released them. They smelled of pine as the pine-box cabin had on warm days....It was safe and we were all together...and we can never go back to it...never....The Judge began to speak.

The sound of horses running. The judge's voice dying away in the midst of a sentence. A horse stopping at the edge of the crowd. A man running to the platform. The Judge standing by the table, untouched water in the pitcher beside him. The man at the edge of the platform. The Judge leaning over to speak to him. The pleated bunting fans of red, white, and blue around the top of the platform with no hands to hold them high.

"There has been trouble," the Judge was saying now, slowly, clearly, "at Tim Connery's place. Will members of the League please meet immediately at the usual place? Please go quietly."

Mary Connery had not fainted. She was just moaning slightly, still seated on the new bench in the midst of her children, her lips trembling. "I knew it would be," she said.

And then she stood, not noticing Sean hanging to her skirts. "I must be for going to Tim himself."

"Ride with me," Amelie cried. "We can go faster in my buggy than in your wagon."

There was not room for all of them in Amelie's buggy. At the hitching-rack, where a bewildered group of people were untying their horses, Amelie turned to Letitia. "Letitia, please ask somebody to see that Mary's children and mine get home. And tell them not to bring them for a while. You don't mind?"

"No." Letitia's stony face was also the brisk school-teacher's now. "Horace went too—but I know Mary must go first; I'll be right along. I'll tend to everything." She was already gathering the frightened children about her.

As Amelie turned her buggy out into the street she had to turn sharply to avoid Dr. Ennis, whose buggy had been hitched next to Amelie's. He was a big Cossack in his tan linen duster, a Cossack with jaws set. He did not look at Amelie as her wheels nearly touched him. But when she last glanced at him he was putting his old pebbly bag into the buggy with exact care.

Sigrid had already turned her buckboard out into the street ahead of Amelie; heedless of her new dress, Anna was climbing to the seat beside her mother, her white ruffles brushing the wheels as the horses started to run, the two golden braided coronets of Sigrid's and Anna's hair shining in the morning sun.

Amelie whipped her own horse until she thought she might have a runaway. She did not care. Past Bailey's store, past Weinstein's, past the station, past the warehouse—what good are meetings now?—past the flour mill, no dancing today on that bare floor, the sieves are set for the harvest.

Edwin. He had gone. He had gone late but he had gone with his neighbors....Tim, younger than any of his children, Mary beside her now...their light down the road...but she must not think of Edwin, or of Tim, or even of Mary beside her murmuring: "I knew it would be," she must think only of this road ahead, only of Sigrid and Anna ahead, not to drive too close to their buckboard...only of the teams behind, to get farther over to the side, for Dr. Ennis is just getting ready to pass...she must think only of this sweaty lathery horse, whip it...faster...hurry....

The horse began to shy. Arne's place. His furniture and Sigrid's in a stack in the middle of the road. Sigrid and Anna had not stopped, only swerving their team to one side a little as they passed their own belongings. A barrel of flour spilling over a rocking-chair piled crazily with great polished copper kettles. The big chest painted with strange blue flowers, the lid torn open, lying on the road, the cream-colored blankets no machine ever loomed spilling out into the dirt—Sigrid Lovenskiold's bridal chest and other Sigrids' before her. Amelie knew without looking what was carved deep into the wood: "Sigrid 1304." Amelie glanced up at the open doorway, the door half-wrenched from its hinges. The house looked empty. The El Dorado Pacific's tenants had not yet moved in. But on the sill stood three new red wrapped cartridges.

Soon now Tim's house next. She must not think of this huddle moaning beside her, but just get her there quickly.

There was already a crowd around Tim's cabin, out in the square yard fenced by the splintery pickets shaped like arrows. A wagon was tied to the fence, and Dr. Ennis's buggy and many saddle-horses tethered. Sigrid, just ahead, leaving the buckboard in the road, was throwing the lines to men who rushed to help her. She and white-ruffled Anna were running into Tim's house.

Amelie knew, a moment later, from the way the men helped herself and Mary out of the buggy, stepping aside, glancing at Mary and away again, that it must be Tim, not Edwin. Amelie and Mary hurried to the steps together, Amelie holding Mary firmly by the arm that was trembling.

"I knew it would be." Oh, stop, Mary.

A man was lying on the porch, groaning, all doubled up, holding his left groin. Ellis, a man Amelie did not know bending over him.

As Amelie looked up she saw there was no door in front of her, but sagging hinges. Tim's door ripped off...where could it be?...

"Please, Mrs. Blansford...Doctor Ennis...for Christ's sake."

This was what they had used the door for. Harry Gordon, flat on the door, the cords in his neck wires to his upraised chin, his lips strained, beseeching: "Oh, Doctor, why did you make them pick me up?...Why didn't you leave me?...This hurts worse...for Christ's sake."

"We couldn't leave you there on the road, son."

Amelie could not see for a moment as she followed them inside. The men who were carrying the door laid it down on a cot, Harry groaning, his face twisted, his eyes never leaving the doctor's face.

"Jesus Christ, help me."

Dr. Ennis leaning over in the old tan duster: "I will help you."

Dr. Ennis turning to Amelie, his eyes big and wide-pupiled—that time he helped Letitia—not noticing Amelie for herself, only for what she could do. "Madam, fetch me some water quickly."

Amelie rushed to the water-bucket on the table and brought back a full dipper.

Edwin standing beside the doctor. "Oh, Edwin, you're all right?"

"Yes, Amelie."

No time for themselves now, not with Harry like this.

When Amelie started to hand the doctor the dipper, he motioned her to hold it a minute. He had four white pellets in his hand and he had screwed the top back on a little bottle that had held them. Looking down at Harry's face, the doctor suddenly unscrewed the bottle again with a swift twist of his brown-stained fingers and shook two more pellets out into his big palm.

"Here, son," he said, and holding Harry's head up with the same strange gentleness with which he had once held Letitia's baby, he put the pellets on Harry's tongue and held the dipper to his lips. "You'll sleep now," he told him.

Harry's mouth, still twisted, relaxed a little, cornerwise. He leaned back against the big hand holding him.

"How long will I sleep?"

"Till morning."

Harry shut his eyes, opened them again to look straight at Amelie.

"Mrs. Blansford—"

"Yes, Harry."

"Please—please...tell Janet I'm sorry about all her furniture. I shouldn't have—brought..."

"Doctor," Edwin was saying in a voice that was not Edwin's at all, only a choked something Amelie could just understand, "don't you think we'd better get a statement?"

Doctor Ennis did not speak for a moment, until he had laid Harry back upon the cot.

"Yes," he bellowed, as if nothing would disturb Harry now, "you'll get a statement, but not from this lad. I'll give you all a statement!"

When he turned, Amelie drew back afraid, for the doctor's eyes were black and staring as he howled: "And I thought this was all over. War again...killing boys...hospitals...amputations...amputations."

"Get him out of here, he's no good to us now."

"No, don't let him go," August called, bending over a bed in the corner. "Come here, please, Doc, we need you."

Only when Amelie turned from Harry did she really see Mary in the corner, kneeling by Tim...and on the same bed Jed Fassett, breathing strangely. No time to separate dead from dying.

"I knew it would be...."

No one noticing Mary—perhaps Doctor Ennis can do something for Jed, his eyes bewildered under his black brows.

"Come on out, Amelie, you've got to know about the others...."

Oh, no others. But there was Pierre, Orrin sitting beside him, where Pierre was crumpled on a quilt, puzzled by this trickle from his mouth that Orrin was caring for....I am glad, Pierre, you bought all those gold crosses at a bargain for your children to put around their necks....They were a bargain....

Oh, no more, Edwin.

She had to have his arms around her now. It was wrong to be so glad with Tim and Harry and Jed and Pierre lying there, but she could not help it. Edwin alive. She was shaking against him.

She looked out the back window and screamed.

"Hush, Amelie, he may live."

But Arne, lying on the ground beside the well in the triangle of the splintery well-sweep, his back turned to her, the shirt ripped away, the skin blown away, surely could not live many minutes. Sigrid, sitting there with his head on her lap, must know it too. She was dry-eyed, one hand upon Arne's cheek, the other on his fair head, still proud. Anna was kneeling beside them, one hand over her mouth, her ruffles a white circle on the ground.

Amelie ran out to them. Arne looked up, his blue eyes brighter than she had ever seen them. He grimaced at her, but she knew it was the old Arne.

"I yust take it back, Mrs. Blansford..." he said.

"Don't talk, please don't talk," Amelie whispered.

"Let him talk," Sigrid said deeply.

"You were right, Edvin." Arne spoke slowly in a light voice, but with something terrible gasping in every word. "We should have waited for the law. You yust can't buck a year. You yust can't buck a railroad. Maybe if we had waited, like what we did for the ditch that time the water got away from us into the hidden river under the ground where we could not see and we yust have to have more assessments and dig another....The Lord never gives you anything outright....We forgot Him and His mountains and how we had to work....You yust have to pay one way—or another—more than you expect."

"There now..." Sigrid said.

Amelie turned away her head. But she could not help seeing, when young Anna in her ruffles flung herself upon her father, there was plenty of red now to wear with the white. And she could not help seeing Sigrid holding Arne as if he were a child against her breast, her blue eyes darkening.

When there was nothing more they could do for Sigrid or Mary, Edwin said: "Let us go home now. I have things to tend to."

But when they reached their own new house he sat on the top step, his head in his hands, save when he looked over at the roof of Tim's place, his field of wheat still shining in the sun, showing in splotches of gold through the young orchard.

"I wish I had been there from the beginning. They promised to wait to hear what the Governor said. But I doubt if anyone could have stopped Tim or Jed, or Arne, either....Arne changed somehow... hearing Cole boast every day about Tim's wheat...."

Edwin stood up.

"Let us tend to what we can, Amelie. The colonel sent four of our men away with the Marshal. They took him out of the county, over to Reesburg to take the train. I guess the colonel's right, it wouldn't be best for the Marshal to go into Nueva Esperanza. But the Marshal will be back. He will come soon. He will arrest me with the others."

"But you didn't have a gun. You didn't plan it."

"I know, only thirteen of us there, only four or five with guns. It wasn't planned. Maybe Jed and Tim…maybe Arne…but not the rest of us. We went because of Cole and because he had bought all those cartridges last week. We were all afraid for Tim today after what Cole had said."

"But the Marshal will know you were always for the law. He will know that you had just come back from seeing the Governor…trying to arrange things peaceably.…How could you be taken?"

"I was there, Amelie. We had taken a pledge to stand together. They were my neighbors. I was one of them."

Edwin and Amelie went into town the next day, for there were things to be tended to for their neighbors' funerals. Even though the trains had stopped running, even though the telegraph office was closed, even though no mails came to the post office and there was talk of soldiers being sent here, their neighbors had to be buried.

When they drove past the railroad station a crowd of men were standing around, some of them League members with pistols at their belts.

"The League's set a guard over the telegraph office and the railroad station, so no El Dorado Pacific property will be damaged. We've got the telegraph operator to come back and he's already sending messages," one of the men told Edwin.

Colonel Becker was walking proudly from the station to the hitching-rack where Edwin was hitching his horses. Amelie saw the colonel carried a white paper in his hand. Edwin was standing still, not speaking, looking at the paper as if he would like to snatch it. But the colonel did not notice.

"How's this, Blansford? What do you think the El Dorado Pacific will think of this:

"*Resolved:* That it is the sense of this people that there is not now, nor has there ever been, any danger in the running of trains or the forwarding of mails by this road, and that it is considered clearly a breach of contract with the U.S. Government on the part of the R.R. authorities in not delivering mails at this time.'"

"The trains will run again," Edwin said, "the El Dorado Pacific just wants to make things out as bad as possible. They're trying to make us out a mob, they know we wouldn't hurt their station or their telegraph dispatcher. That's the last thing we intend to do."

"You didn't come to the League meeting last night," the colonel reproached Edwin.

"No, I couldn't, I was taking turns sitting up at Tim's and Arne's place."

"Well, see what you think of this—this is the message that's going to the Secretary of the United States Senate—the telegrapher is punching it now. Listen:

"Secretary of the U.S. Senate:

"The journals of the Senate and House will show that we have done all in our power for the investigation of our case. Seven citizens have been murdered. We pray that our case be heard. We hold the El Dorado Pacific Railroad Company responsible for their blood and for all future trouble in the Nueva Esperanza country. Answer if received.

Signed by the order of the Land League,
Homer Becker"

"Why, that's just fine, Colonel."

But Edwin turned away from the colonel and his papers.

"Let's go, Amelie."

For Mary had asked Edwin to buy a new Sunday suit. "Fit for his burying. His old one is not for being good enough to be put in the ground," Mary had said.

When Harry Gordon was buried in the two days set aside for the funerals, Janet was the only one who did not go to the services for her husband. She did not seem to understand at all what had happened. Janet had gone back to her dusting.

But everyone else was there, Amelie decided. On all four sides of the space fenced in from the fields to the west of Nueva Esperanza, buggies and horses and wagons and surreys formed a black square—the hitching-racks along the road could not hold them all.

"They say there's six hundred people here today—they've come from Visalia and Fresno and all up and down the valley...the telegraph operators have sent out messages and they say the San Francisco papers are full of it...and Washington too...."

San Francisco...Washington....

No longer just Arne and Harry and Tim and the others who had lived on crow meat and dug an impossible ditch and turned the water from the Sierras from a river to their liking. But lying here in this earth they themselves had helped to fence, their questioning and their bewilderment persisted...past their neighbors to others in other cities...other lands...other races they had never seen.

At Arne's funeral, with Sigrid standing motionless and Anna ten years older, the smaller children looking so like Arne with their sandy hair and blue eyes—Mary Connery, Rhoda, Letitia standing bareheaded by the open grave that would soon be heaped like these new others in the row—the Reverend Mr. Gilmer looking toward the east where the Sierras that Arne had loved were very near on this clear day, said:

"We are left to bury our dead today, tomorrow we consign others to the tomb; it may be that at the end of this trouble someone will be left to bury us."

In the quiet air when he had done, another sound intruded. Hatless men turned, and women. On the shining tracks on the earthwork curving through the wheat-field across from the cemetery gate, thrusting cam-shaft gleaming, the locomotive screeching a whistle at the cemetery crossing, a brakeman standing in the open doorway of the baggage car, the passenger coach windows alternating shutters of light and shadow, the day's train tore east to west in continuing echoing power. It was soon far distant from the living and the dead in this small space of common ground fenced in by near neighbors, for decency and for love and for honor, from the larger fields.

The El Dorado Pacific had resumed its regular schedule.

C. C. Post
"We Intend to Hold Them"

In his version of the gunfight, C. C. Post doesn't bother to disguise Walter Crow's name. Instead, his narrative declares Crow to be a "pretended" buyer of land, a "tool" of the railroad. Meeting the marshal at the Hanford depot, Crow and his crew set off to dispossess his neighbors from their land, even as they gather in celebration at the local picnic. In this telling of the event, Crow mortally wounds the gallant Erastus Hemmingway in a scene designed to suggest cold-blooded murder rather than a tragic mistake, an interpretation that preserves for readers the untarnished image of the Mussel Slough farmers.

The first year after the completion of the main irrigating ditch, the settlers had set apart the eleventh day of May as a day of general rejoicing, and thanksgiving for the harvest which followed the coming of the waters, and through all their troubles they had regularly observed it, their festivities usually taking the form of a picnic, which was attended by everybody, regardless of age or sex, and it was this eleventh day of May, this festival day in 1880, that the corporate conspirators fixed upon for the consummation of their scheme for possessing themselves of the homes of these people.

In order to secure fit tools for this purpose, the company had made pretended sales of the homes of a portion of the settlers to men of known desperate character, among others to one named Crow, a noted desperado and crack-shot; and it was these men whom the United States marshal was ordered to take upon his raid of eviction.

The marshal left San Francisco before day and arrived at Hanford, the station nearest the Slough lands, at seven o'clock in the morning.

Here he was met by Crow with his gang of desperadoes armed to the teeth, and all started together in wagons.

Crow carried two bulldog revolvers and a knife in his belt, and had a repeating rifle and a double-barreled fowling piece in the wagon in which he rode, and all bristled with deadly weapons, principally revolvers and knives.

As was anticipated by the marshal, they arrived at the first house in the Slough settlement after its occupants had left for the picnic.

Without ceremony the door of this peaceful dwelling was broken down and everything in it pitched into the highway.

This done, they placed three No. 10 cartridges upon the doorstep as an indication of the fate which awaited the honest settler and his family if they dared replace their household goods and resume the occupancy of their home.

They then started in the direction of the next settler's claim, intending to proceed in the same manner with each of twenty-five houses against whose owners the marshal had writs of ejectment.

But they were not destined to proceed so far.

Unknown to them the gang had been seen to leave Hanford by one who, surmising the nature of their errand, hastened to notify the settlers of what was about to be attempted.

Mounting a horse he rode with all speed, and, approaching the picnic grounds, came first upon several parties who had driven a little way back from the immediate scene of festivities in order to find a suitable place for leaving their teams and wagons.

Among them were Erastus Hemmingway and his neighbor, Mr. Johnson.

To these men he communicated what he had observed, and his belief regarding the intention of the marshal and his gang of desperate characters.

All listened eagerly to the information brought by their friend, and then held a hurried consultation among themselves.

Erastus, Johnson, and one of the others, were armed with a single revolver of small calibre each. The rest were without weapons of any kind.

They did not like to return to the picnic grounds and frighten the women and children with an announcement of what they believed was taking place; neither did they propose that their homes should be ravished and they make no effort to defend them.

It was finally agreed that Hemmingway, Johnson, and those who were with them, should hurry across country to a point in the road about a mile away, over which the marshal and his crowd must pass, while the friend who had brought the information should quietly notify others and leave them to follow or wait for a report from those who were in advance, as they thought best.

Hurrying across the fields, this little body of men came out into the road by which the gang were proceeding, just in advance of the marshal and his party, as they approached the cottage of the second victim marked upon their list for eviction.

Seeing them, the marshal halted and got down from the wagon in which he was riding. Crow and the others did the same.

Approaching to within a few feet of the marshal, Erastus demanded to know if it were true that they had come to evict the settlers, and was told that they had.

"You will not be allowed to do so," replied Hemmingway; "we redeemed these lands from the desert and gave them all the value they possess. They belong to us and we intend to hold them."

The marshal replied that "he was doing only what the law and the court required of him, but that rather than use force he would abandon the attempt."

But Crow and his gang thirsted for blood, and had been ordered to prevent any abandonment of the object for which they were sent.

Scarcely had the words of the marshal issued from his mouth when Crow drew his revolver and fired at Erastus, thus giving the signal to the others of the gang, who at once followed his example and emptied their revolvers into the bodies of the innocent and almost defenseless men in front of them.

Crow's first shot was aimed at Hemmingway's heart and missed it by but a few inches. The bullet entered his left breast and passed entirely through his body, but though mortally wounded he succeeded in drawing his own revolver, and, firing, killed one of the desperadoes on the spot.

One other of the gang was wounded by a shot fired by Johnson, who was himself instantly killed by the second volley of the desperadoes.

Two others of the settlers were killed outright and three wounded; the latter by shots from the fowling piece of Crow, who fired at them as they fled, and but for the fact that the horses attached to the wagon, in which lay the villain's revolving rifle, took fright and ran away, not one of them would have escaped death.

Terror-stricken the bleeding men sped on in the direction of the picnic grounds, but had gone but a little distance when they met a score of neighbors, who, having been told the rumor of attempted evictions, had not waited for word from the first party, but followed on after, leaving their panic-stricken families to hitch up the teams and follow by the longer way of the road.

To these men the news of the awful tragedy just enacted was communicated, and a portion hurried forward while others returned to find the families of the dead and wounded men, if perchance they had not yet left the grounds, and prepare them as best they could for the worst that could occur.

Meantime the marshal and his brutal allies had beat a hasty retreat.

The former avoided Hanford and reached another station, where he took the train for San Francisco.

Crow, attempting to follow on after his horses, was found next day dead by the roadside, a bullet through his heart, one hand clasping a bulldog revolver and the other his double-barreled shotgun.

Erastus Hemmingway and the other murdered and dying victims of the conspiracy were tenderly lifted from the ground and carried to their homes.

Lucy, with her mother and two children—a second child, a girl, having been born to them—reached home in advance of those who brought her wounded husband.

They had heard the most terrible rumors, and were tortured by the most horrible fears, but were in ignorance of what had actually occurred until the men came bearing the bleeding body with its unconscious face and laid it at their feet.

To those who cannot imagine the agony of these loving hearts no description which the writer can give would convey any meaning whatever.

Erastus lived until morning.

He was unconscious during the whole time, and died without a word or look of recognition of those about him, while wife and mother and children poured forth their anguish in tears and sobs as they watched the pulsing of the heart grow fainter and fainter and felt the hands which they clasped become colder and colder, as the death-damp gathered upon the brow of him they loved.

Section IV:

The Truth that Will Prevail

Who shot first?

Eyewitness testimony couldn't settle the matter, and each faction had much to gain in the mind of the general public if it could duck responsibility for the outcome of the bloody battle and throw blame on someone else. No wonder that crack marksman Walter Crow—who stood at the center of the battle and who had been the most lethal killer by far—was cast in all manner of roles according to the needs of whomever was telling the tale: some said he was a U.S. marshal; a few said he was an innocent, though determined, local farmer; others said he was a tool of the railroad. In the end, five settlers were convicted of obstructing Marshal Poole in the course of his official duty, and the railroad saw its reputation for rapaciousness and greed—already considerable in the public imagination—grow even more unsavory. Although eventually most of the Mussel Slough land disputes were settled—partly the result of a price compromise between the Southern Pacific and the settlers, partly the result of the Southern Pacific's relentless defense of its property rights—the story of the gunfight still evoked powerful local feelings years later. The memory of the tragedy was even kept alive in plans for a memorial and, for a time, in solemn anniversary services held at the gravesides of the slain Mussel Slough farmers.

Like every other interested party, the Mussel Slough novelists each had their own colorful version of the real-life events and characters, using them to create muckraking fiction. By keeping alive the essential conflict between the Jeffersonian farmers and the railroad capitalists, by putting their own spin on these historical figures and events, the early Mussel Slough novelists aimed to fuel sympathy for progressive causes in California; accurate history was someone else's job. According to San Joaquin Valley historian Wallace Smith, the denouement of the

Mussel Slough gunfight was "long and tedious. It did not come until Hiram Johnson, an implacable foe of the Southern Pacific and all other autocratic corporations, was elected governor of California in 1910."[1]

Novelists, reporters, political cartoonists, pamphleteers, lawyers and judges all had their unique take on the story, but in the end, it is the novelists who most effectively embedded the event in our collective memory. And even if the details are just plain wrong—or perhaps skillfully embellished—the truth that will prevail lives in novels more than history books. At least, that's how it seems.

In this section, anger gives way to confusion and resignation, but in the end, "all things, surely, inevitably, resistlessly, work together for the good."

May Merrill Miller
"The United States Versus Ralph Walker"

After twenty-eight days of trial in a San Francisco courtroom, the defense rests in the settlers' prosecution for conspiracy and resisting a federal officer. The men are acquitted of the first charge but convicted of the second. San Francisco citizens organize a meeting to express their support of the Nueva Esperanza settlers and their righteous indignation against the railroad. Such sentiments seem of little use, however, as Edwin and Amelie visit their jailed neighbors, trustworthy men who stood on their principles. But in Amelie's judgment, these people were not the outright martyrs extolled in the oratory of the San Francisco firebrands; they were "hasty men, mistaken men."

The prosecution had taken over three weeks, the defense less than one. Twenty-eight days since the trial started. Today the District Attorney for the United States and Mr. Loring for the defendants would argue before the jury.

Edwin could sit beside Amelie now—the case was completed. Amelie thought the jury would make short work of it when she saw Mr. Loring, speaking earnestly, striding up and down. "We have shown you there was no possibility of concert, therefore the charges of conspiracy are preposterous. The very day of this tragedy the

---

[1] Wallace Smith, *Garden of the Sun: A History of the San Joaquin Valley* (Los Angeles: Lymanhouse, 1939), 288.

members of the League were assembling at a meeting to hear a judge give an opinion on their legal rights....

"We have shown you the character of this assassin Cole. We have shown you by the words of many witnesses the threats Cole made.... We have shown you that these peaceful defendants were engaged in a controversy over their lands and that they had engaged counsel to represent them....Gentlemen of the jury, is there anything reprehensible in that?...

"We have drawn a careful line between the characters of Cole and Ellis and this gentleman, the United States Marshal. We have drawn a line between the defendants and Fassett and Connery, who attempted to resist the Marshal. It is unfortunate that these mistaken individuals attempted to resist him, but where are those individuals now?—they are dead and buried—mistaken they were, thinking by so doing they could keep lands they regarded as their own.

"We have shown you that these defendants who still live acted in self-defense because they thought one of their number would be killed, and subsequent events have proved their fears to be well founded.

"Ministers of the gospel, attorneys at law, merchants, all have testified these defendants were respectable husbandmen interested only in keeping their homes by legal means. Gentlemen of the jury, I ask for a verdict of acquittal on both charges."

Amelie settled back in her chair....This would soon be over and the men freed. Of course the District Attorney had exaggerated.

But something cold and sharp cut into her mind when the Judge looked down at the jury and in the room that was growing dim—for it was five o'clock and the gray fog was thick in the streets and clouded the window—leaned over his bench beneath the great flag on its one standard, undimmed even in this dusk, and said, slowly, sternly: "Jurors, you are not to allow yourselves to be governed by sympathy or any other consideration except by testimony. You have nothing to do with the merits of the El Dorado Pacific Railroad Company as to the titles of their lands. There was but one way to contest this case and prevent the writ from issuing, and that was by an appeal to the Supreme Court of the United States. When the writ was issued on a judgment it was the duty of the Government to execute it, and if a successful resistance is made thereto by force, then anarchy necessarily ensues....If you gentlemen, in your judgment, beyond a reasonable doubt, believe these parties or any of them guilty, and you fail to give effect to that judgment, you prove recreant to your duties as citizens and violate your oaths as jurors. Mr. Marshal, take charge of the jury."

When at nine o'clock the foreman of the jury said they could agree in five minutes but announced a little later no verdict could be reached at present, the jury was locked up for the night and Edwin and Amelie returned to Aunt Nora's.

When Edwin brought Amelie the news the next day that all of the six men were released from the charge of conspiracy but found guilty of resisting a marshal, Amelie said weakly: "Oh, Edwin, I did hope they would be acquitted."

But Edwin said briefly with that same calmness with which he had announced the verdict given to Mr. Turner after Martin's murder: "They couldn't do anything else....If only Tim had waited, if only Cole had not baited Tim, if only the men had got the Marshal out of the way of the horses and the shooting between Tim and Cole, then it would have been just self-defense. But they didn't wait to let the Marshal read his paper—the jury couldn't do anything else."

Amelie wanted to go home that very day—this was the 23rd and Christmas so near—but Edwin said they must stay for the mass meeting that night.

The announcement was in every paper, on every wall:

MEETING OF THE CITIZENS OF SAN FRANCISCO
In Behalf of the
NUEVA ESPERANZA SETTLERS

The Citizens of San Francisco are respectfully solicited to meet at Platt's Hall, on Wednesday evening, December 23, 1880, at 7:30 o'clock, to express sympathy for the Nueva Esperanza settlers and to protest against any further evictions by the El Dorado Pacific Railroad Company.

Hon. Elbert Deschault and other prominent speakers will address the meeting.

LET ALL LOVERS OF LIBERTY TURN OUT

DEC. 23RD   BY ORDER OF THE COMMITTEE

The mass meeting at Platt's Hall—the largest in San Francisco— was not at all like the trial. No judge, just a chairman and an enthusiastic crowd filling back aisles and ready to agree to almost anything before the meeting started.

Behind the speaker's table was a huge map of California, crude but accurate enough. There was Tulare Lake and the two lines of the El Dorado Pacific—the one actually built through Nueva Esperanza and the other the original grant, a dotted line that missed Nueva Esperanza by a hundred and forty miles and ran continuously to the coast instead of stopping altogether at the foothills, as the actual line did, leaving a white gap between Nuron and Los Pinos.

It was exciting to hear it all again—to follow the pointer of the speaker indicating that blank space over the mountains where the railroad was never finished, asserting, in his opinion: "Ladies and gentlemen, the El Dorado Pacific never fulfilled its contract and is holding half of California by fraud.

"The question of corporations is one the public is getting aroused to," he shouted. "It's greater than States' Rights. If the El Dorado Pacific treats these poor Nueva Esperanza settlers this way, they'll soon treat every producer in the State of California the same. Talk of the oppressions of Ireland! Why, they are nothing compared to what these honest settlers have suffered at the hands of this company. Will the citizens of California see their own so treated without a protest? I call upon you to send a resolution to the Chief Executive of the United States asking his official clemency for these settlers who fought only to defend their homes!"

A standing vote seemed to please everyone, giving them a chance to clap and stretch.

Amelie was startled, when each new resolution was read, at all the attention and oratory her neighbors were receiving.

"*Resolved:* By the people of San Francisco in mass meeting assembled, that we denounce as criminal the attempt on the part of the El Dorado Pacific Railroad Company to evict from their homes and firesides the hundreds of families in the Nueva Esperanza District, and call upon the good people of the civilized world to join us in denouncing these unparalleled acts of wrong.

"*Resolved:* That we, the citizens of San Francisco, will render to these persecuted and oppressed settlers of Nueva Esperanza our moral and financial support in the further prosecution of their rights before the courts of our country."

Amelie thought it sounded hopeful, but when she glanced at Edwin he did not even seem interested, only weary.

In the midst of the applause a man in the back of the room shouted, waving a paper: "No! Those are only meant for babes; we must have meat for men! I have some here:

"*Resolved:* That the history of railroad tyranny, monopoly and extortion, east and west, proves that the State must either own and control the railroads, or the railroads will own and control the State: that in order that such control by the State may not result in an increase in the number of political bummers in Government employ, parties must be abolished and the people enabled to secure direct and proportional representation, until which they are not morally bound by laws which they had no part in enacting.

"*Resolved:* That the Democratic and Republican parties are responsible for outrages against which they have never raised a remonstrance."

"But it isn't over, Edwin," Amelie whispered, laying a hand on his arm as he rose.

"It might as well be—when folks get to blaming the Democratic and Republican parties for everything, it's time to go home."

When Edwin went to the jail the next morning, Amelie insisted on going with him.

"You can't, Amelie."

"I've got messages. Rhoda, Stella..."

Amelie thought she was prepared for the sight of Ralph and Orrin and the others, but she wasn't. Not bars and the remembered stale stench of Gratiot Street.

Her neighbors. In jail. She was ashamed. They were not martyrs, as was proclaimed by one orator after another at the mass meeting last night where thousands gathered. She did not believe it. They had been hasty men, mistaken men. She knew those who were left of her neighbors had gone to help Tim...but they had confronted a United States Marshal as well...the Judge's words...these kind, well-known faces before her...something was wrong, for both were true.

Amelie felt Edwin's arm shaking as he held her own. He had been so calm all along. But as he sank down on the bunk beside Orrin, Edwin's lips were twisted and his face bleak and naked.

It was Orrin and Ralph who comforted him, not he them.

"Never mind, Edwin."

Edwin was not looking at Ralph or Orrin or these bars, but far past them. "God damn the El Dorado Pacific to hell. I wish we had some money to fight them. They just waited till this happened...now we can't go on...If we had money for lawyers we could....Nothing's proved—that railroad can lie for years unfinished over those mountains, only a few miles over the ridge from Faltham to Los Pinos...but they'll leave the round-tables at each end, the ties will rot, they'll never lay another, not while we live or our children....

"No one will ever know if the land is theirs or ours, but we'll pay for it....Our case will never get to the high court now. They had us beaten before we started, a handful of Sandlappers, and them with money to buy off our lawyers...money to wait when we couldn't.... Nobody cares if the El Dorado Pacific is rich or not. I admire folks who can see ahead. I watched that other railroad climbing the Carson—that company deserved what they made and this one too. But not to take advantage of others....Not to use laws like bullets against folks, reaching for writs the way Cole loaded cartridges...."

"Never mind, Edwin, please."

But Edwin went on in the gasps of a man who drinks deeply after a long thirst. "We'll never see it—or those windbags at the mass meeting last night with all their resolutions—I hear they're sending a petition to the legislature and thousands will sign—but it's the beginning: people will remember us....Some day in California plain folks will get together and fight the El Dorado Pacific with laws in the legislature— laws to stop them when they don't keep their promise—laws to protect folks who deal with them—laws fair to both sides. The law is all right today, it's good like the El Dorado Pacific's '67 survey was on paper, but it isn't enough alone—it takes men too, men to follow it and build it and not stop for mountains and make the two ends come together so folks can travel on it....It will happen in California, God, I'd like to be here to see it...."

Edwin brushed his hands across his eyes and stood unsteadily. Then he smiled.

Amelie, watching, loved him.

"Well, how I do go on!—it's you fellows have to stay here. Maybe I ought to keep you company."

"Shucks, now—if we'd just listened to you we wouldn't be here."

"I brought you some tobacco. They wouldn't let me come here before, not while I could be called as witness."

"We know."

"Did they do anything else at the mass meeting, Ed?"

"They passed the hat. They took up quite a lot—it will help Sigrid and Mary and Minna and your womenfolks while you're here and maybe give a start to those who haven't any money to begin paying for the land."

"We'll have to pay the full price?"

"Yep."

The jailer had come with his keys.

Orrin stood before Amelie. He held something in his palm. A silver dollar.

"Mrs. Blansford—it's 'most Christmas. I know it isn't much, but please make it go as far as you can for the twins."

◆

Henry E. Highton
"LETTER TO THE PRESIDENT,"
SAN FRANCISCO, 1881

Accompanying the petitions for the pardon of the convicted Mussel Slough settlers, the following letter has been sent to the President by the settlers' attorney:

SAN FRANCISCO, FEBRUARY, 1881

Sir:—As one of the counsel for the defense, I took a leading part in the recent trial of these five men in the circuit court of the United States for this district, which resulted in their conviction of the offense of having obstructed the U.S. Marshal in the execution of final process, in a certain action of ejectment brought by the Southern Pacific Railroad Company against two settlers in the Mussel Slough country, named Brewer and Storer. They were each sentenced to imprisonment in the county jail of Santa Clara County for eight months and to pay a fine of three hundred dollars, together with the costs of prosecution, aggregating nearly four thousand dollars. The infliction of this sentence, or of any considerable part of it, would reduce their families, which are numerous and respectable, to irretrievable ruin.

These men are members of the settlers league of Tulare and Fresno Counties, an organization of about four hundred men, seeking, legally and constitutionally, to protect their homes against the demands of the Southern Pacific Railroad Company. The indictment against them contained two counts—one, for an alleged conspiracy, practically affecting all the members of the league, and involving a possible penalty in each case of ten thousand dollars fine, and two years imprisonment, and the other for actual resistance or obstruction, to which the lesser penalty is attached. They were acquitted on the first count and convicted on the second by a jury composed of respectable men, who nevertheless, with two or three exceptions from the nature of their business and associations, had very little sympathy with the trials and struggles of American settlers against railroad corporations.

The charge of the court upon the subject of conspiracy was extremely elaborate, searching, and complete. It certainly gave the jury the opportunity to find the fact of conspiracy at any moment down to the actual collision in which five of the settlers lost their lives. The verdict of acquittal therefore may be fairly taken as evidence that, until the fight was commenced, there was no unlawful concert of action between these men, and that they had formed no intention of obstructing the U.S. Marshal in the execution of the writ. Without great elaboration it would be impossible for me to present fully the reasons for my opinion that the difficulty was precipitated by Walter J. Crow and M. D. Hartt, two grantees nominally of the Southern Pacific Railroad Company, to one of whom the Marshal was to have delivered possession of the *locus in quo*. Omitting any discussion of this point, therefore, I have to say that these five men took no part in the physical struggle, and that their offense at most was technical and venial. Braden and Purcell were unarmed, Pryor and Patterson had such small weapons as were usually carried in that region, Doyle was not on the ground, and all of them left effective weapons at their houses. In the face of the verdict that he was not a party to any conspiracy, it is inconceivable by me that Doyle could have been rationally found guilty of any obstruction whatever, technical or otherwise; Braden and Purcell actually did nothing— they neither spoke nor acted, Pryor merely remonstrated with Crow, and, when the fight commenced, without any complicity on his part, his horse ran away, and he was not even in the contest. Patterson simply endeavored to maintain the peace and to quell the disturbance, and undoubtedly saved the Marshal's life from an infuriated crowd which embraced none of the defendants. Under these circumstances, it is evident to me, without touching other disputed questions, upon which my opinion and feelings, in common with the great mass of more disinterested citizens throughout the state, are very firm and deep, that the authority of the government has been sufficiently vindicated, and that justice and policy alike require the unconditional pardon of these vicarious sufferers for the alleged sins of a whole community. When William IV of Great Britain was on his death bed his last official act was the pardon of a condemned criminal, and of this act it has been remarked that "even a far nobler reign than his would have received new dignity, if it closed with a deed of mercy." I respectfully submit to your Excellency that there could be no more appropriate finish to a peaceful and successful administration than to restore five Americans of more than average intelligence and worth, of pure lives, industrious habits, or patriotic instincts, and whose situation is unfortunate rather than criminal, to their homes, their families and their friends. Such an act would be peculiarly consistent with the spirit of our institutions, could never be construed into an approval of lawlessness, and would deserve and receive the just commendation of the American people, and especially of those residing in the western extremity of the republic.

I have the honor to be with great respect,

> Your obedient servant,
> Henry E. Highton

To his Excellency Ruthford B. Hayes, President of the United States.

William C. Morrow
"A Very Long Journey"

After the gunfight, a warrant has been issued for the arrest of John Graham, but he resolves to leave for San Francisco, still seeking answers in the mystery of his father's murder. In the meantime, his grandmother hears rumors that she will be evicted from their home and she embarks on "a very long journey" to save their land, a trip that is for her the last chapter in the long-running melodrama of the land dispute.

An idler at San Francisco might have seen, if he had noticed, a feeble, tottering old woman, covered with dust from a long journey, and nearly falling with weakness at every step, slowly picking her way along the noisy streets. The idler might have seen at a glance that she was frightened and shy, and not in the least accustomed to the bustling crowds that hurried past her, scarce noticing her feebleness and confusion. He might have seen her timidly inquiring the way to a certain rich man's house, and continually going astray from the directions that were kindly though roughly given her. He might have noticed the infinite pains that she took to follow the directions closely, and the repeated failures that she made, and the many apologies that she offered for troubling people so often.

But at last her old heart bounded with joy as she found herself ascending the broad stone stairs that led to the door—so feeble and weary with long walking and hunger that the climbing was hard work for her: so hard, indeed, that she was forced to crawl on her hands and knees.

A lackey answered her timid summons; and when he saw the dusty, decrepit old woman at the door, he brusquely demanded:

"Why didn't you go around to the kitchen?"

"I didn't think of that, sir," she said humbly.

"Well, clear out, then!" he commanded, as he was shutting the great door.

"O, but, sir!" she cried, in such agony that his hand was stayed, and he looked at her with considerable curiosity. "O, sir, please tell the master that I want to see him on a very important matter."

"Bah!" ejaculated the servant, as he shut the door with a bang.

The poor old woman sat down and cried like a child; and how long she sat there she did not know; but presently the lackey again appeared, and his indignation and astonishment at seeing the poor old woman at the door were so great that it was with difficulty he repressed a desire to kick her.

"What! you here still?" he demanded.

"I couldn't help it, sir. I couldn't leave without seeing the gentleman."

"Do you want money?"

"Money!" exclaimed the old lady, proudly drawing herself up to her full height. "Money! No; I want to see him about a very important matter."

The servant—not a bad fellow at heart—became interested, and he said:

"If you'll tell me what it is, I'll let him know."

"O, I want so much to speak to him myself. I *must* speak to him. You couldn't make him understand."

"Now, look here, old woman," said the man, "it's no use cutting up like that. You needn't think you can run this house, you know. The boss won't come down unless he wants to. Say your say, and I can tell him what it is; and then if he wants to waste any of his valuable time on you, why, it's none of my lookout, you know."

"Well, then, tell him," said the old lady, "that I have come to beg for my home. They are going to turn me out."

"What has he to do with that?"

"O, they say that he has a great deal to do with it. You know my grandson bought the place, and it will be so hard for us to give it up."

"O, he did?"

"Yes, sir."

"Well, I'll tell the boss; but you needn't think it's going to do you any good."

In a short while the servant returned, with a message to the effect that the master was too busy to see her, and that in any event it would be impossible for him to do anything, as the law had taken its course, and interference was simply out of the question. What irony was that!

This crushed out the last hope that the timid, feeble old woman had. She picked her way down the broad stairs, hardly knowing whither she went, so benumbed with grief was she. She tottered down the sidewalk. Then she could not keep her wits about her very well. After a long time she found herself on a railroad train; and then she remembered that some men had been talking to her, and that one of them had brought her something to eat, and that they asked her a great many questions which she could not understand, and that then they placed her in a carriage, which seemed to roll along the street for days and days, and that soon it halted, and a man helped her out very kindly and gently, and told her not to be afraid, as nobody would hurt her, and that then he assisted her upon the train, and spoke concerning her to a man wearing a cap with a gold band around it, and dark blue clothes trimmed with brass buttons. All these things flitted like shadows through her failing memory, and she half believed that it had all been a dream. And then the dull pain that came upon her at the rich man's house returned, and seemed to be gnawing her heartstrings loose.

Poor, simple old woman! The only brave thing she had ever attempted in all her life to do brought her only bitterness and despair: and it brought more than that, for her mind was shaken.

For hours and hours—and perhaps for days and months and years, for all she knew—the train bore her over the dusty plains—on and on, she thought—always on and on, stopping now and then to take breath for further effort—on and on, puffing and groaning and rattling and grinding—always, and it seemed eternally, carrying her away and away, on the dreary road that leads from time to eternity.

But at last the man with a cap having a gold band came to her and told her he would help her off the train. She thought it was about time; for in a vague sort of way she had been dying all that time—all those hours and perhaps days and months—dying a slow and painless death, and that at last she had reached the haven of rest. And then the dream seemed more real than ever; for when she alighted, she recognized the broad plains and some houses she knew. She felt sure that she was dead, and that her spirit had returned to get John and take him to heaven.

Where was John? She asked that question of a familiar spirit—face that she saw, and the voice that belonged to the spirit—it was such a tender, pitying, manly voice—told her that John had gone far away.

Ah, John! you should not have disappointed her thus. She was sure that you would be there to meet her with your grave smile of welcome, and your strong grasp of her trembling old hand. Ah, John! it was very, very cruel of you to go so far away, and not be there to welcome your old grandmother, who had always loved you with the deepest affection, John.

The kind spirit whom she had addressed offered to take her out in his wagon to her home. At first she thought she could walk the distance, as it was only a few miles away, especially as she was a spirit, and would not be fatigued by the walk; but perhaps her spirit was old and feeble, as well as the body she had left at the rich man's door; for her spirit tottered, and could not walk a dozen steps. But the other spirit— the one with the kind, manly voice, and whom she had known when she was alive—picked her up with perfect ease—for she was merely a spirit, weighing nothing—and placed her in the wagon, and drove away.

It was a sweet and restful ride for a spirit to take. There was very little noise and very little dust, and spirits were not continually coming and going, and slamming doors. It is true that the sun was hot and the plains were barren; but for all that they were very beautiful, for everything is beautiful to a spirit. Sometimes she tried to speak, although she knew that spirits could not talk in an audible voice; and when she did, her voice sounded to her as if it were a long, long way off, and talking from the body that she had left behind. And then she would not talk again, because it was wrong for a spirit to put a voice into the body that it had left.

The spirit in whose wagon her spirit rode told her that he would take her on to his house, but she said she wanted to go home, as John might be there, and he would want to see her. It was a kind spirit that talked to her and tried to cheer her; but although she tried hard to be cheerful, she failed, and could only cry a little now and then.

Soon they came to her house. A great change had taken place there. She saw all her household goods in the road, where they had been recently put. And they were all covered with dust. In particular, one famous quilt, which she had made with her own hands, a great, great many years ago, and which she had treasured from year to year—a many-colored quilt of the finest silk—lay all in a shapeless bundle in the dirt. If she had not been a spirit she would have felt aggrieved at this; but of what use were all those cherished things now?

The spirit with whom she rode begged her not to get out, telling her that her house had been taken from her in her absence, as were those other homes on the day when they had that great fight; but she did not think that any one could rob a poor old woman of her home; and she begged so piteously that he tenderly lifted her from the wagon.

She hobbled to the door, and there she was met by a man whom she had never seen. If John had been there he would have recognized in the intruder the man who discovered him digging for the treasure at the foot of Lone Tree.

"Oh!" he said, in his whining, nasal voice, "you're the old 'un thet was a-holding this place, ain't yer? Well, I guess you'll have to clear out and take yer duds with yer, as the rightful owners of this here house has throwed yer things out and placed me in possession."

"That's an infernal shame!" growled the man in the wagon.

"Well, what could a feller do? Yer see, I wanted a place, and I've got as much right to a home as any of yer; and I paid 'em ther price for his place. The old 'un here wouldn't have a place that doesn't belong to her, would she?"

"I'm not complaining," meekly said the old lady. "I haven't any use for a house now; but I thought maybe John was in there."

"Ha! ha! There's no John in here, I can tell yer, old critter. Yer'll have to go somewhere else if yer want to see yer John. Likely as not he'll be in prison soon."

The man in the wagon jumped to the ground, and grasped his whip in such a manner that the stock could be used to dangerous advantage, and then threateningly advanced on the man in the door. But that discreet person suddenly closed the door and securely bolted it on the inside, while the old lady's angry champion hurled these insults at him:

"You low-lived coward! You *would* stand in with them robbers to drive a poor old woman out on the plains, when her mind is already shaken with trouble!" And then he turned toward Mrs. Graham just in time to see her fall unconscious to the ground. He raised her head, and anxiously spoke to her, but no answer came. She was at the end of her long and dreary journey at last.

"Do you think John will come?" she presently asked in a whisper.

"He will meet you in heaven," said the man, as the tears streamed down his rough but kindly face, and silently fell upon the ground.

Then he placed the gaudy old quilt in the bottom of the wagon, and tenderly picked her up in his great strong arms and laid her thereon.

She smiled sweetly; and then, with the name of John upon her lips, her sweet spirit took its flight to heaven, and the journey was at an end.

◆

John Vance Cheney
"THE MAN WITH THE HOE, A REPLY"
FROM THE NEW YORK *SUN*, 1900

"Let us a little permit Nature to take her own way: she better understands her own affairs than we."

—Montaigne

Nature reads not our labels, "great" and "small";
Accepts she one and all

Who, striving, win and hold the vacant place;
All are of royal race.

Him, there, rough-cast, with rigid arm and limb,
The Mother moulded him,

Of his rude realm ruler and demigod,
Lord of the rock and clod.

With Nature is no "better" and no "worse,"
On this bared head no curse.

Humbled it is and bowed; so is he crowned
Whose kingdom is the ground.

Diverse the burdens on the one stern road
Where bears each back its load;

Varied the toil, but neither high nor low.
With pen or sword or hoe,

He that has put out strength, lo, he is strong;
Of him with spade or song

Nature but questions,—"This one, shall he stay?"
She answers "Yea," or "Nay,"

"Well, ill, he digs, he sings;" and he bides on,
Or shudders, and is gone.

Strength shall he have, the toiler, strength and grace,
So fitted to his place

As he leaned, there, an oak where sea winds blow,
Our brother with the hoe.

No blot, no monster, no unsightly thing,
The soil's long-lineaged king;

His changeless realm, he knows it and commands;
Erect enough he stands,

Tall as his toil. Nor does he bow unblest:
Labor he has, and rest.

Need was, need is, and need will ever be
For him and such as he;

Cast for the gap, with gnarled arm and limb,
The Mother moulded him,—

Long wrought, and moulded him with mother's care,
Before she set him there.

And aye she gives him, mindful of her own,
Peace of the plant, the stone;

Yea, since above his work he may not rise,
She makes the field his skies.

See! she that bore him, and metes out the lot,
He serves her. Vex him not

To scorn the rock whence he was hewn, the pit
And what was digged from it;

Lest he no more in native virtue stand,
The earth— sword in his hand,

But follow sorry phantoms to and fro,
And let a kingdom go.

Frank Norris
"Prodigious Mechanism of Wheels and Cogs"

After the gunfight, the League has gone to pieces. Magnus Derrick is no longer its leader and he is about to lose his ranch. Meanwhile, Presley travels to San Francisco, where he visits with the capitalist Cedarquist. Despondent over the injustices suffered by his friends, on impulse Presley decides to confront Shelgrim, president of the Pacific and Southwestern Railroad. The head of the Octopus, Shelgrim is not what Presley expects.

Why not see, face to face, the man whose power was so vast, whose will was so resistless, whose potency for evil so limitless, the man who for so long and so hopelessly they had all been fighting. By reputation he knew him to be approachable; why should he not then approach him? Presley took his resolution in both hands. If he failed to act upon this impulse, he knew he would never act at all. His heart beating, his breath coming short, he entered the building, and in a few moments found himself seated in an ante-room, his eyes fixed with hypnotic intensity upon the frosted pane of an adjoining door, whereon in gold letters was inscribed the word, *"President."*

In the end, Presley had been surprised to find that Shelgrim was still in. It was already very late, after six o'clock, and the other offices in the building were in the act of closing. Many of them were already deserted. At every instant, through the open door of the ante-room, he caught a glimpse of clerks, office boys, bookkeepers, and other employees hurrying towards the stairs and elevators, quitting business for the day. Shelgrim, it seemed, still remained at his desk, knowing no fatigue, requiring no leisure.

"What time does Mr. Shelgrim usually go home?" inquired Presley of the young man who sat ruling forms at the table in the ante-room.

"Anywhere between half-past six and seven," the other answered, adding, "Very often he comes back in the evening."

And the man was seventy years old. Presley could not repress a murmur of astonishment. Not only mentally, then, was the President of the P. and S. W. a giant. Seventy years of age and still at his post, holding there with the energy, with a concentration of purpose that would have wrecked the health and impaired the mind of many men in the prime of their manhood.

But the next instant Presley set his teeth.

"It is an ogre's vitality," he said to himself. "Just so is the man-eating tiger strong. The man should have energy who has sucked the life-blood from an entire People."

A little electric bell on the wall near at hand trilled a warning. The young man who was ruling forms laid down his pen, and opening the door of the President's office, thrust in his head, then after a word exchanged with the unseen occupant of the room, he swung the door wide, saying to Presley:

"Mr. Shelgrim will see you, sir."

Presley entered a large, well lighted, but singularly barren office. A well-worn carpet was on the floor, two steel engravings hung against the wall, an extra chair or two stood near a large, plain, littered table. That was absolutely all, unless he excepted the corner washstand, on which was set a pitcher of ice water, covered with a clean, stiff napkin. A man, evidently some sort of manager's assistant, stood at the end of the table, leaning on the back of one of the chairs. Shelgrim himself sat at the table.

He was large, almost to massiveness. An iron-grey beard and a mustache that completely hid the mouth covered the lower part of his face. His eyes were a pale blue, and a little watery; here and there upon his face were moth spots. But the enormous breadth of the shoulders was what, at first, most vividly forced itself upon Presley's notice. Never had he seen a broader man: the neck, however, seemed in a manner to have settled into the shoulders, and furthermore they were humped and rounded, as if to bear great responsibilities, and great abuse.

At the moment he was wearing a silk skull-cap, pushed to one side and a little awry, a frock coat of broadcloth, with long sleeves, and a waistcoat from the lower buttons of which the cloth was worn and, upon the edges, rubbed away, showing the metal underneath. At the top this waistcoat was unbuttoned and in the shirt front disclosed were two pearl studs.

Presley, uninvited, unnoticed apparently, sat down. The assistant manager was in the act of making a report. His voice was not lowered, and Presley heard every word that was spoken.

The report proved interesting. It concerned a bookkeeper in the office of the auditor of disbursements. It seems he was at most times thoroughly reliable, hardworking, industrious, ambitious. But at long intervals the vice of drunkenness seized upon the man and for three days rode him like a hag. Not only during the period of this intemperance, but for the few days immediately following, the man was useless, his work untrustworthy. He was a family man and earnestly strove to rid himself of his habit; he was, when sober, valuable. In consideration of these facts, he had been pardoned again and again.

"You remember, Mr. Shelgrim," observed the manager, "that you have more than once interfered in his behalf, when we were disposed to let him go. I don't think we can do anything with him, sir. He promises to reform continually, but it is the same old story. This last time we saw nothing of him for four days. Honestly, Mr. Shelgrim, I think we ought to let Tentell out. We can't afford to keep him. He is really losing us too much money. Here's the order ready now, if you care to let it go."

There was a pause. Presley all attention, listened breathlessly. The assistant manager laid before his President the typewritten order in question. The silence lengthened; in the hall outside, the wrought-iron door of the elevator cage slid to with a clash. Shelgrim did not look at the order. He turned his swivel chair about and faced the windows behind him, looking out with unseeing eyes. At last he spoke:

"Tentell has a family, wife and three children....How much do we pay him?"

"One hundred and thirty."

"Let's double that, or say two hundred and fifty. Let's see how that will do."

"Why—of course—if you say so, but really, Mr. Shelgrim—"

"Well, we'll try that, anyhow."

Presley had not time to readjust his perspective to this new point of view of the President of the P. and S. W. before the assistant manager had withdrawn. Shelgrim wrote a few memoranda on his calendar pad, and signed a couple of letters before turning his attention to Presley. At last, he looked up and fixed the young man with a direct, grave glance. He did not smile. It was some time before he spoke. At last, he said:

"Well, sir."

Presley advanced and took a chair nearer at hand. Shelgrim turned and from his desk picked up and consulted Presley's card. Presley observed that he read without the use of glasses.

"You," he said, again facing about, "you are the young man who wrote the poem called 'The Toilers.'"

"Yes, sir."

"It seems to have made a great deal of talk. I've read it, and I've seen the picture in Cedarquist's house, the picture you took the idea from."

Presley, his senses never more alive, observed that, curiously enough, Shelgrim did not move his body. His arms moved, and his head, but the great bulk of the man remained immobile in its place, and as the interview proceeded and this peculiarity emphasised itself, Presley began to conceive the odd idea that Shelgrim had, as it were, placed his body in the chair to rest, while his head and brain and hands went on working independently. A saucer of shelled filberts stood near his elbow, and from time to time he picked up one of these in a great thumb and forefinger and put it between his teeth.

"I've seen the picture called 'The Toilers,'" continued Shelgrim, "and of the two, I like the picture better than the poem."

"The picture is by a master," Presley hastened to interpose.

"And for that reason," said Shelgrim, "it leaves nothing more to be said. You might just as well have kept quiet. There's only one best way to say anything. And what has made the picture of 'The Toilers' great is that the artist said in it the *best* that could be said on the subject."

"I had never looked at it in just that light," observed Presley. He was confused, all at sea, embarrassed. What he had expected to find in Shelgrim, he could not have exactly said. But he had been prepared to come upon an ogre, a brute, a terrible man of blood and iron, and instead had discovered a sentimentalist and an art critic. No standards of measurement in his mental equipment would apply to the actual man, and it began to dawn upon him that possibly it was not because these standards were different in kind, but that they were lamentably deficient in size. He began to see that here was the man not only great, but large; many-sided, of vast sympathies, who understood with equal intelligence, the human nature in an habitual drunkard, the ethics of a masterpiece of painting, and the financiering and operation of ten thousand miles of railroad.

"I had never looked at it in just that light," repeated Presley. "There is a great deal in what you say."

"If I am to listen," continued Shelgrim, "to that kind of talk, I prefer to listen to it first hand. I would rather listen to what the great French painter has to say, than to what *you* have to say about what he has already said."

His speech, loud and emphatic at first, when the idea of what he had to say was fresh in his mind, lapsed and lowered itself at the end of his sentences as though he had already abandoned and lost interest in that thought, so that the concluding words were indistinct, beneath the grey beard and mustache. Also at times there was the faintest suggestion of a lisp.

"I wrote that poem," hazarded Presley, "at a time when I was terribly upset. I live," he concluded, "or did live on the Los Muertos ranch in Tulare County—Magnus Derrick's ranch."

"The Railroad's ranch *leased* to Mr. Derrick," observed Shelgrim.

Presley spread out his hands with a helpless, resigned gesture.

"And," continued the President of the P. and S. W. with grave intensity, looking at Presley keenly, "I suppose you believe I am a grand old rascal."

"I believe," answered Presley, "I am persuaded—" He hesitated, searching for his words.

"Believe this, young man," exclaimed Shelgrim, laying a thick powerful forefinger on the table to emphasise his words, "try to believe this—to begin with—*that Railroads build themselves*. Where there is a demand sooner or later there will be a supply. Mr. Derrick, does he grow his wheat? The Wheat grows itself. What does he count for? Does he supply the force? What do I count for? Do I build the Railroad? You are dealing with forces, young man, when you speak of Wheat and the railroads, not with men. There is the Wheat, the supply. It must be carried to feed the People. There is the demand. The Wheat is one force, the Railroad, another, and there is the law that governs them—supply and demand. Men have only little to do in the whole business. Complications may arise, conditions that bear hard on the individual—crush him maybe—*but the Wheat will be carried to feed the people* as inevitably as it will grow. If you want to fasten the blame of the affair at Los Muertos on any one person, you will make a mistake. Blame conditions, not men."

"But—but," faltered Presley, "you are the head, you control the road."

"You are a very young man. Control the road! Can I stop it? I can go into bankruptcy if you like. But otherwise if I run my road, as a business proposition, I can do nothing. I can *not* control it. It is a force born out of certain conditions, and I—no man—can stop it or control it. Can your Mr. Derrick stop the Wheat growing? He can burn his crop, or he can give it away, or sell it for a cent a bushel—just as I could go into bankruptcy—but otherwise his Wheat must grow. Can anyone stop the Wheat? Well, then no more can I stop the Road."

Presley regained the street stupefied, his brain in a whirl. This new idea, this new conception dumfounded him. Somehow, he could not deny it. It rang with the clear reverberation of truth. Was no one, then, to blame for the horror at the irrigating ditch? Forces, conditions, laws of supply and demand—were these then the enemies, after all? Not enemies; there was no malevolence in Nature. Colossal indifference only, a vast trend toward appointed goals. Nature was, then, a gigantic engine, a vast cyclopean power, huge, terrible, a leviathan with a heart of steel, knowing no compunction, no forgiveness, no tolerance; crushing out the human atom standing in its way, with nirvanic calm, the agony of destruction sending never a jar, never the faintest tremour through all that prodigious mechanism of wheels and cogs.

C. C. Post
"It Could Not Be Told Otherwise"

At this point in Driven from Sea to Sea, *John Parsons has died of grief and Erastus Hemmingway has perished in the Mussel Slough gunfight. C. C. Post then concludes his propagandistic novel with a rhetorical flourish, pleading the truthfulness of his story and abjuring all responsibility for presenting such a sorrowful tale because, "as it is a true story, it could not be told otherwise than it has been."*

The story "Driven from Sea to Sea" is finished,—no, not finished. John Parsons and Erastus Hemmingway are dead. One sleeps with his crippled child upon the mountain side; one lies buried in the valley, side by side, with his neighbors, who fell like him, the victims of the rapacious greed of corporate conspirators on that fatal morning of May, 1880; but Martha Parsons and Lucy Hemmingway still live, and living still contend with a corporation for the shelter above their heads and the heads of orphaned children. With them battle others whose homes and farms are in jeopardy from the same source.

Occasionally some settler, driven from his home, made desperate by long-continued suffering, by wrongs oft repeated, takes vengeance upon the immediate author of his woes; and some man, some tool of the corporation sent to hold possession of the land from which the settler has been evicted, is found dead upon the spot where the wrong was done. Even as you read these lines and wonder if such things are possible, honest settlers, not alone in California, but in any of a dozen different States, it may be, are being driven from their homes, their altars overthrown, their household gods destroyed, their lives sacrificed, their wives widowed and their children made orphans.

No, the story is not yet finished; but so far as told it is a true story. All of the main incidents have taken, place substantially as related. They are part of the history of our country; have occurred to our own citizens, beneath the shadow of our own flag.

Had it been other than a true story it might have ended with a brighter picture; with the brightest and best of all pictures—the picture of a loving and honored old couple enjoying the last years of their well-spent lives amidst scenes of plenty and beauty, the work of nature and their own hands; with loving children and laughing babies, the children of their children about them.

As it is a true story it could not be told otherwise than as it has been, and if the pictures presented have been sorrowful instead of pleasant ones, and if the reader has been forced to weep, when, like the writer, he would prefer laughter to tears, it is not the writer's fault.

If sometime the people shall make it possible to write a story in which, without being untrue to life as the great mass of the people live it, the pleasant pictures shall crowd out and force us and them to forget the sorrowful ones, then will the writer of this be only too glad to write the sequel of "Driven from Sea to Sea; or, Just a Campin'."

J. G. P.
"TO THE MUSSEL SLOUGH MARTYRS," N.D.

I.

Sons of Tulare! though from a prison cell you hail,
Your bark through life serenely yet will sail;
While the tyrants who forged your fetters and sealed your fate
In sackcloth and ashes will repent, but too late.

II.

The Shroud supplants the Ermine, and we hear the funeral bell;
Satan will monopolize their carcasses in a fiery hell.

The modern Neros laugh, while weeping widows sigh,
"But every dog will have his day" in "the sweet bye and bye."

III.

You were torn from your homes by tyranny's hand,
And by a vile tribunal dispatched to a distant land;
But not disgraced, for, like the martyrs of old,
You've passed thro' the crucible, now shine like gold.

IV.

Which lies unnoticed 'neath the ground,
But brightly glistens in a kingly crown.
So, while Freedom was shrieking in Tyranny's doom,
You were dearer to us in the midst of your gloom.

V.

As the diamond, unobserved in its casket of sand,
Resplendently shines in man's skillful hand,
So each pure link in love's golden chain
Shines brighter now, you are with us again.

VI.

You've passed from that prison with no stain on your brow,
We honored you then, we honor you now.
The crime you've committed we cannot discern,
And your names are still cherished in love's golden urn.

VII.

You've enriched this valley and made its fertile soil,
And tho' the bands of monopoly, like the serpent's coil,
Are still winding their unhallowed lengths thro' your beloved land,
Their course will yet be stayed by God's eternal hand.

VIII.

The Federal Court, with a heart by hatred fired,
Kept you bound 'till the last hour expired,
For which their hearts will surely bleed,
While at the Throne of Mercy they'll vainly plead.

IX.

The Devil will receive them from the hands of God,
And pierce them through with his burning rod;
While for every victim slain and every widow's sigh,
The Railroad and its Court will be punished from on high.

x.

For the 11th day of May and the Court's unjust decree
Will live thro' endless ages on the pages of history.
Then, noble martyrs! with souls full of love and hearts full of
    glee,
We welcome you back to the land of the brave and the home of
    the free.

Charles Russell
"Speaking of Widows and Orphans"

Charles Russell was a pioneer muckraking journalist who—like Ambrose Bierce before him—harbored a special enmity for the railroads. In his retelling of the Mussel Slough gunfight, Russell doesn't hesitate to place blame squarely upon the shoulders of Walter Crow for commencing the gun battle. He makes no mention of the horse that caused the marshal to stumble, which was the incident in witnesses' accounts that originally caused the confusion that led to gunfire.

What went on in the minds of the railroad managers is only to be surmised, but from subsequent events the conclusion seems reasonable that after so many years of autocratic rule they were greatly nettled by this active and so far successful opposition. The settlers believed that, following the usual custom, both sides should now halt to await the Supreme Court's decision. As to this the railroad company had another opinion. Ignoring the pending litigation, it sharked up from the north two hardy men to whom it promised land without charge if they would succeed in breaking the settlers' position. One of these men, Walter J. Crow, was reputed to be among the best rifle and revolver shots in the state, and the settlers thought they knew the purpose for which he was employed. The antecedents of the other, M. D. Hartt, are not so well known.

Hartt and Crow went into the region, and soon after, with other men that had obtained land from the railroad, they exhibited this notice, which they said they had received:

Tulare County, April 24, 1880.

You are hereby ordered to leave the country.

BY ORDER OF THE LEAGUE.

The Settlers' League did not send out these notices and had no knowledge of them. At the same time reports were sent abroad that bands of armed and masked men were riding up and down the district making threats and committing outrages, although the residents were not aware of such matters.

Next, the railroad company went into the Federal Court, secured writs of ejectment, placed them in the hands of A. W. Poole, United States Marshal of the district, and demanded that he serve them at once, remove the settlers, and put Hartt and Crow in possession.

The marshal, of course, was obliged to comply, and on Monday, May 10, 1880, he went to Hanford, Tulare County, the trading town that had grown up near the settlers' lands.

Major T. J. McQuiddy, president and leader of the Settlers' League, upon which he had always urged moderation and patience, learned that night of the marshal's arrival and understood well enough his errand. With the secretary of the league Major McQuiddy drew up the following address:

To the United States Marshal:—

Sir: We understand that you hold writs of ejectment issued against settlers of Tulare and Fresno counties, for the purpose of putting the Southern Pacific Railroad Company in possession of our lands, upon which we entered in good faith and have by our own patient industry transformed from a desert into valuable and productive homes.

We are aware that the United States District Court has decided that our lands belong to said Railroad under patent issued by the United States Government.

We hereby notify you that we have had no chance to present our equity in the case nor shall we be able to do so as quickly as our opponents can complete their process for a so-called legal ejectment, and we have therefore determined that we will not leave our homes unless forced to do so by a superior force. In other words, it will require an army of 1,000 good soldiers against the local force that we can rally for self-defense, and we further expect the moral support of the good, law-abiding citizens of the United States sufficient to resist all force that can be brought to bear to perpetuate such an outrage.

Three cases have been appealed to the United States Supreme Court and we are determined to submit to no ejectment until said cases are decided.

We present the following facts:

First—These lands were never granted to the Southern Pacific Railroad Company.

Second—We have certain equities that must be respected and shall be respected.

Third—The patents they hold to our lands were acquired by misrepresentation and fraud, and we, as American citizens, cannot and will not respect them without investigation by our government.

Fourth—The Southern Pacific Railroad Company have not complied with their contract both with our people and with our government, and therefore for these several reasons we are in duty bound to ask you to desist.

BY AUTHORITY OF THE LEAGUE.

Early the next morning before this could be delivered to him, the marshal hired a buggy and accompanied by W. H. Clark, the railroad's grader or appraiser of lands, he drove three miles northeast to the nearest of the farms covered by the writs of ejectment the farm of W. B. Braden, a member of the League.

In another buggy close behind came Hartt and Crow, heavily armed with revolvers, rifles and shotguns, the shotguns being loaded with small bullets or slugs instead of shot.

It happened that on this day the League was having a picnic some miles away; whether this fact influenced the action of the railroad company and its traveling batteries I do not know. Braden was at the picnic; no one was in the little cottage. The marshal entered, carried out all the household goods, piled them in the road, and formally declared Hartt to be in possession of the premises. [Four loaded cartridges were left on Braden's doorstep, probably as an indication of what would be the result of any resistance on his part.]

This was about nine o'clock in the morning. The marshal and Clark, closely followed by Hartt and Crow, drove to the next place, the farm of one Brewer, over the border of Fresno County, and about three and a half miles from Braden's. They encountered on the road a settler named J. H. Storey, an old friend of Marshal Poole's, and Poole reined in for a time while the two talked. Storey said the settlers hoped for a compromise with the railroad company and he would try to arrange one.

When they drove on, Clark, the grader, reproved the marshal for talking with Storey because Storey was the partner of Brewer, whom they had come to dispossess.

About ten o'clock they arrived at Brewer's place. He was harrowing in his field. Both buggies drove into the yard, past the house, and about two hundred yards west into the field. At this moment there appeared about fifteen of the settlers in a group, some mounted, some on foot, advancing toward them. The settlers carried no visible arms; among them all were only five small pocket pistols. Marshal Poole descended from his buggy and went forward, saluting them courteously. The foremost of the settlers addressed him quietly, asking the marshal not to serve any writs until the case then pending in the Supreme Court should be decided. He also handed to the marshal the address that Major McQuiddy had drawn up.

Marshal Poole read the document and said his duty was to serve the writs then and there. The settlers replied without vehemence that they would not allow him to serve them.

They now closed about the marshal and demanded that he give up his revolver and surrender to them, whereupon he would be conducted in safety to a station whence he could leave the county. He said he would yield to force and go away but he would not give up his revolver, although he promised not to use it. Two of the settlers, Archibald McGregor and John E. Henderson, were then told off to guard the marshal and Clark to the railroad station at Kingsburg.

All this Hartt and Crow watched narrowly from the other buggy about seventy-five feet away. As the conference with the marshal ended, Hartt reached down and seized a rifle.

"Let's shoot," said he.

Without shifting his watchful gaze from the group of settlers, Crow put a hand upon his companion's arm.

"Not yet," said he, "it isn't time."

James Harris, from the group about the marshal, rode up to Hartt and Crow and cried:

"Give up your arms!"

He was within a few feet of the buggy. Crow laid his hands upon a shotgun before him. He raised it deliberately; he fired it into Harris' face.

Henderson spun around at the sound and whipped from his pocket a small caliber revolver. He caught a glimpse of the body of Harris slipping to the ground. He spurred forward, trying to fire his revolver at Crow. The hammer clicked on the cartridge but the arm was not discharged. Hartt started to descend from the buggy. As he leaned over the wheel Henderson's revolver worked at last and the bullet struck Hartt in the abdomen. At the same instant Crow, from his raised gun, shot Henderson dead.

Crow leaped to the ground with a revolver in one hand and carrying other weapons. He was firing rapidly into the group of settlers. Iver Kneutson was shot dead before he could draw his revolver. Daniel Kelly fell from his horse with three bullets through his body. Archibald McGregor, who was armed with only a penknife, was shot twice through the breast. As he ran screaming toward a pool of water, Crow at one hundred and seventy paces shot him in the back. He fell over and lay still. Crow fired his shotgun and Edward Haymaker, also unarmed, fell, struck in the head.

All this happened, as it seemed, in an instant. A stupefaction had fallen upon the spectators; they could but stand and stare. J. M. Patterson awoke first. He bounded forward crying, "This has gone far enough! It must stop!" One or two ineffectual shots were fired. As they rang out, Major McQuiddy, who all the morning had been trying to overtake the marshal, hurried upon the scene and took charge of the disorganized settlers.

Crow still stood there, weapons in hand, menacing the crowd. McQuiddy spoke rapidly to the marshal, protesting against any further action. As the two advanced, Crow suddenly doubled forward and dodged past the corner of the barn toward a field of standing wheat.

"Don't let that man escape!" shouted McQuiddy, and as Crow disappeared into the tall grain some one—just who is not likely ever to be known—followed upon his trail.

McQuiddy now turned to the wounded and ordered them to be carried to Brewer's house while messengers rode for surgeons. The bodies of Harris, Henderson and Kneutson were placed upon the porch; they were dead. Within the house Kelly, McGregor and Hartt were moaning and twitching with agony. Two doctors were brought from the village and found that all were mortally hurt except Haymaker. [McGregor and Kelly died before morning and Hartt on the 12th.]

This made six persons done to death that morning—on the Southern Pacific's corruptly obtained and wrongly held grant from the public domain.

Very soon there was another. Crow, dodging through the wheat, was making for the house of one Haas, his brother-in-law, and likewise an opponent of the settlers. As he ran he came to the irrigation ditch and turned off along its course; a ditch tender working below saw him running. At a mile and a half from Brewer's there was a bridge where the road crossed the ditch. Major McQuiddy had sent men on horseback to try to catch Crow. These were watching for him at the bridge. Haas and his hired man drove up from the other direction in a wagon containing six guns and a supply of ammunition.

"Where's Crow?" asked Haas, seeing the group by the bridge.

At that instant a cry arose, for Crow broke into sight along the ditch. He stopped, dodged back, and whipped up his rifle, aiming it at George Hackett. Before he could fire, a shot rang behind him. He swayed, turned a little and pitched over on his face—dead. He had been shot through the chest.

◆

Ambrose Bierce
"AN HONORING WORD FOR WALTER CROWE"
FROM THE SAN FRANCISCO *WASP,* 1881

The people of Mussel Slough are subscribing and soliciting subscriptions for a monument to the memory of those who fell by the hand of Walter Crowe while resisting an officer in the discharge of his duty. If their neighbors believe that these men are martyrs to principle; that they died in defence of their homes; it is right that they should erect above their ashes a memorial to do them honor. It is admitted that their cause has engaged the honest sympathies of the people. It is not denied that the corporation evicting them is a heartless, shameless and monstrous tyranny. Let the monument rise as a lasting protest against that corporation's conscienceless exaction, and a rebuke to the political methods that gave its managers the wealth they did not earn and the power they abused.

But Walter Crowe—did he not fall in defence of *his* home? Had he not the law upon his side, and dares any man impugn his motive in delivering battle to such fearful odds? Are his surviving antagonists ungenerous enough to wish that the splendor of his terrible courage shall perish from the obscure spot which it illuminated as with a blaze of light from heaven? That amazing performance, the death struggle of Walter Crowe— the startling terrors of his departure from this life, baptized with the blood of men, saluted with the wails of widows: and orphans—the grim nobility of this dead hero lying in state and no man daring to approach the body—this needs no monument to fix its memory in hearts that honor daring. But can the people of Mussel Slough afford to expose this immortal memory to the insult of commemoration by Leland Stanford and Charles Crocker?

Is there no better man than I to speak an honoring word for Walter Crowe? Is there no pen with enough of courage and honesty behind it to write a line in his praise? Do the gentlemen of the press fear to imperil their interest or influence by making and demanding recognition for this bravest of Americans? Will God not raise up an historian to relate, a poet to celebrate, his valor? Are Mr. Morrow's duties on the Visalia *Delta* so engrossing that he cannot set his grimly powerful pen to this congenial theme and make himself immortal? If I had his talent I would be ashamed to lack the will. I would apologize for silence and pray for opportunity.

Littleton Dalton and Frank F. Latta
"On Walter Crow"

In an extended interview with historian Frank Latta for his book Dalton Gang Days, *Littleton Dalton (1857–1942)—a member of the famed Dalton family of outlaws—told what he knew of the Mussel Slough gunfight, which included a spirited defense of the character of Walter Crow.*

I had an intense interest in the Mussel Slough Tragedy, as we called it; so I was anxious to hear [Littleton Dalton] tell what he knew about it. Possibly he could clear the tangled story that had grown up since 1880 about the part Walter Crow had played in the battle.

Walter was one of the finest rifle shots in California. He did most of the shooting at Mussel Slough. And certainly Mussel Slough was a tragedy.

Eight men lost their lives as a result of the battle, which lasted less than three quarters of a minute. Five men were killed instantly and three died soon afterward.

Every man died who was shot or who was armed and, with one exception, every man died who fired a shot. For length of time and percentage of casualties, it was one of the bloodiest battles of human history. Because of my own wide acquaintance with the Crow family and my admiration for many of its members, even yet it is a difficult subject for me to approach.

Having studied the Mussel Slough battle for more than fifty years, I am as well prepared to appreciate the accuracy of Lit's statement as anyone who has written of that affair. His is the only story that checks with the records, the inquest reports, which describe how each man was shot. Lit's story is an accurate, unvarnished account. While manuscript for this publication was being prepared, a wild story of the Mussel Slough battle was published in the San Joaquin Valley newspaper of largest circulation. Among other impossibilities, it portrayed the noted train bandit, Chris Evans, as taking an active part in the shooting.

We looked at Lit's fine old gold hunting case watch. It was noon. Even though I hated to break the spirit of reminiscence Lit had fallen into, I proposed that we go back to Hanford for dinner. But he decided the matter himself.

"Let's get that Mussel Slough battle off our chest and then go over to Visalia. We can eat any time. I want to show you where Grat broke jail."

So we again settled back against the barn, and the shadow crept to our feet and up our legs until, when the story was done, it was gone, and for an hour we had been basking in a mellow, afternoon April sun.

The S. P. had begun selling land to settlers at Mussel Slough several years before I went to Benedict's. I received several of their advertising circulars. They quoted timber land at five dollars an acre and valley land at two-fifty, a quarter down and seven years in which to complete payment. I didn't buy because everyone told me the railroad title was no good, and I believed them. I don't believe yet that it was good. I'll tell you why.

The land grant to the S. P. was made with the understanding that by July of 1878 they would complete a railroad from San Francisco to Los Angeles. They were to get every odd numbered section of land for a distance of ten miles on each side of the completed road. Everybody expected the road to be built down the coast.

But the coast route didn't look good to the railroad men. Half of their land would be in the Pacific Ocean and the other half was already given away in Spanish Land Grants. They fooled around for several years and finally began connecting the end of the railroad to Gilroy with the railroad at Goshen, in Tulare County. They began at each end and built as far as Tres Pinos and Huron. Then they quit. They haven't *yet* completed the road.

During this time and for years afterward, the S. P. encouraged settlers to go on the land, with the understanding that it would sell for the same price as the open government land. Several years after settlers had moved on the land, and while I was at Benedict's, the railroad company sent land graders in to put a price on each separate piece of land. The prices established ranged from fifty dollars an acre down to ten. There wasn't an acre graded under ten dollars. The government land sold for a dollar and a quarter an acre. The settlers were being made to pay for their own improvements.

While the S. P. was delaying, homes were built and other improvements were made. Dan Rhoades built an irrigation ditch to his place, and when I arrived, many of the ranches were irrigated by three large ditches. Then the railroad began demanding a share of the crops.

The Settlers' League sent representatives to Governor Stanford and to Washington, but got a glassy-eyed brush-off. You can imagine how those settlers felt. They were the most desperate people I have ever seen. If one of them tried to borrow my rifle or Ben's, there must have been a hundred.

After I left Benedict's, things moved fast. Judge Terry, of San Francisco, wrote an opinion concerning the Mussel Slough trouble and made arrangements to come to Hanford to deliver it. The date was set for May 11, 1880, and the settlers planned a picnic where they would listen to Terry read his opinion.

On the same day, the United States Deputy Marshal, A. W. Poole, began to dispossess settlers and put buyers in possession. One of the buyers was M. J. Hart, who had for some time been Southern Pacific station agent at Goshen. Another was Walter Crow. I knew both Hart and Crow well.

Walter Crow had been raised on the east side of the San Joaquin River, west of Modesto. His father was a brother to the Crows after whom the town of Crows Landing was named. He was one of the most expert rifle shots in California, or anywhere else, for that matter. When a young man he used to bring in bags of wild ducks and geese, shot on the wing with a thirty-two calibre single-shot rim-fire rifle. In addition, he was a quiet man, was absolutely fearless and could not be bluffed or imposed upon.

Marshal Poole and land-grader Clark took Crow and Hart to the Braden place. Braden was not at home and they hauled his furniture out and put it in the road. Hart was put in possession. Then they drove on to the next place, which Brewer and Storer held in partnership. Poole and Clarke were traveling in a buggy and Crow and Hart in a wagon. On the way the party met several people who carried to the picnic the news of what was going on. About a dozen men, some armed with revolvers, rode as fast as they could to the Brewer and Storer place. They arrived just as the marshal and his party had entered the premises.

Poole met Storer and talked with him. Storer rode out into the field where his partner, Brewer, was plowing, in order to talk the matter over with him. They stopped at the far side of the field, diagonally across from the house. While Poole was waiting for Storer and Brewer to come in from the field, the settlers rode up and met the party. Poole stood about fifty yards from the wagon where Hart and Crow were sitting. Part of the settlers surrounded Hart and Crow and began to abuse them for buying land and helping dispossess the settlers.

There has been a lot of talk about who started the fight and who fired the first shot. I can answer those questions. It was Jim Harris. I knew him well. He was a hot-headed, ignorant, overbearing fellow and a coward to boot. He was always pulling a gun and threatening to shoot someone. Once, in Hanford, I saw him pull a gun on Cornelius

Patrick. Patrick was unarmed, but he walked up to Harris and told him to put the gun up or he would beat him to death. Harris did put the gun up, and he left the place, too.

Harris rode to the marshal, pulled his gun and demanded that the marshal give up his gun. The marshal said nothing, but he looked Harris over and didn't give up his gun. At this time Poole was talking to some of the settlers about fifty yards away from Crow and Hart. Jim Patterson asked Archibald McGregor to guard Poole and let Poole keep his gun.

Harris rode over to where Crow and Hart were sitting in the wagon. He was mad because he saw he had made a fool of himself trying to bluff the marshal, so he began to curse Crow and Hart. Crow was a man who would stand just about so much abuse and no more. He challenged Harris to shoot, telling him he should keep the front sight filed off his gun. Harris still had his revolver out, and he threw it down on Crow and fired. He overshot and hit Hart in the groin. There was never one of the witnesses of the battle that I talked to who disagreed with the account which I have just given you about how the first shot was fired. Jim Harris started the shooting, but Crow finished it, all but killing himself. Things happened fast and furious, for it was over in less than three quarters of a minute, all but the killing of Crow.

Crow had a revolver strapped on him, but didn't use it at first. He jumped from the wagon, grabbed his shotgun from the back of the wagon, and blew Harris off his horse.

As soon as Crow emptied the shotgun, he yelled to Hart to bring him the rifle. In his wounded condition, Hart was having a hard time to control the team. He was suffering too much to know what he was doing, but he did manage to get out of the wagon and hand Crow another gun. During this time he held to the lines and kept the team from running away.

When Crow tried to use the second gun, he saw it was not his rifle, but another shotgun and it was empty. By this time there was a terrible uproar and several of the settlers were shooting at Crow. But he held his ground and stood there facing the crowd as cool as if he was at a turkey shoot. He broke the shotgun open, reached in his pocket, took out two shells, loaded the gun, and shot Ivar Knudsen off his horse.

The killing of Knudsen was an entire mistake. I never heard any-one who was there say anything different. In the excitement of the moment Crow didn't recognize him. Knudsen was a friend of Crow, he was unarmed and had a large family of children. Crow thought that Knudsen was Mike White. White was a deadly enemy of Crow. White and Knudsen were the same size, wore the same kind of beard and looked so much alike that few persons could tell them apart a few yards away.

Next Crow shot Kelley. By then the shotgun was empty and Crow held it in his left hand while he drew his revolver and shot Haymaker, Henderson, and McGregor, who were still about fifty yards away, guarding Marshal Poole.

By this time Hart gave up trying to hold the team and collapsed on the ground. The team started to run away. Crow still wanted his rifle, so he ran after the team. But they had too much of a start and were traveling too fast for him to catch them. He did get to the rear of the wagon and actually put his hand on the stock of his winchester, but at that moment he lost his footing and fell.

I have heard it said that Crow ran from the scene of the shooting and hid as soon as it was over. That is all pure fiction. Crow never ran from anything in his life. In fact, he did just the opposite. He got up from the ground, picked up his shotgun, loaded it and walked back to the crowd.

By this time everyone who had been armed was lying on the ground and the marshal ran to Crow, asking him to get on a horse and make a run for it. The marshal knew that Crow had been attacked and had only shot to defend himself. Crow refused to take a horse and started afoot to walk across the fields to his father-in-law's place, where there was a [bullet-proof] brick house and where he had plenty more guns and ammunition.

In the meantime, more of the settlers were coming up to the scene of the shooting and one of these, Caleb Flewelling, caught Crow's team, took Crow's own rifle and shot him with it. Flewelling was too far away for Crow to use either the shotgun or the revolver on him. Crow still had both of these guns and they were both loaded when his body was picked up.

Well, Crow, Henderson, Harris, and Knudsen had all been killed instantly. Kelly and Hart died during the night and McGregor next morning. Haymaker lingered some time. But when Haymaker died, Caleb Flewelling was the only man left who had fired a shot that day....

◆

Ambrose Bierce
"AFTER MUSSEL SLOUGH"
FROM THE SAN FRANCISCO *WASP*, 1881

"These mounds are green where lie the brave
Who fought and fell at Hanford;
O, point me out, I pray, the grave
Of Leland Stanford."

"'Twas here he fell"—the Granger thus
Replied, with tears in torrents—
"'Twas here he fell afoul of us
With writs and warrants.

"Our fallen brave sleep well; each keeps
This ground, where none besets him.
And well the fallen Stanford sleeps—
When conscience lets him."

◆

Frank Norris
"That Terrible Dance of Death"

Having helped enforce the railroad's will upon the settlers, having taken advantage of their plight in order to gain for himself control of their land and crops, the hateful S. Behrman—perhaps the most venal of all the characters drawn by the Mussel Slough novelists—meets a fitting death.

Upon descending from his train at Port Costa, S. Behrman asked to be directed at once to where the bark "Swanhilda" was taking on grain. Though he had bought and greatly enlarged his new elevator at this port, he had never seen it. The work had been carried on through agents, S. Behrman having far too many and more pressing occupations to demand his presence and attention. Now, however, he was to see the concrete evidence of his success for the first time.

He picked his way across the railroad tracks to the line of warehouses that bordered the docks, numbered with enormous Roman numerals and full of grain in bags.

The sight of these bags of grain put him in mind of the fact that among all the other shippers he was practically alone in his way of handling his wheat. They handled the grain in bags; he, however, preferred it in the bulk. Bags were sometimes four cents apiece, and he had decided to build his elevator and bulk his grain therein, rather than to incur this expense. Only a small part of his wheat—that on Number Three division—had been sacked. All the rest, practically two-thirds of the entire harvest of Los Muertos, now found itself warehoused in his enormous elevator at Port Costa.

To a certain degree it had been the desire of observing the working of his system of handling the wheat in bulk that had drawn S. Behrman to Port Costa. But the more powerful motive had been curiosity, not to say downright sentiment. So long had he planned for this day of triumph, so eagerly had he looked forward to it, that now, when it had come, he wished to enjoy it to its fullest extent, wished to miss no feature of the disposal of the crop. He had watched it harvested, he had watched it hauled to the railway, and now would watch it as it poured into the hold of the ship, would even watch the ship as she cleared and got under way.

He passed through the warehouses and came out upon the dock that ran parallel with the shore of the bay. A great quantity of shipping was in view, barques for the most part, Cape Horners, great, deep sea tramps, whose iron-shod forefeet had parted every ocean the world round from Rangoon to Rio Janeiro, and from Melbourne to Christiania. Some were still in the stream, loaded with wheat to the Plimsoll mark, ready to depart with the next tide. But many others laid their great flanks alongside the docks and at that moment were being filled by derrick and crane with thousands upon thousands of bags of wheat. The scene was brisk; the cranes creaked and swung incessantly with a rattle of chains; stevedores and wharfingers toiled and perspired; boatswains and dock-masters shouted orders, drays rumbled, the water lapped at the piles; a group of sailors, painting the flanks of one of the great ships, raised an occasional chanty; the trade wind sang æolian in the cordages, filling the air with the nimble taint of salt. All around were the noises of ships and the feel and flavor of the sea.

S. Behrman soon discovered his elevator. It was the largest structure discernible, and upon its red roof, in enormous white letters, was his own name. Thither, between piles of grain bags, halted drays, crates and boxes of merchandise, with an occasional pyramid of salmon cases, S. Behrman took his way. Cabled to the dock, close under his elevator, lay a great ship with lofty masts and great spars. Her stern was toward him as he approached, and upon it, in raised golden letters, he could read the words "Swanhilda—Liverpool."

He went aboard by a very steep gangway and found the mate on the quarter deck. S. Behrman introduced himself.

"Well," he added, "how are you getting on?"

"Very fairly, sir," returned the mate, who was an Englishman. "We'll have her all snugged down tight by this time, day after to-morrow. It's a great saving of time shunting the stuff in her like that, and three men can do the work of seven."

"I'll have a look 'round, I believe," returned S. Behrman.

"Right-oh," answered the mate with a nod.

S. Behrman went forward to the hatch that opened down into the vast hold of the ship. A great iron chute connected this hatch with the elevator, and through it was rushing a veritable cataract of wheat.

It came from some gigantic bin within the elevator itself, rushing down the confines of the chute to plunge into the roomy, gloomy interior of the hold with an incessant, metallic roar, persistent, steady, inevitable. No men were in sight. The place was deserted. No human agency seemed to be back of the movement of the wheat. Rather, the grain seemed impelled with a force of its own, a resistless, huge force, eager, vivid, impatient for the sea.

S. Behrman stood watching, his ears deafened with the roar of the hard grains against the metallic lining of the chute. He put his hand once into the rushing tide, and the contact rasped the flesh of his fingers and like an undertow drew his hand after it in its impetuous dash.

Cautiously he peered down into the hold. A musty odour rose to his nostrils, the vigorous, pungent aroma of the raw cereal. It was dark. He could see nothing; but all about and over the opening of the hatch the air was full of a fine, impalpable dust that blinded the eyes and choked the throat and nostrils.

As his eyes became used to the shadows of the cavern below him, he began to distinguish the grey mass of the wheat, a great expanse, almost liquid in its texture, which, as the cataract from above plunged into it, moved and shifted in long, slow eddies. As he stood there, this cataract on a sudden increased in volume. He turned about, casting his eyes upward toward the elevator to discover the cause. His foot caught in a coil of rope, and he fell headforemost into the hold.

The fall was a long one and he struck the surface of the wheat with the sodden impact of a bundle of damp clothes. For the moment he was stunned. All the breath was driven from his body. He could neither move nor cry out. But, by degrees, his wits steadied themselves and his breath returned to him. He looked about and above him. The daylight in the hold was dimmed and clouded by the thick chaff—dust thrown off by the pour of grain, and even this dimness dwindled to twilight at a short distance from the opening of the hatch, while the remotest quarters were lost in impenetrable blackness. He got upon his feet only to find that he sunk ankle deep in the loose packed mass underfoot.

"Hell," he muttered, "here's a fix."

Directly underneath the chute, the wheat, as it poured in, raised itself in a conical mound, but from the sides of this mound it shunted away incessantly in thick layers, flowing in all directions with the nimbleness of water. Even as S. Behrman spoke, a wave of grain poured around his legs and rose rapidly to the level of his knees. He stepped quickly back. To stay near the chute would soon bury him to the waist.

No doubt, there was some other exit from the hold, some companion ladder that led up to the deck. He scuffled and waded across the wheat, groping in the dark with outstretched hands. With every inhalation he choked, filling his mouth and nostrils more with dust than with air. At times he could not breathe at all, but gagged and gasped, his lips distended. But search as he would, he could find no outlet to the hold, no stairway, no companion ladder. Again and again, staggering along in the black darkness, he bruised his knuckles and forehead against the iron sides of the ship. He gave up the attempt to find any interior means of escape and returned laboriously to the space under the open hatchway. Already he could see that the level of the wheat was raised.

"God," he said, "this isn't going to do at all." He uttered a great shout. "Hello, on deck there, somebody. For God's sake."

The steady, metallic roar of the pouring wheat drowned out his voice. He could scarcely hear it himself above the rush of the cataract. Besides this, he found it impossible to stay under the hatch. The flying grains of wheat, spattering as they fell, stung his face like wind-driven particles of ice. It was a veritable torture; his hands smarted with it. Once he was all but blinded. Furthermore, the succeeding waves of wheat, rolling from the mound under the chute, beat him back, swirling and dashing against his legs and knees, mounting swiftly higher, carrying him off his feet.

Once more he retreated, drawing back from beneath the hatch. He stood still for a moment and shouted again. It was in vain. His voice returned upon him, unable to penetrate the thunder of the chute, and horrified, he discovered that so soon as he stood motionless upon the wheat, he sank into it. Before he knew it, he was knee-deep again, and a long swirl of grain sweeping outward from the ever-breaking, ever-reforming pyramid below the chute, poured around his thighs, immobilising him.

A frenzy of terror suddenly leaped to life within him. The horror of death, the Fear of The Trap, shook him like a dry reed. Shouting, he tore himself free of the wheat and once more scrambled and struggled towards the hatchway. He stumbled as he reached it and fell directly beneath the pour. Like a storm of small shot, mercilessly, pitilessly, the unnumbered multitude of hurtling grains flagellated and beat and tore his flesh. Blood streamed from his forehead and, thickening with the powder-like chaff-dust, blinded his eyes. He struggled to his feet once more. An avalanche from the cone of wheat buried him to his thighs. He was forced back and back and back, beating the air, falling, rising, howling for aid. He could no longer see; his eyes, crammed with dust, smarted as if transfixed with needles whenever he opened them. His mouth was full of the dust, his lips were dry with it; thirst tortured him, while his outcries choked and gagged in his rasped throat.

And all the while without stop, incessantly, inexorably, the wheat, as if moving with a force all its own, shot downward in a prolonged roar, persistent, steady, inevitable.

He retreated to a far corner of the hold and sat down with his back against the iron hull of the ship and tried to collect his thoughts, to calm himself. Surely there must be some way of escape; surely he was not to die like this, die in this dreadful substance that was neither solid nor fluid. What was he to do? How make himself heard?

But even as he thought about this, the cone under the chute broke again and sent a great layer of grain rippling and tumbling toward him. It reached him where he sat and buried his hand and one foot.

He sprang up trembling and made for another corner.

"By God," he cried, "by God, I must think of something pretty quick!"

Once more the level of the wheat rose and the grains began piling deeper about him. Once more he retreated. Once more he crawled staggering to the foot of the cataract, screaming till his ears sang and his eyeballs strained in their sockets, and once more the relentless tide drove him back.

Then began that terrible dance of death; the man dodging, doubling, squirming, hunted from one corner to another, the wheat slowly, inexorably flowing, rising, spreading to every angle, to every nook and cranny. It reached his middle. Furious and with bleeding hands and broken nails, he dug his way out to fall backward, all but exhausted, gasping for breath in the dust-thickened air. Roused again by the slow advance of the tide, he leaped up and stumbled away, blinded with the agony in his eyes, only to crash against the metal hull of the vessel. He turned about, the blood streaming from his face, and paused to collect his senses, and with a rush, another wave swirled about his ankles and knees. Exhaustion grew upon him. To stand still meant to sink; to lie or sit meant to be buried the quicker; and all this in the dark, all this in an air that could scarcely be breathed, all this while he fought an enemy that could not be gripped, toiling in a sea that could not be stayed.

Guided by the sound of the falling wheat, S. Behrman crawled on hands and knees toward the hatchway. Once more he raised his voice in a shout for help. His bleeding throat and raw, parched lips refused to utter but a wheezing moan. Once more he tried to look toward the one patch of faint light above him. His eye-lids, clogged with chaff, could no longer open. The Wheat poured about his waist as he raised himself upon his knees.

Reason fled. Deafened with the roar of the grain, blinded and made dumb with its chaff, he threw himself forward with clutching fingers, rolling upon his back, and lay there, moving feebly, the head rolling from side to side. The Wheat, leaping continuously from the chute, poured around him. It filled the pockets of the coat, it crept up the sleeves and trouser legs, it covered the great, protuberant stomach, it ran at last in rivulets into the distended, gasping mouth. It covered the face.

Upon the surface of the Wheat, under the chute, nothing moved but the Wheat itself. There was no sign of life. Then, for an instant, the surface stirred. A hand, fat, with short fingers and swollen veins, reached up, clutching, then fell limp and prone. In another instant it was covered. In the hold of the "Swanhilda" there was no movement but the widening ripples that spread flowing from the ever-breaking, ever-reforming cone; no sound, but the rushing of the Wheat that continued to plunge incessantly from the iron chute in a prolonged roar, persistent, steady, inevitable.

---◆---

Dr. Lowe
"WHY CAME WE HERE?"

Why came we here?
Why drop the sympathizing tear?
Other graves there are around,
Marking places in this ground.
Then why, oh! why, should these graves here
Seem to us so doubly dear?

Fresh in the memory are the lives of those,
Whose bodies in these graves repose.
Fresh in our memory is the noble stand
That the departed ones took in defending their land.
Fresh are these memories, and that is why,
Around these graves we breathe a sigh.

They fell, but not in the din of battle,
Midst the cannon's roar and the musket's rattle.
They fell by a cold blooded murderer's hand,
Urged to the deed by the usurper of our land.
In their death, we clearly see,
That we must work for liberty.

The tyrant now is forging a chain,
To fetter those whom he has not had slain.
Then let us not inactively sit down,
Like a stupid cur or a worthless hound,
But let us up and be shiny and to the cause awake,
For the good of our country, and for posterity's sake.

These graves before us do plainly say,
Fight the oppressor in every fine way.
To your homes, to your country, prove worthy men,
Then God his blessings to you will send.
Look to Him for assistance; let the Lord be your guide,
You'll then conquer your enemies, and o'er all evil will ride.

Hanford, Cala., May 11, 1881

Composed by Dr. Lowe and read at the graves of the settlers who were assassinated by the minions of the Southern Pacific railroad company on May 11, 1880.

Sources

The following sources have been cited in the text or have been of significant help in its formation. Not included in this list are the many newspaper articles, local histories, and assorted general references that have been consulted for background.

Adams, Frank. *Irrigation Districts in California. Bulletin* 21. *Reports of the Division of Engineering and Irrigation*. Sacramento: State of California Department of Public Works, 1929.

Anonymous. "Subsidy: A Goat Island Ballad." *(San Francisco) California Mailbag*. 1872. Reprinted in *Songs of the American West*, edited by Richard E. Lingenfelter, et al. Berkeley: University of California Press, 1968.

American Society of Mechanical Engineers. "The Fresno Scraper." Fresno, CA: American Society of Mechanical Engineers, 1991.

Bederman, David J. "The Imagery of Injustice at Mussel Slough." *Western Legal History* 1 (1988): 237–269.

Bierce, Ambrose. "After Mussel Slough." *(San Francisco) Wasp*, 1881. Reprinted in *The Ambrose Bierce Satanic Reader*, edited by Ernest Jerome Hopkins. Garden City, NY: Doubleday, 1868, 195.

——. "An Honoring Word for Walter Crowe." *(San Francisco) Wasp*, 1881. Reprinted in *The Ambrose Bierce Satanic Reader*, 27.

——. "Ode to the Central Pacific Spade." *(San Francisco) Wasp*, 1884. Reprinted in *The Ambrose Bierce Satanic Reader*, 205.

——. "Poem on Railroad Control." *(San Francisco) Wasp*, 1885. Reprinted in *The Ambrose Bierce Satanic Reader*, 208.

Bishop, William Henry. "Southern California II." *Harper's* (November 1882): 863–882.

Brown, J. L. *The Mussel Slough Tragedy*. 1958. Reprint, Lemoore: Kings River Press, 2001.

——. "More Fictional Memorials to Mussel Slough." *Pacific Historical Review* 26 (1957): 373–376.

Brown, Richard Maxwell. *No Duty to Retreat*. New York: Oxford University Press, 1991.

Brown, Robert R. *History of Kings County*. Hanford, CA: n.p., 1940.

Browne, Carl. "The Affair of May Last, Marshal Poole reading evictions; his tools firing on the Settlers." Illustration. *(San Francisco) Daily Graphic*, n.d.

———. "The Mussel Slough Eviction." Illustration. *(San Francisco) Daily Graphic,* 11 December 1880.

———. "Portraits of the Mussel Slough Settlers." Illustration. *(San Francisco) Daily Graphic,* 18 December 1880.

———. "Revised Design for the Proposed Monument in Memory of the Victims to Corporate Greed." Illustration. *(San Francisco) Weekly Graphic,* 28 July 1881.

Chambers, Mary E. "Pioneers in Mussel Slough: A Lady's Experience." *Visalia (California) Weekly Delta,* 4 June 1880.

Cheney, John Vance. "The Man with the Hoe, a Reply." New York *Sun,* 1900. Reprinted in Vol. 4, *The World's Best Poetry: Of Fancy, Of Sentiment,* edited by John R. Howard et al. Philadelphia: John D. Morris, 1904, 395–397.

Clark, Gordon W. "A Significant Memorial to Mussel Slough." *Pacific Historical Review* 18 (1949): 501–504.

Clendenning, John. *The Life and Thought of Josiah Royce.* Madison: University of Wisconsin Press, 1985.

Conlogue, William. "Farmers' Rhetoric of Defense: California Settlers Versus the Southern Pacific Railroad." *California History* 78.1 (1999): 40–55, 73–76.

Daggett, Stuart. *Chapters on the History of the Southern Pacific.* 1922. Reprint, New York: Augustus M. Kelley, 1966.

Dalton, Littleton Dalton. Interview in *Dalton Gang Days,* by Frank F. Latta. Santa Cruz: Bear State Books, 1976. Reprinted by permission of Monna Latta Olson, Trustee of the Latta Family Trust, which holds all copyrights issued to Frank Latta in the years 1976 through 1980.

Deverell, William. *Railroad Crossing: Californians and the Railroad, 1850–1910.* Berkeley: University of California Press, 1994.

Featherstone, M. S. "The Mussel Slough Tragedy." Typescript, 1881. California State Library, California Section.

George, Henry. *Our Land and Land Policy.* San Francisco: White and Bauer, 1871.

Glasscock, C. B. *Bandits and the Southern Pacific.* New York: Frederick A. Stokes, 1929.

Graham, Don. "Frank Norris." *Encyclopedia of Western Literature.* Fort Worth: Texas Christian University Press, 1985.

Hanford Carnegie Museum. "The Old Oak Tree." Photograph. 1 December 1995.

Hart, James D. "Two Great Battles." Review of *First the Blade* by May Merrill Miller. *Saturday Review of Literature,* 15 October 1938, 15.

———. *A Companion to California.* New York: Oxford, 1978.

Haslam, Gerald. *The Other California.* Santa Barbara: Capra Press, 1990.

Henderson, George L. *California and the Fictions of Capital.* New York: Oxford, 1999.

Highton, Henry. "Letter to the President." San Francisco, February 1881. "Mussel Slough Scrapbook 93.4," no item number. Kings County Museum, Burris Park, CA.

Hutchison, Claude B., ed. *California Agriculture.* Berkeley: University of California Press, 1946.

Jefferson, Thomas. *Notes on the State of Virginia.* Edited by William Peden. New York: W. W. Norton, 1954.

J. G. P. "To the Mussel Slough Martyrs." Circa 1881. "Mussel Slough Scrapbook 93.4," Item 72. Kings County Museum, Burris Park, CA.

Keller, George Frederick. "The Curse of California." *(San Francisco) Wasp,* 19 August 1882.

——. "Trouble in Tulare: A Railroad Monster on the Rampage." *(San Francisco) Wasp,* n.d.

Kings County Centennial Committee. *Kings County: A Pictorial History.* Hanford, CA: County Government Center, 1992.

Larimore, John A. "Legal Questions Arising from the Mussel Slough Land Dispute." *Southern California Quarterly* 58 (1976): 75–94.

Lewis, Oscar. *The Big Four.* New York: n.p., 1938.

Limerick, Patricia Nelson. *The Legacy of Conquest: The Unbroken Past of the American West.* New York: W. W. Norton, 1987.

Lindley, Daniel. *Ambrose Bierce Takes on the Railroad: The Journalist as Muckraker and Cynic.* Westport, CT: Praeger, 1999.

Lowe, Dr. "Why Came We Here?" Manuscript. "Mussel Slough Scrapbook 93.4," Item 62. Kings County Museum, Burris Park, CA.

——. *The Lands of the Southern Pacific Railroad Company.* San Francisco: Southern Pacific Railroad, 1880.

Markham, Edwin. "The Man with the Hoe." *San Francisco Examiner,* 1899. Reprinted in Vol. 4, *The World's Best Poetry: Of Fancy, Of Sentiment,* edited by John R. Howard et al. Philadelphia: John D. Morris, 1904, 393–394.

Martin, Ronald E. *American Literature and the Universe of Force.* Durham, NC: Duke University Press, 1981.

Maxwell, Hu. *Evans and Sontag: The Famous Bandits of California.* 1893. Reprint, Fresno: Pioneer Publishers, 1981.

Mayfield, Thomas Jefferson. *Indian Summer: Traditional Life Among the Choinumne Indians of California's San Joaquin Valley.* Berkeley: Heyday Books, 1993.

McAfee, Ward. *California's Railroad Era, 1850–1911.* San Marino, CA: Golden West Books, 1973.

McKee, Irving. "Notable Memorials to Mussel Slough." *Pacific Historical Review* 17 (1948): 9–27.

U.S. Deputy Marshal, Los Angeles. 12 May 1880. Letters from 15 February 1878 to 15 September 1881. U.S. Marshal Records, Northern District of California, RG 527. National Archives and Records Administration, San Bruno, CA.

Michaels, Walter Benn. "Corporate Fiction: Norris, Royce, and Arthur Machen." *Reconstructing American Literary History.* Edited by Sacvan Bercovitch. Cambridge, MA: Harvard University Press, 1986, 189–219.

Miller, May Merrill. *First the Blade.* New York: Knopf, 1938.

Morris, Roy, Jr. *Ambrose Bierce: Alone and in Bad Company.* New York: Crown, 1995.

Morrow, William C. *Blood-Money.* San Francisco: F. J. Walker, 1882.

Morsberger, Robert E. "The Inconsistent Octopus." *Western American Literature* 16 (1981): 105–113.

Mowry, George E. *The California Progressives.* Berkeley: University of California Press, 1951.

Muir, John. "Tulare Levels." *San Francisco Bulletin,* 17 November 1875.

———. *The Mountains of California.* 1894. Reprint, New York: Penguin, 1985.

Mussel Slough Monument Committee. "To the Lovers of Liberty Everywhere." Illustration. Hanford, CA, 25 October 1881.

Nordhoff, Charles. *California for Travelers and Settlers.* New York: Harper and Brothers, 1872.

Norris, Frank. *The Octopus: A Story of California.* New York: Doubleday, Page, 1901.

———. *The Responsibilities of the Novelist and Other Literary Essays.* 1903. Reprint, New York: Haskell House Publishers, 1969.

One of the Nineteen. "The Mussel Slough Difficulty: Something from One of the Settlers Who Is Not a Land Leaguer." *(San Francisco) Argonaut,* 23 April 1881.

Orsi, Richard J. "The Octopus Reconsidered: The Southern Pacific and Agricultural Modernization in California." *California Historical Quarterly* 54 (1975): 196–220.

Pisani, Donald J. *From the Family Farm to Agribusiness: The Irrigation Crusade and the West, 1850–1931*. Berkeley: University of California Press, 1984.

Pizer, Donald. *Realism and Naturalism in Nineteenth-Century American Literature*. Carbondale, IL: Southern Illinois University Press, 1984.

Post, C. C. *Driven from Sea to Sea; or, Just a Campin'*. Philadelphia and Chicago: Elliot and Beezley, 1884.

Preston, William L. *Vanishing Landscapes: Land and Life in the Tulare Lake Basin*. Berkeley: University of California Press, 1981.

Redding, B. B., and Jerome Madden. "Railroad Lands." Flyer. San Francisco: Central Pacific Railroad and Southern Pacific Railroad Land Departments, 1 July 1876. "Mussel Slough Scrapbook 93.4," no item number. Kings County Museum, Burris Park, CA.

Rice, Richard, William A. Bullough, and Richard J. Orsi. *The Elusive Eden: A New History of California*. 3rd ed. New York: Knopf, 2002.

Robinson, W. W. *Land in California*. Berkeley: University of California Press, 1948.

Royce, Josiah. *The Feud of Oakfield Creek: A Novel of California Life*. Boston: Houghton Mifflin, 1887.

——. *The Letters of Josiah Royce*. Edited by John Clendenning. Chicago: University of Chicago Press, 1970.

Ruggles, Lyman Brown. "Settlers' Ditch Song." *(Alta, CA) Advocate*, n.d. Reprinted in W. Smith, *Garden of the Sun*.

Russell, Charles Edward. *Stories of the Great Railroads*. Chicago: Charles H. Kerr, 1912.

"Railroad Robbers." *San Francisco Chronicle*. 24 August 1879.

Saunders, Richard. *Ambrose Bierce: The Making of a Misanthrope*. San Francisco: Chronicle Books, 1985.

Selvin, David. *Sky Full of Storm: A Brief History of California Labor*. Berkeley: Center for Labor Research, 1966.

Settlers' Committee. "The Struggle of the Mussel Slough Settlers for their Homes! An Appeal to the People. History of the Land Troubles in Tulare and Fresno Counties. The Grasping Greed of the Railroad Monopoly." Pamphlet. Visalia, CA: Delta Printing Establishment, 1880.

Slotkin, Richard. *The Fatal Environment: The Myth of the Frontier in the Age of Industrialization, 1800–1890*. New York: Atheneum, 1985.

Smith, Henry Nash. *Virgin Land: The American West as Symbol and Myth*. Cambridge, MA: Harvard University Press, 1950.

Smith, Wallace. *Garden of the Sun: A History of the San Joaquin Valley, 1772–1939.* Los Angeles: Lymanhouse, 1939.

Starr, Kenneth. Introduction to *The Octopus* by Frank Norris. New York: Penguin, 1986.

Stedman, J. C., and R. A. Leonard. *The Workingman's Party of California.* San Francisco: Bacon and Company, 1878.

Sullivan, Jack, ed. *The Penguin Encyclopedia of Horror and the Supernatural.* New York: Viking, 1986.

Thompson, Thomas A. *Official Historical Atlas Map of Tulare County.* Tulare, CA: n.p., 1892.

Wister, Owen. *Roosevelt: The Story of a Friendship.* New York: Macmillan, 1930.

About the Editor

Terry Beers is an associate professor of English at Santa Clara University and the author of *A Thousand Graceful Subtleties: Rhetoric in the Poetry of Robinson Jeffers* (1995) and *Unfolding Beauty: Celebrating California's Landscapes* (2000). General editor of the California Legacy Project, he lives in northern Monterey County, where he runs sled dogs.

A *California Legacy* Book

Santa Clara University and Heyday Books are pleased to publish the California Legacy series, vibrant and relevant writings drawn from California's past and present.

Santa Clara University—founded in 1851 on the site of the eighth of California's original twenty-one missions—is the oldest institution of higher learning in the state. A Jesuit institution, it is particularly aware of its contribution to California's cultural heritage and its responsibility to preserve and celebrate that heritage.

Heyday Books, founded in 1974, specializes in critically acclaimed books on California literature, history, natural history, and ethnic studies.

Books in the California Legacy series appear as anthologies, single author collections, reprints of important books, and original works. Taken together, these volumes bring readers a new perspective on California's cultural life, a perspective that honors diversity and finds great pleasure in the eloquence of human expression.

Series editor: Terry Beers
Publisher: Malcolm Margolin
Advisory committee: Stephen Becker, William Deverell, Charles Faulhaber, David Fine, Steven Gilbar, Ron Hansen, Gerald Haslam, Robert Hass, Jack Hicks, Timothy Hodson, James Houston, Jeanne Wakatsuki Houston, Maxine Hong Kingston, Frank LaPena, Ursula K. Le Guin, Jeff Lustig, Tillie Olsen, Ishmael Reed, Alan Rosenus, Robert Senkewicz, Gary Snyder, Kevin Starr, Richard Walker, Alice Waters, Jennifer Watts, Al Young.

Thanks to the English Department at Santa Clara University and to Regis McKenna for their support of the California Legacy series.

CALIFORNIA
LEGACY

Related California Legacy Books

Unsettling the West: Eliza Farnham and Georgiana Bruce Kirby
in Frontier California
JoAnn Levy

California Poetry: From the Gold Rush to the Present
Edited by Dana Gioia, Chryss Yost, and Jack Hicks

Mark Twain's San Francisco
Edited with a new Introduction by Bernard Taper

The Journey of the Flame
Walter Nordhoff

California: A Study of American Character
Josiah Royce

Death Valley in '49
William Lewis Manly

Eldorado: Adventures in the Path of Empire
Bayard Taylor

Lands of Promise and Despair: Chronicles of Early California, 1535–1846
Edited by Rose Marie Beebe and Robert M. Senkewicz

The Shirley Letters: From the California Mines, 1851–1852
Louise Amelia Knapp Smith Clappe

Unfolding Beauty: Celebrating California's Landscapes
Edited with an Introduction by Terry Beers

And many others.

For more California Legacy titles, events, or other information,
please visit www.californialegacy.org. If you would like to be added
to the California Legacy mailing list, please send your name,
address, phone number, and email address to:

> California Legacy Project
> English Department
> Santa Clara University
> Santa Clara, CA 95053